A GREENHORN NATURALIST IN BORNEO

A GREENHORN NATURALIST IN BORNEO

HANS BREUER

Whittles Publishing

Published by

Whittles Publishing Ltd,
Dunbeath,
Caithness, KW6 6EG,
Scotland, UK

www.whittlespublishing.com

Printed in the UK by Severn, Gloucester

© 2023 Hans Breuer
ISBN 978-184995-508-9

For my parents, Hans and Ingrid Breuer,

who have always encouraged my inner Wild Man of Borneo.

CONTENTS

AUTHOR'S NOTE

Taxonomy: As scientific names are forever in flux, I have always tried to use the most recently published nomenclature. I am aware that this could merely add fuel to the fires of the raging taxonomy wars, but I couldn't face the daunting task of creating a gigantic footnote to every single name in order to appease all the participants in this dialogue.

Weights and measures: I have standardized mostly on imperial, but have retained millimeters where appropriate. If you think in metric, I have in the more important places inserted a footnote with the conversion.

If you'd like to contact me about this book or anything else that you feel is relevant, feel free to email me: Hans Breuer hansbreu63@gmail.com

PUBLISHER'S NOTE

Language: As Hans Breuer's English is of the international/US variety and his writing is so wonderfully idiosyncratic (as you're about to find out), we've broken the mould of our UK English style in order to retain nearly all of his preferred spellings, vocabulary, punctuation and syntax. *Vive la différence!*

FOREWORD

Like an enticing offering of nectar seducing insects, the intoxicating allure of pitcher plants has led countless wayward naturalists to Borneo, many never to return home. It was under this shared botanical inebriation that Hans and I first crossed paths many years ago at the Sarawak Nepenthes Summit, though little did either of us realize that this would launch his eight-year sojourn on the island. Just as an insect teeters on the brink of a pitcher's watery precipice, once Hans had tasted the enchantment of Borneo's mythical rainforests, there was no turning back.

I have had the great fortune of enjoying Hans's company on more than a few outings in Borneo, and can say with conviction that if you ever find yourself knee-deep in a leech-infested swamp photographing pitcher plants, his boundless enthusiasm is a great asset to have at your side. Hans is gifted with the ability to point out the whimsical side of nature explorations, a trait that shines through in his writing and makes for fond recollections long after the leech bites have faded away. Certainly, few people may be able to see the humor in being rushed by an indignant king cobra, but Hans thrives on such experiences and his love and deep respect for all things in nature is evident in his colorful descriptions of wild creatures.

The great tropical island of Borneo has had a long history of exploration by famous naturalists. The written accounts of 19th-century legends such as Alfred Russel Wallace and Odoardo Beccari describe a land that had scarcely been seen by Western scientists, with forests stretching unbroken from coast to coast, and teeming with a multitude of species that had never been named. In *A Greenhorn Naturalist in Borneo*, Hans shows that despite the clearly diminished expanse of the Bornean rainforest today, not only does it still harbor incredible beauty and countless untold stories, but the spirit of exploration is alive and well in the 21st century. His unflagging fascination with the myriad discoveries of his jungle forays shows us that being a greenhorn naturalist is not always so much about how deep one delves into the jungle, but more about how one takes the time to cherish the miracle of even small discoveries in an urban backyard.

This book comes at a crucial time when Borneo's rainforests are poised on the brink. The once vast and seemingly impenetrable jungles have now been felled, burned, drained, and over-hunted, and it is becoming clearer than ever before that decisive action must be taken on our part if this unique wilderness and the countless species found therein are to persist into the future. The encouragement of a reverence for nature, sometimes as simple as Hans sharing the incredible wonder of a living snake with schoolchildren, is a fundamental prerequisite for the development of a conservation mindset—and ultimately the only way effective conservation can be achieved. (NB It is worth mentioning that direct handling of wildlife is prohibited under Malaysian ordinances, even when the goal is merely to relocate a threatened species to a safe area.)

Whether you are savoring Hans' great storytelling from the comfort of an armchair or in the midst of planning your own adventure to Borneo, I am confident that in reading this book you will not only be entertained but also be inspired to look deeper into the true value of these irreplaceable rainforests.

Chien Lee
Honorary Research Fellow
Institute of Biodiversity and Environmental Conservation
Universiti Malaysia Sarawak
March 2022

Map of Borneo
Credit: Addy Siong Teck Meng.

1 THE ROAD TO THE RAINFOREST

It is a cursed evil to any man to become as absorbed in any subject as I am in mine.

Charles Darwin

For many sociopolitical pundits, a leisure greenhouse is the embodiment of *petite bourgeoisie*; a compromise for people who fancy plants but are intimidated by their natural habitats or cannot afford a proper garden.

I am not one of those people. I love the outdoors and own a proper garden. Yet once I too owned a greenhouse, and it stood on the roof of my garage on the island of Taiwan.

On a dark and steamy night in 1989 I had arrived in Formosa, as Taiwan used to be known to early Portuguese explorers and the asparagus canning industry. I had come to enroll at a college in Taipei for a two-year course in Mandarin, part of the curriculum at the university in my native Germany where I majored in Chinese Studies.

By the time I finished the course, I already knew that the average German employer back home would be inclined to view my proficiency in written and spoken Mandarin as an utter waste of youth. Taiwan, on the other hand, offered a plethora of business opportunities for multilingual foreigners, and I embraced my good fortune. Instead of returning home to finish my degree, I opted to stay there and start a career as a translator and interpreter. Despite the exotic setting, I was soon ensnared in a quiet, desk-bound life, puttering down Humdrum Highway at a safe and sensible speed. A parallel storyline saw me marry a local lady, raise two boys, and purchase, fix up, and move into a little house in the country north of Taipei.

I worked from home, and my days were cast in an iron mold of routine: rise at seven, take kids to school, read emails over breakfast, then translate until my wife Lisa had returned from the market and cooked lunch. Lunch was followed by a siesta, after which I picked up the boys at school, translated some more until dinner, and typically finished the day nodding off with a book on my face.

On weekends I disappeared into my greenhouse, Lisa withdrew under the bougain-villeas with a gardening magazine, and the boys would treat our four dogs to a spa package by dumping the mutts in the kiddie pool and blasting them with a garden hose.

A formulaic suburban existence like millions of others.

If it hadn't been for that greenhouse.

From the outside, my greenhouse blended in nicely with all the other lower-middle-class trappings that surrounded it. Our backyard was the stage for my wife's horticultural expressions. The front yard was occupied by our four fiercely territorial dogs, and this had forced me to erect the greenhouse on top of our garage. Steel tubing covered with double-layered shade netting formed a 14-foot-tall arch across the roof, leaving just a small deck outside the shade house door. Taiwan's northern half enjoys a subtropical climate, and the purpose of the construct, rather than raising temperatures inside, was to protect the plants from too much sun while welcoming the rain. Aside from this small difference, it was by and large the same arrangement found in various modifications around the yards of tomato enthusiasts and begonia lovers from Stockholm to Tasmania.

My greenhouse, however, held nothing as mundane as veggies or flowers. Far from it. Beneath those shady covers reigned the Dark Side of Gardening, manifested as a primordial, hostile jungle. The air was hot and gelatinous. Snarls of vines, hanging from light fixtures and sprinkler pipes, snaking along the walls like tentacles, were ready to strangle anything foolish enough to ignore them. Hordes of gaping traps, wickedly camouflaged and baited with sweet, sticky knockout juice, lay in wait for unsuspecting prey. The heady aroma of digestive fluids fused with the pong of rotting cadavers. It was Mordor-on-the-Green; a floral abattoir where innocent creatures met their agonizing end in an orgy of silent screams.

Or at least, that was the consensus among the local insect community. My green-house, you see, was devoted to the cultivation of the most formidable group of life forms ever to populate the Kingdom of Plants: the carnivorous tropical pitcher plants of the genus *Nepenthes.*

My interest in this eccentric family of climbing vines had started on my 40th birthday, when a friend with a small collection of flesh-devouring plants presented me with a *Nepenthes × ventrata*, known in grower circles as the flower shop pitcher plant. *N. × ventrata* is a hybrid specifically developed for hardiness and a forgiving attitude toward casual windowsill growers and people with brown thumbs. Except for a few finicky ultra-highland species that require scorching days and icy nights, most *Nepenthes* are easy to care for, given the proper conditions.

But proper conditions for tropical pitcher plants are the opposite of everything you know about tulips. *Nepenthes* have learned to deal with a minimum of nutrients, so your typical rich gardening substrate will first make them gag and then snuff them. These creatures have evolved in locations with hard, nutrient-deficient soil and

Right side of the greenhouse

dramatic daily rainfalls. Due to the soil's inability to store any useful amount of water, the rains run off as fast as they have arrived. In a captive setting this means the plants crave frequent watering, but since they are highly susceptible to root rot, they need fast-draining substrates devoid of any nutritional value, like sphagnum moss and coco peat. And never put your neps in a cool and dry room unless you're in urgent need of herbarium specimens.

The largest carnivorous plants on Earth are found among the almost 180 kinds of *Nepenthes* in tropical Asia. Carnivorous colossi like the awe-inspiring *N. rajah* and *N. truncata* produce cavernous vessels that may occasionally contain half-digested rat carcasses. While these are extreme examples, even the average representative of the genus has little trouble gobbling up small lizards. (Indeed, one of my regular morning tasks in the greenhouse was to fish drowned geckos from pitchers where they had perished overnight while prowling for freshly trapped bugs. Leaving them in the traps would first lead to a decomposed gecko, and then to a decomposing plant.)

All carnivorous plants evolved their predatory ways in response to habitats like bogs and infertile sandy soils, where nutrients are extremely limited yet sunlight and water are abundant. Seeking alternative sources for nitrogen, phosphorus, and other substances essential for survival, the plants found them in the bodies of animals, mostly invertebrates, and developed fiendish modifications to attract, snare, and digest them. The Venus flytrap, the one plant of prey most people will instantly recognize, jams its quarry between two jaw-like appendages that snap shut at lightning speed. On the leaves of sundews, glistening glue drops will ground all bugs dumb enough to mistake them for nectar and small enough to get stuck. The leaves slowly envelop their meal, while the plant, just like any regular stomach, secretes enzymes and employs microorganisms to facilitate digestion. Bladderworts get their name from the tiny vacuum sacs growing around their roots and stems. When minute organisms like protozoa bump against such a bladder, they trigger a booby trap that sucks them inside and slams the door shut again, the entire process taking less than one hundredth of a second.

And many genera, including *Nepenthes*, use pitcher traps. These *periuk kera* (monkey cups, their Malay name, as monkeys were once thought to drink rainwater from them) vary in size and shape, but they all share a common strategy that is as simple as it is effective: their upright urns, with a generous opening at the top and filled with digestive fluids, act as pitfall traps. Most pitcher plants equip their killing jars with half-opened lids that keep rainwater from diluting the digestive liquid and serve as landing platforms for winged creatures. Different advertising schemes, from enticing scents and delicious nectar to optical signals, are employed to pique the interest of passing insects in the hope the bugs will pay the plant a quick visit, amble around the pitcher rim, and lose their footing on the slippery lining. After the victim has fallen into the digestive juices, the strong viscosity of these enzyme cocktails helps immobilize it. Should the doomed bug, against all odds, heroically struggle back out of the goop, any attempts at scaling the walls back to freedom will be sabotaged by a coat of slick wax crystals. There is only one direction for the prey: down. Score one for the plant—the tables have turned; now the cabbage is eating the rabbit.

⁎ ⁎ ⁎ ⁎ ⁎ ⁎

The hybrid I had received from my friend had been conceived to survive massive violations of every rule meant to keep its kind alive and happy. *Nepenthes* are generally tough, and can, in the care of skilled gardeners, attain extraordinary life spans. Specimens collected during the 18th and 19th centuries for the Royal Botanic Gardens at Kew were still happily sucking down ants and gnats when German bombs brought them to an untimely end during World War II.

Being anything but a skilled gardener, I murdered my little *N. × ventrata* within a fortnight, and entirely without the help of an air raid. At the time we had not yet moved to the countryside, but were living in an apartment in Taipei. I had hung the plant in my unsuitably cold and dry air-conditioned office, watered it only once a week, and generously added fertilizer, a substance about as beneficial to the health of these peculiar creatures as hydrochloric acid. But I was nothing if not dedicated. After my first

Nepenthes had shuffled off its mortal coil, I felt like I had lost a favorite dog. I had never kept as much as a potted fern in a corner of the bathroom, let alone tended a garden. Yet that little pitcher plant had stealthily but steadily weaseled its way into my heart.

What ignites and fuels passion for a nature-related hobby? Often it is a desire for perfection in form or function. Collectors of butterflies or seashells may seek to invite beauty and grace into their homes, looking to offset their own ordinary existence with a touch of the sublime. Some plant lovers may quest for immaculate petunias or award-worthy pumpkins, but the majority are perfectly content with the simple, yet deep, enjoyment that the splendor in the grass and the glory in the flower bring into their lives.

Nepenthes are such spectacular and perplexing creatures, they even bewitched the great Carl Linnaeus, inventor of the binomial taxonomy system biologists use to this day to classify every life form on our planet. Linnaeus coined the name for the genus after seeing an herbarium specimen for the first time. The plant brought to his mind a scene from Homer's *Odyssey* in which Helen of Troy dispenses a drug called *nepenthe* (without grief) to her battle-weary guests as an anesthetic and general happy pill:

> Then Helen, daughter of Zeus, turned to new thoughts. Presently she cast a drug into the wine whereof they drank, a drug to lull all pain and anger, and bring forgetfulness of every sorrow.

Linnaeus was positively giddy about the dried creeper:

> If this is not Helen's Nepenthes [*sic*], it certainly will be for all botanists. What botanist would not be filled with admiration if, after a long journey, he should find this wonderful plant. In his astonishment past ills would be forgotten when beholding this admirable work of the Creator.

Some, maybe all, of the above applied to me one way or another—but there was more. The precise reasons for why anybody lusts after anything are often impossible to identify, let alone understand. True love always contains a substantial element of mystery, of something you can't quite put your finger on, and will never be able to explain. Sonny Barger, a founding member of the Hells Angels, once defined love as "the feelin' you get when you like somethin' as much as your motorcycle." Or your pitcher plants, I guess.

I recalled Linnaeus' words to dull my own pain when I drove to the Taipei Weekend Flower Market a few days after my first *Nepenthes* had died. I was wildly determined to treat the next one with respect and honor, while trying to rationalize away a distressing awareness that my passion was fast approaching addiction. In spite of the alarm bells going off, I felt supremely alive and right and whole.

I was familiar with the sensation; it was an old friend. Playing blues guitar. Learning Mandarin. Weightlifting. Those were other stages in my life that had started by my unexpectedly falling head over heels about the subject. Many of my previous obsessions had quickly taken over a disproportionate chunk of my life and ultimately ended in disaster, or at least multiple abdominal hernias. I knew I was well on my way toward another severe infatuation, but in true self-enabler fashion I decided to hang back and see where the ride would lead me this time. How life-changing could it be? After all, it had just been a plant.

And now I needed another one. Pronto.

ⁿ   ⁿ   ⁿ   ⁿ   ⁿ   ⁿ

After bringing home the second *Nepenthes*, another *N. × ventrata*, I hung it from the balcony railing, far away from any desiccating air-conditioning unit. That bought the plant another month before it expired—from too much sun. Clearly, I needed to re-read my copy of *The Savage Garden*, a guide to the cultivation of killer flora, in particular the passages discussing shade netting and filtered sunlight. The following weekend found me at the Taipei Flower Market again, where I bought yet another *ventrata* from the same vendor, who made no effort to hide his euphoria at my burgeoning enslavement. I applied the wisdom from *The Savage Garden* with more care this time, and miraculously the third plant not only survived but gave birth to new pitchers, a sure sign of happiness. The triumph emboldened me, and before long I came home from the flower market toting a bag with three additional *Nepenthes*, each of them a different species. The vendor had promised me they would grow into fabulous specimens, if I only kept them in a tank. ("Tank," in grower vernacular, is shorthand for "empty aquarium repurposed as an artificial high-humidity environment for carnivorous plants via the addition of high-yield light fixtures.")

I started canvassing local pet shops and recycling centers for discarded fish tanks. I studied which color temperatures of fluorescent tubes benefited my plants. I learned how to keep the humidity on par with that of a busy Turkish steam bath. Soon, my office was crammed from floor to ceiling with brightly lit terrariums full of murderous vegetation jostling cheek by jowl for a go at our houseflies. My Saturday pilgrimages to the flower market were now routine, and my collection grew with amazing speed. Out of curiosity, I would sporadically buy a non-nepenthic carnivore—a Venus flytrap, perhaps, or a sparkling sundew—but it would soon end up forgotten in a corner of its enclosure, overshadowed, outgunned, and out-awesomed by the mighty pitcher plants. My grow list was now longer than my arm, and already I had begun to worry about the spatial limits of our little apartment in the Taipei outskirts.

As luck would have it, our two rowdy preschoolers were also outgrowing not only the confines of our living space but also the patience of our long-suffering neighbors. And so we decided to look for a place in the countryside, one with ample space for a proper greenhouse.

We began hunting the coast north of Taipei for suitable real estate, and it didn't take us long to decide on an elderly little house with pleasing views of the ocean and the mountains. There was a freestanding garage with a flat roof perfect for a greenhouse that would not only hold my current collection of a few dozen plants, but also offer comfortable space for expansion into the triple digits. As soon as the moving dust had settled, I set out on my scooter to reconnoiter the district for applicable greenhouse architecture and associated architects. The lightweight, but tough-looking shade houses at a nearby chili farm caught my fancy, and within the week the man who had built those pepper hotels was standing atop my garage, scratching his naked beer gut and hectoring his crew like galley slaves, his flying spittle testament to his strong work ethos.

Seeing the greenhouse go up gave me great satisfaction. I sensed I was finally entering the big leagues. Now there would be room for hundreds and hundreds of pitcher plants! I would grow specimens that would forever remain daydreams for those apartment dwellers with their puny tanks. I would exchange cuttings with other growers, create new hybrids, and name them after subjects dear to me: *Nepenthes* Lisa Liang ... *Nepenthes* Peking Duck ... *Nepenthes* Muddy Waters ... the possibilities were only limited by my own imagination.

The construction crew worked fast and efficiently, and before the week was over I stood inside the finished, if still empty, structure, testing the automatic sprinklers, installing humidity gauges and thermometers, and grinning like a briar-eating mule. My dream had come true—I had pulled off my escape from the boundaries of indoor growing.

In the weeks to come, I moved my plants from the office to the greenhouse, placed them in just the right spots, and raided the local garden supply stores for everything my pitcher plant empire would need. Hundreds of fast-draining pots in all available sizes. Boxes of tags, labels, and markers, to properly identify all my future creations. Enough sacks of substrate to fortify Omaha Beach. And when everything was in place, I perfected the tableau with a *pièce de résistance* that advertised my agrarian sophistication as well as my love for la Ilha Formosa, the Beautiful Island: a Taiwanese coolie hat.

I was now master of all that I surveyed, the king of my very own potted rainforest. Never one to balk at hubris, I was entirely convinced that one day I would own maybe not the biggest, but surely one of the most acclaimed pitcher plant collections in Taiwan—why, in all East Asia! Consequently, the next move would be to amass the grandest specimens available. With 90 percent of the greenhouse still empty, it would be a challenge, but I could not imagine a more fulfilling way to spend my free time.

First step: source sources. In those days, two *Nepenthes* nurseries were doing business in Taiwan. The operation in Hualien County on the scenic east coast was a tourist bus destination with a café hidden inside a vast tropical greenhouse. There you could quench your thirst with iced tea served in actual *Nepenthes* pitchers (debugged before being served), while you marveled at the starship flotilla of carnivorous vines swinging from the low ceiling in thousands of pots. An ingenious idea, and a novel experience for anyone without previous knowledge of these plants—but for the true aficionado the whole setup was a letdown, since every pot housed the same variety: *Nepenthes × ventrata*, the flower shop pitcher plant, developed for spontaneous casual buyers like those bussed to the joint every weekend.

The other commercial *Nepenthes* grower was based near the port of Kaohsiung, impractically located 200 miles away, on the southern tip of the island. Unlike the tourist trap in Hualien, Mr. Lin's *Nepenthes* nursery offered a goodly choice of species and hybrids. The logistics, though, were less agreeable. For a shopping excursion to Kaohsiung, one could choose between a long, uncomfortable road trip or just half a day by train. Rail travel seemed the obvious choice, but even in first class the return trip presented daunting challenges. First you needed to seize a few overhead luggage racks to stow your bounty of large, unwieldy vines potted in leaking containers. In the unlikely event of success, you had to keep all those pitchers in an upright position, and all those grabby tendrils from interfering with the humans sitting below. The task required not only an acrobat's dexterity but also a good deal of tolerance on the part of the other passengers who as a rule did not enjoy a mugful of half-digested ants pouring down their collars at every sharp bend. Commercial air travel back to Taipei was out for the same reasons. So I began to look into acquisition strategies closer to home.

Growing *Nepenthes* from seeds is a tedious undertaking; they can take years to germinate and develop into maturity. The problem is circumvented by stuffing stem cuttings into suitable substrate, where they take root within a much more acceptable time frame. And that, I decided, would be my ticket to world dominance.

For some time already, I had been active on a Taiwanese online forum for carnivorous plant lovers, where I had gained a modicum of recognition. Not through my horticultural accomplishments—I was still as green as a spring onion—but simply by being the only foreigner I collected brownie points by actively participating in the Mandarin-only discussions. Chinese native speakers as a whole respect non-Chinese people who make an effort to learn their language, especially the written form, and my communication attempts, clumsy as they were, earned me special treatment. Locals who would never unlock their greenhouse for a compatriot they had only just met on the internet threw open the doors to their collections for me. There I witnessed truly marvelous plants, their humbling splendor the result of many years of experiments and experience. Of course, I wanted cuttings of all of them, but I had nothing to trade. All I had was a greenhouse and a handful of half-mature plants far from ready for the pruning shears. But typical Taiwanese kindness and generosity didn't let this shortcoming stand in the way of my expanding collection. One of my new friends was the proud master of a gargantuan *Nepenthes bicalcarata*, an impressive member of the genus that sports two saber-tooth spines projecting downward from the pitcher lid like rattlesnake fangs. Noting how I gawked with childlike awe at this behemoth coiling out onto the roof from its indoor greenhouse, he grabbed the closest gardening tool, hacked a foot-long side shoot off the plant, and put it in my hot little hand with a gentle smile. His peers displayed the same largesse, and within months, the cuttings corner in my greenhouse had doubled my total plant count.

I felt it was time to give back to the community.

* * * * * *

Much like Korea and Japan, Taiwan had realized early that English skills are a crucial tool for an export-oriented economy, and now English language schools, catering to anyone from kindergartners to CEOs, are a huge industry. But since English has no colonial legacy in Taiwan and is mostly acquired in the classroom, many Taiwanese are not at ease with actually speaking it. Confucian values further compound the dilemma. The widely prevailing motto "if in doubt, shut your snout" is a considerate, but counterproductive, notion for practicing oral language skills, as is the idea that making mistakes in the classroom (a necessary part of any effective learning process) will result in loss of face for student and teacher alike.

The resulting communication barrier was cause for constant dismay among those of my Taiwanese buddies wishing to buy plants from exotic (i.e., non-Chinese-speaking) countries, and I saw a chance to compensate for all the altruism I had been shown; I would use my language skills to assist with the import of plants my friends and I lusted after. A handful of international nurseries specialize in *fleurs du mal*, and some even produce nothing but *Nepenthes*. Their websites are at the top of every fanboy's bookmark list (yes, most growers are male), and hardcore carnie buffs will log on in the morning and check for new plants in the sales catalog before even brushing their teeth. I would help my Taiwanese co-addicts get their hands on that titillating greenery that they so far knew only from photographs.

I had recently discovered an English-language online forum for the cultivation and science of the genus *Nepenthes*, and it had quickly become my spiritual home. The forum was the brainchild of a young German horticulturalist, Volker Heinrich, who had decided to ditch the Holy Trinity of his birthplace (beer, bratwurst, BMW) and relocate to the mountains of Mindanao to start the largest carnivorous plant nursery in the Philippines. Far from being a mere gardening geek with a greenhouse pallor, Volker regularly leads botanical expeditions in his adopted homeland, and has co-discovered and co-described several new *Nepenthes* species, including *N. attenboroughii*, a stupendous giant named after legendary television nature program presenter Sir David Attenborough, himself a noted Nepenthophile.

Compared to the multitudes cultivating roses or hydrangeas, *Nepenthes* hobbyists and commercial nurserypeople as a group fail to show up even as an ink stain on the horticultural map. There are probably more people growing *Lithops*, that floral version of the Pet Rock. In general, fringe hobbyist communities dabbling in exotica like paleolinguistics or giant tropical leeches are tiny tribes. This breeds a strong us-against-them mentality which strengthens the bonds between the tribe members. Professionals and academics from unconventional disciplines are also more likely to mingle with citizen scientists and private fanciers.

Volker's forum was no exception; the place vibrated with people from all walks of life. Video game programmers from San Francisco, car mechanics from rural Sweden, Parisian accountants, and Sumatran botanists all hung out at the virtual hothouse. Ideas, plants, and techniques were shown off, swapped, and compared, and the amateurs sat at the feet of the pros, inhaling every morsel of expertise the gods deigned to share.

And share they did. Every day, *Carnivorous Plants in the Tropics* was the first website I logged on to over breakfast, and the last one I closed at bedtime. The site provided a great wealth of technical and scientific wisdom – and, even better, a great wealth of knowledge about sourcing plants for my collection. Both nurseries and connoisseurs kept creating new hybrids at an exciting rate. The shops all shipped overseas, and the collectors were all keen to add to their grow lists by offering seeds and cuttings for trade. Soon I was knee-deep in international business. Many of my older plants had grown to cutting size—some had even flowered and grown seeds—and hardly a week went by without a plant shipment or two arriving at or leaving our house. Some of the parcels came from hobbyists, while others were of commercial origin. Before any overseas plant purchase, I would ask my Taiwanese friends if they wanted to join in on a collective order. Some would always be game. As soon as their wish lists had arrived in my inbox and their money in my bank account, I placed the order and wired the funds, and two weeks later, we all met at my house and huddled in awe around the freshly unboxed plants. These new arrivals were true highlights of my existence, not unlike Christmas merging with Chinese New Year, only much better, and twice a month. I did not reap any monetary benefits from these deals, but by silent agreement I kept all the freebie plants the vendors would customarily throw in as bait for future orders. The larger the order, the more freebies I received, and we always ordered large.

Life was good. Unless, of course, you were the type that fretted about legalities. Island nations like Taiwan worry about invasive life forms to the point of paranoia. Among the top bugaboos are nematodes, a.k.a. roundworms, in particular the parasitic kind. These thread-like, soil-dwelling microorganisms often measure less than a millimeter, and prey on a broad variety of vegetal matter. Nematodes can wreak agricultural havoc, and governments around the world go out of their way to keep the bugs beyond their borders. One acre of arable soil, calculated to a depth of 8 inches,[1] may contain 3 billion

---

1 20 cm

nematodes. Plant roots tend to grow in soil, and in most countries, including Taiwan, the import of any rooted plant without explicit permission is therefore absolutely *verboten.*

I had been happily importing *Nepenthes* for almost a year, had never heard about nematodes, and exhibited the same blissful obtuseness toward the laws created to keep those pests out of the country. This all changed one dark day when I found a pink postcard in my mailbox, dispatched by the Customs Administration of the Republic of China on Taiwan. After a warm greeting, the card informed me that the CAROC/TW had received a parcel from abroad, addressed to Mr. Hans Breuer in Sanchih Township, a parcel that—so sorry!—contained plant matter requiring official import documentation to enter Taiwanese territory. In the unfortunate case that I was unable to produce such documentation—really sorry now!—the postcard invited me to select one of two courses of action and inform the Customs Administration about my choice: (A), have the authorities return said plant matter to sender, postage courtesy of CAROC/TW; or (B), have the authorities incinerate said plant matter at their earliest convenience. Should I not reply to the pretty postcard within ten days, said authorities would automatically assume I had favored option (B) and act accordingly. Unspeakably sorry. Please advise.

I was shattered. What in the holy name of St. Fiacre[2] had happened? I was dimly aware that there were some kinds of import restrictions, but I had never taken the legal aspect seriously. There had never been any reason to; all previous parcels had made it to my doorstep without a hitch. There were two dozen plants in this shipment, which would now be either fed to the flames or sent back on a ten-day journey to the vendor, which meant certain death by dehydration. I felt a nauseous mix of anger and incomprehension, and immediately consulted my fellow nep-heads. One of the *Nepenthes* forum regulars, Amos, was a former officer of the Taiwanese Special Forces, a man with a bad case of wanderlust. A decade earlier, he had left his native island to find a home in the tropics for himself and his pitcher plant collection, and had settled in the town of Kuching, the capital of Sarawak, one of the two Malaysian states on the island of Borneo. There he ran a profitable nursery for orchids, bromeliads, and a wide selection of flesh-munching veggies. Now he cleared up my fog of ignorance:

> That has happened to all of us. Yes, you need import permits for Taiwan.
> It's an island, and they're scared of nematodes and other invasive pests.
> But customs are always overworked and undermanned and can't open
> every box that comes in. The best they can do are spot checks, and one
> of those has hit you now. Relax and get used to it. There will be more
> confiscations, but you can reduce the chances of those happening. Next
> time, tell the vendor to write 'silk scarves' on the mailing label and have
> him wrap the box in Hello Kitty gift paper.

---

2 Patron saint of gardeners and venereal diseases. No, I'm not making this up.

I tried to find solace in the fact that I was not alone in my torment, but gained little succor. Too depressed to do anything of value, I clicked on random forum postings, and eventually arrived at a long, photo-intensive entry chronicling the poster's recent trip to Borneo, where he had spent three weeks in the company of some of the world's most exquisite wild *Nepenthes*. The man had a knack for camera work, and there were dozens of beautifully rendered photos of mouth-watering plants in their native habitats. Gorgeous specimens with pitchers like drinking horns painted by acid-addled Vikings grew on moss-covered walls twinkly with dew. Bomb-shaped traps in camouflage nestled in long, windswept grasses in front of montane vistas. Shrouded in frayed wisps of fog, otherworldly plants sat between hardscrabble bushes hugging the stark ground in wild bonsai gardens. There were entire *Nepenthes* colonies strangling trees, their pitchers hanging from the host plants like flesh-eating Yuletide ornaments. It was pure plant porn, but instead of soothing my pain like Helen's *Nepenthe*, it just intensified my sadness. Normally, images like these were a source of daily joy for me; they also lived in the books and the nature show DVDs on my shelves, and their posters covered my office walls. But now they merely amplified my grief and brought about self-pity of the worst kind.

"Why do I have to put up with all this crap?" I mewled. "All that hassle, all those efforts and expenses, just to get the plants to thrive, and now the added anxiety about customs waylaying me? I've just about had it with the whole scene. What I really should do is ditch it all and move to Borneo where I don't even have to build a greenhouse. They grow by the goddamn roadside down there, and far better than they ever will on my stupid garage roof!"

⌃   ⌃   ⌃   ⌃   ⌃   ⌃

The Beat poet Allen Ginsberg advised, "Follow your inner moonlight. Don't hide the madness." The seed for my personal brand of moonlit madness sown by my first pitcher plant had germinated, and now it was pushing its way through to the surface. Like a blade of grass growing through tarmac, it had already opened a tiny fissure. In time, aided by other events, this hairline crack would widen into a great cleft and split off the entire promontory I stood on, sending me into the unknown.

But for the moment, the concept of relocating to Borneo was just what it would sound like to any sane person: an impossible escapist fantasy that would surely, once I calmed down, retreat into the dimension of the irrational. Even in the realm of the speculative, the very thought of moving your entire family to a rainforest island for no better reason than the frivolous enjoyment of things that could hardly be considered essential for one's material well-being was beyond decadent. The idea ranked right up amongst other perennially popular sky-pies born from the existential frustration frequently experienced by overworked middle-agers. Like quitting your 30-year job as a tollbooth operator to cruise the world on a catamaran for a decade or two, then retire on some sunny island where the climate agrees with your arthritis, and where the only problem left in life is whether to eat the crabs or the oysters first. Even if you did afford the idea some closer inspection, there would be social hell to pay. We all have the occasional weak moment and hallucinate about getting away from it all—but woe betide those who dare and do it. Their friends and family will immediately condemn them to pariah status for committing the ultimate sin: helping themselves to happiness.

I was neither man nor mad enough for such a tectonic life change. Hypothetically, I could live anywhere I wanted, earning my rice online as I did. As long as I had access to broadband and a power outlet I could live in a tree in New Guinea. But nobody in their right mind would live in a tree in New Guinea. Or move to Borneo, for that matter. Did they even have broadband in Borneo? Besides, what would my family do down there, anyway? Did they have schools in the jungle? Even if, how would the kids get there? They would probably need to leave the house three hours before sunrise to paddle raging whitewater streams and bushwhack through dense jungles full of tigers, snakes, and yellow fever, just to be on time for class.

Or would they?

I didn't know. In fact, there was a whole lot I didn't know about the world's third largest island, and what I did know was grievously selective. Sure, I knew about *Nepenthes*. Of roughly 180 species worldwide, the largest contingent grew in Borneo, among them outlandish creatures straight from the set of *Avatar: Revenge of the Shrubbery*. Many of those species are endemic to the island (i.e., not found anywhere else in the world), with Mount Kinabalu, at 13,435 feet[3] the highest mountain in the region, particularly renowned for its peerless flora. I also knew a few other random factoids about Borneo. It's twice the size of Germany, and bigger than Texas. The equator bisects the island. The nations of Indonesia, Malaysia, and Brunei share the territory, with Indonesia ruling the lower two thirds, Malaysia's two states of Sarawak and Sabah clinging to the north coast, and Brunei sitting like a tiny oyster pearl right on the border between the two Malaysian states. Apart from this basic information—stuff any moderately attentive high school student could tell you—I knew next to nothing about Borneo.

What I *perceived* about it, though, was its mysteriousness. Borneo's near-mythical status in Western minds has long obsessed nonlocals for a multitude of reasons. For me specifically, the island was the near-prehistoric homeland of my little meat-eating friends, a place that ran off the edge of my imagination. Just looking at these bizarre plants, even as they stood in the artificial setting of my greenhouse manacled to their polyethylene pots, gave rise to romantic musings about their mystical home. What sort of alien place would produce such unreal life forms that defied all conventional

---

3 4,095 meters

understanding? It was a fantasy world, yet it existed.

One of my former university professors was an expert on classical Chinese literature. A native German, he had always mulishly refused to visit Communist China; to him, the modern version of his beloved and long-gone Chinese world was a horrible degradation of all the cultural values he held dear. While not quite as quixotic as my teacher, I, like him, suffered from a remarkable lack of realism, but on the matter of Borneo. Like all *Nepenthes* fans, I had a powerful desire to visit the Old Country of my darling carnivores at least once in my life. But please, only the nice parts, because the other parts were just too sad to handle. Hardly a day passed without a media report on the cataclysmic dimensions of Borneo's deforestation. Here was the world's oldest rainforest, dating back 140 million years. The home of over 220 species of mammals, 622 species of birds, and an estimated 15,000 species of *known* plants, not to mention the unknown ones, and the millions of known and unknown invertebrates. The Four Horsemen of the Ecopocalypse—river pollution, soil erosion, climate change, and monocultures—were trampling this unique natural treasure into the ground, the newspapers and magazines said. So did the TV programs, the radio talk shows, and the internet. The home planet of my little aliens was being flayed into a red moonscape, just so we could all have hardwood floors and printer paper, and the gaping red wounds were everywhere, clearly visible from the air. So they all said. It was all too depressing to face, and much like my old professor, I dealt with it in my own peculiar way.

* * * * * *

The word "escapism" has never sounded dirty to me and, as a devotee of books by and about Victorian explorer-naturalists, I have tended to brighten my eco-blues by diving deep into the lives of my 19th-century idols. To a great extent, these lives had been spent in Borneo when it was still green and pristine. These folks populated a pantheon of real-life superheroes who braved hardships of the greatest order, all in the name of the discovery and decipherment of our natural world.

They were women like Marianne North, a botanical artist from a wealthy English family who taught herself painting and, eschewing marriage and a cushy life in Britain's aristocracy, spent the years between 1869 and 1885 traveling to some of the globe's most remote corners in search of new plants, which she depicted with enormous abundance and tenacity. After her return to England, this strong-willed character managed to persuade the rigidly science-minded patriarchs at the Royal Botanic Gardens at Kew to build a gallery at the gardens solely dedicated to her art. Several plant species are named in her honor, including the imposing *Nepenthes northiana*.

They were men like Alfred Russel Wallace, the Father of Biogeography and co-postulator of the theory of evolution, who spent ten lonely, malaria-racked years in the Malay archipelago, catching birds and butterflies to sell to museums and collectors

Nepenthes
northiana by
Marianne North

in England, and communicating with his customers through letters that took months to reach London. His goal was neither fame nor fortune, but to support his literally feverish quest to find out "not only how and why do species change, but how and why do they change into new and well-defined species."[4]

They were plant hunters employed by British nurseries, naturalists from the Royal Zoological Society, enterprising veterans from colonial armies, and all manner of freelancing nutcases pursuing all kinds of head trips. Theirs was a wild, romantic world full of great dangers and miseries, but full also of even greater promises and discoveries—discoveries that were still possible to be made by the naked human eye.

---

4 Alfred Russel Wallace, *My Life: A record of events and opinions*, 1905

It was a world represented by maps that often showed more white space than anything else, and where "Here Be Dragons" was not considered a droll grammatical mishap but a serious warning, to be taken lightly at your own peril.

I tried to re-experience some of that glory vicariously, through my plants. By toil and suffering, my Victorian idols had discovered for science the ancestors of the individuals that now inhabited my greenhouse. Sometimes I would just stand in my greenhouse, eyes closed, and imagine myself on some storm-lashed high plain on Mount Kinabalu, surrounded by acres of breathtaking flora.

Not surprisingly, my favorite section of the pitcher plant forum was "*Nepenthes in the Wild*" where members posted photos and reports from trips they had taken in search of pitcher plants *in situ* in their countries of origin. I could disconnect from reality for hours by reading and re-reading travel accounts and ogling the accompanying photos. Despite all the horror stories about the Rape of Borneo and its status as one of the world's most imperiled ecosystems, there still seemed to be quite a few locations with wild *Nepenthes* in the settings where the Victorians had found them. It gave me reason for cautious optimism, and in the face of all environmental odds, I clung to this little seedling of hope, dreaming that someday I might also have the chance to see Borneo's pitcher plants for myself, and that maybe—just maybe!— that world remained a tiny little bit as it was back in the days of North, Wallace, and their contemporaries.

And so I dreamed on, year in, year out, hoping against hope, wishing I could see Borneo firsthand, while being utterly terrified of what I might actually find there.

*   *   *   *   *   *

On the morning of October 17, 2006, after years of my waffling and whining, the Fates threw me a bone the size of a T-rex femur. That day, I logged on to the pitcher plant forum to find this post:

> Hi all,
>
> I thought this would be an excellent place to make the first formal announcement of the 2007 Sarawak Nepenthes Summit, which will be held in Kuching in August next year.
>
> In addition to being the first-ever carnivorous plant conference held in Borneo, this event will offer *Nepenthes* enthusiasts a chance to meet many of the leading researchers from around the world, hear firsthand accounts of the latest discoveries, and participate in memorable field trips to some truly outstanding sites in the rainforests of Sarawak.

I pinched myself, read the post again, then re-pinched, harder. The message came from the offices of one Chien C. Lee, long-time contributor to the forum and one of its most distinguished members. Born in California to a Sicilian-American mother and a Cantonese martial arts instructor, Chien had shown a keen interest in the natural world from a young age. Collecting beetles and growing carnivorous plants throughout high school had led to regular work as a naturalist and educator in the Golden State's national parks. After earning an ecology degree in college, he had emigrated to Borneo in his early twenties, accepting an offer to supervise the tissue culture program at a pitcher plant nursery in Kuching. Over time, Chien's interest in everything nature— nature photography, natural sciences, the outdoor lifestyle—fused into a multifaceted career. Apart from organizing and guiding scientific expeditions and specialized trips all over the tropics, Chien has built a reputation as a top-shelf nature photographer as well as an advisor and facilitator for media crews visiting Borneo. He spends his free time researching selected aspects of the region's flora and fauna, often discovering new species in the process. Dr. Matthew Jebb, director of the National Botanic Gardens of Ireland, calls him a "latter-day Alfred Wallace."

On his website Chien confesses a broad interest in everything the island has to offer: "Borneo is a fantastic place to live if you've got an insatiable interest in nature. It's easy for a photographer to get spoiled by the overwhelming diversity of subjects every time you're out." But for all his immense knowledge of all things tropical, Chien's love for pitcher plants has always loomed paramount. So it came as no shock to anyone when his passions eventually culminated in the ambitious idea for an international convention on the genus, the Sarawak Nepenthes Summit 2007.

I was in seventh heaven. A multi-day conference on my favorite life forms! Outings into the rainforest to see wild *Nepenthes*! A chance to meet all those brilliant botanists whose books I revered, and all those horticultural geniuses whose plants I envied! And it would all happen in Borneo! This was too once-in-a-lifetime to pass up. All my fears of the ecological holocaust I might confront in Borneo went straight out the window. I would see Borneo, I would see it in the company of like-minded nepsters, and I would enjoy the hell out of it!

Fearful that tickets would sell out within hours, I ordered my attendance kit straight away. As evidence of my eagerness, it bore the serial number 0001. Thirty minutes later I had also booked a hotel room, secured round trip air tickets Taipei–Kuching, and made an appointment for malaria prophylaxis.

Now all that was left to do was to wait ten months.

2 FIRST CONTACT

There are two kinds of adventurers: those who go truly
hoping to find adventure and those who go secretly hoping
they won't.

William Least-Heat Moon, Blue Highways[5]

The blond dreadlocks of the Swedish backpacker snoring on my shoulder half-
obscured my view through the cabin window, but what I could see of the land below
kept feeding coins into my mind's jukebox, which was playing Wagner's "Ride of the
Valkyries" on an infinite loop. My overtaxed nervous system was failing miserably to
cope with the tension. Our flight from KL (Kuala Lumpur appears to be the written
form only; saying it out loud will immediately out you as a tourist) to Kuching had
already passed over the Borneo coast, but we had yet to spot major signs of civilization
below. The coastline was carpeted with a nearly unbroken avocado skin of mangroves
and trunkless nipah palms resembling 30-foot feather boas stuck into the gray mud
by a giant's hand. Twinkling lines snaked through the green expanse in wild bends,
now looping back onto themselves, now straightening again. Presently, the Airbus
roughly aligned its descent with the thickest of those lines. This was *Sungai Sarawak*,
the Sarawak River. As we lost altitude, the river gained in size, and so did the butterflies
in my stomach.

Almost a year had passed since my registration for the Nepenthes Summit. I had
spent those months preparing for the trip, but at the first glimpse of the island my
excitement deserted me; the idea of finally setting foot on the miraculous world I had
glorified from afar for so many years unnerved me. Visions of the wonders I was about
to discover were clouded by fears of being unprepared for possible heartbreaks. In
concert with conflicting images and reflections about the land below, they created an
inner typhoon that made me crave a stiff dose of valium.

Kuching International is a small but modern airport, and we deplaned via a jet bridge rather than taking the stairs down to the tarmac. This was disappointing, since I had briefly considered stepping onto the airfield with the appropriate gravitas, dropping to my knees, and smooching the ground of the Holy Land. But maybe it was for the best. Public display of strong emotions might violate certain moral codes dear to the locals; and in Sarawak, where "the locals" is shorthand for a hodgepodge of over 40 ethnic groups with an eclectic variety of dos and don'ts, it was probably prudent to spoon out the madness in cautious portions.

I had flown from Taipei to Kuala Lumpur International Airport and passed through immigration onto Malaysian territory. After the domestic flight from KL, which is of course the capital of Malaysia, to Sarawak, a member state of the Malaysian Federation, I found to my bafflement that everyone—even the Malaysian passengers—entering Sarawak had to pass through immigration again. A fellow traveler solved the riddle for me: Sabah (the former British North Borneo) and Sarawak used to be colonies governed separately from British Malaya, on the Malaysian peninsula, and they did not join the independent Federation of Malaya upon its foundation in 1957. That changed in 1963, when both states became part of the new Federation of Malaysia, together with Malaya and (for just two years) Singapore. In exchange for increasing Malaysia's territory by a cool 150 percent (over 76,000 square miles) with a single stroke, Sabah and Sarawak, now jointly known as East Malaysia, were allowed to retain a higher degree of local government and legislative autonomy than the peninsular states in West Malaysia. And this included the right to screen visiting countrymen upon arrival. Granted, it was mostly a formality—a smile, a little blue rectangle slammed into the passport—but the whole concept struck me as odd. My new friend gave me a wistful look and indicated that this would not be the last oddity in East Malaysian politics I would encounter.

My befuddled frown was quickly smoothed out by the giant hot towel that slapped me in the face as I left the hyper-airconditioned terminal. Kuching had recently been voted Southeast Asia's Most Livable Town. One of the reasons was a variety of parameters that keep the temperatures on the pleasant side; they seldom exceed 91°F, and rarely drop below 75°F.[6] Few buildings are taller than four stories, which prohibits the convection-oven conditions that prevail in the high-rise canyons of tropical megalopolises like Bangkok and Mumbai. Often there is also a nice breeze. The Kuching-based British naturalist Sir Hugh Low wrote in 1848 that Borneo's climate is not "so inconveniently oppressive to Europeans as a hot summer day in England."

Unless Sir Hugh was a closet masochist or a compulsive prankster, this sounded to me like the perfect environment for an out-of-shape German hobby gardener. But it's not the heat alone that people who hate tropical weather complain about. It is the

---

6 33°C and 24°C.

extreme humidity—a humidity that saps your energy to the marrow, turns the air into gel, and makes you watch in horror as streams of life-giving salt water leave your body. Located just over 100 miles north of the equator, Kuching has an average humidity of 85 percent, with a few days a year even climbing above 100 percent.

Back home in Taiwan, the Tropic of Cancer divides the land into a subtropical north and a tropical south, which lies just inside the outer rim of the tropics proper. After 18 years on that island, I had thought I was ready for Borneo's climes. How foolish the notion! At the end of the 15 seconds it took me to carry my duffel bag from the terminal door to the taxi stand, Sir Hugh's "exceedingly healthy" climate had wrapped me up and steamed me like a dumpling. For once, I was grateful for the deplorable regional habit of cranking all air conditioners within reach to Polar Bear Enclosure. (Failing to bring a thick sweater and ski mittens to shopping malls and movie theaters in tropical Asia bears the risks of pneumonia and the loss of digits to frostbite.) My taxi driver, an elderly fellow of Chinese descent, had his infirm A/C on the customary arctic settings. I gyrated my mass into embarrassing positions, the better to benefit from the thin streamlets of exquisitely icy air coming from the dashboard, all the while making wanton noises of high satisfaction and looking like a water buffalo wallowing in a mud pit. Meanwhile, my back, out of coolness's reach, was super-glued with sweat to the plastic seat covers.

The brief ride to my hotel across town was uneventful, though as it was rush hour this quiet little burg surprised me with ferocious snarl-ups only thought possible in post-apocalyptic traffic war zones like Los Angeles. The streets were shaded by wide, blooming trees, and lined with red calla lilies and bushes bejeweled with small pink flowers. Armies of workers in leather aprons and Tuareg-style head wraps weed-whacked the roadside grass into submission. The roads were populated with the usual emerging-nation mix of Japanese 4×4 pickups, locally made compact cars, and antique trucks kept alive with dogged resolve since the days of the British Raj. Flocks of two-stroke mopeds, another Southeast Asian traffic staple, flowed amongst the larger vehicles. Now and again, a Ducati or Harley would lend an exotic highlight to the two-wheeled swarms, and by the end of the short drive we had also passed a Lamborghini Murciélago, two Ferraris, and a generous helping of German luxury cars. Kuching may be small, but it will routinely remind you of its position as Sarawak's political and economic power base.

I had booked accommodation at the Singgahsana Lodge, a boutique backpacker joint strategically located by Kuching's Waterfront. After checking in, I explored the city's sights, strolling through the picturesque streets, visiting museums, galleries, and antique shops, and pausing only every other hour for a quick espresso.

No, wait. That's not what happened.

What happened was that I went straight up to my room, shut the curtains, revved up the air conditioner until hoarfrost formed on the window, and then flopped onto the bed for a long nap. Ralph Waldo Emerson told us that "nature punishes any neglect of prudence," and it would have been an act of pure madness to expose myself once more to the outdoor sauna before the late afternoon brought temperatures down to a survivable level. And even then, I would only sneak out for a quick nosh next door before rushing back to my cool cave.

An hour later I awoke in the dark, shivering like a wet chihuahua, and guiltily aware of the impossibility of experiencing my beloved Borneo without leaving my hotel room. Surely other persons of size must have survived the climate before I arrived, I told myself with insincere bravery. Matter of fact, some of the locals in the streets had reminded me of "before" images in weight-loss ads, and those chaps looked perky enough despite the heat. Moreover, I was hungry, and since the hotel had no restaurant I steeled myself for the Great Schvitz Outside, put on my favorite sun cap—the one with the Royal Botanic Gardens at Kew logo – and eased myself back into the superheated air.

In less than a minute my clothes were pasted onto my skin, but by then I had stopped noticing—the magic of the Kuching Waterfront will do that to you. Running along the Sungai Sarawak where it sidles up to the city, this promenade oozes nostalgic charm and awakens in the visitor a melancholy for days long gone. Broadly crowned trees cool vacationers and locals strolling between the jetties and the flowerbed arrangements; snack and drink vendors hawk exotic treats. On the other side of the river looms a humongous wizard's hat that holds beneath its golden gleam the Sarawak State Legislative Assembly. Between the Waterfront and the Malay *kampungs* (villages) on the far bank, traditional wooden river taxis, *tambangs*, provide ferry services. The vessels are small, and passengers crouch beneath low, curved canopies. At the prow stands the barefooted boatman, a gnarled, sunburnt fossil like the craft he pilots, with two steering paddles and a frayed hemp rope that governs the outboard engine in the stern. From dawn to dusk he boldly defies heat and rain, his only defense a tattered straw hat. In jarring contrast to the medieval mood projected by this ancient mode of transport, the tambang roofs advertise root beer, life insurance, and Air Asia.

Now we turn away from the boats, the river, and the State Assembly, and rest our backs against the handrail that keeps us from falling into the muddy drink. Block your mind to the cars and motorbikes, and the smartphones in everyone's hands. Ready? Welcome to the 19th century. Main Bazaar, the street running along the Waterfront promenade, has not undergone any substantial alterations since the first White Rajah, James Brooke, colonized Sarawak in 1841. Chinese shophouses dominate the image, solid bastions against the tropical elements with their shady arcades and tall, louvered window shutters. Their narrow doorways lead into foyers funneling into passages crammed with artful disarrays of antiques, dried fruit, chainsaws, bush knives, cheap and expensive jewelry, garments of limitless colors, and pretty much everything else

Kuching Waterfront
(photo, Elliot Pelling)

you will ever need for your daily doings. Sidewalk vendors offer Sarawakian specialties like banana fritters made from truncheon-sized fruits, and limitless varieties of *kek lapis*—layer cake so sweet you can almost feel your fingertips tingle with diabetic shock as you sample it. A few card-table enterprises sell traditional marital aids. Men afflicted with the six-thirty syndrome, as the Chinese call that embarrassing condition when gravity claims one's manhood, can purchase organic picker-uppers fresh from the jungle. At *gambir Sarawak* stalls, tourists stock up on powdered tree bark said to fight premature happy endings. The most peculiar of these products, however, is meant for the sole pleasure of the fair sex. This timeless toy is called Eye of the Goat. Eric Hansen, the man who walked across Borneo and back and lived to write a book about it, described it for us in *Stranger in the Forest*:

> Mata kambing, literally the eye of the goat, is mainly used by the coastal Malays and Iban.[7] From a freshly killed goat you carefully cut out the eyelash and surrounding connective tissue. When detached, it forms a natural ring with upper and lower bristly eyelashes radiating outwards. You stretch this over a stick about the same circumference as your penis.

---

7 The Iban are one of the tribes of Sarawak.

Then let it dry. Directions for use: First soak the mata kambing in warm water until soft and pliable. Then slip it over the head of the penis. It should fit snugly without cutting off circulation. This goat eyelash tickler is also available commercially.

The humanity inhabiting this stage is just as timeless: Malay matrons in batik robes and headscarves; whippy *orang ulu* men from upriver rainforest tribes, swirly tattoos hugging their bodies; bushy-bearded Qur'an scholars, all serene smiles and flowing attire; Chinese shopkeepers, resplendent in white ribbed tank tops and horn-rimmed spectacles, lolling on rattan chairs; and you could swear that from the corner of your eye you just spied a Victorian naturalist in pith helmet, monocle and a lettuce-crisp linen suit turning the corner toward the Sarawak Museum.

Scents and sounds lend additional dimensions to the scene: there's chatting and yelling and laughing and bantering in a dozen languages. Somewhere in the maze of shoulder-wide alleys behind the shophouses a muezzin calls from the wooden Indian mosque, the sound billowing out into the main street like a drop of ink into water. A million aromas compete with the audio track at various levels of intensity: from overripe fruit and river sewage to an incomprehensible variety of herbs and spices—powdered, whole, dried, fresh, jellied. Your mucous membranes are infiltrated by eyewatering offerings of *belacan* (fermented shrimp paste), *ikan bilis* (tiny salted fish) and a bevy of other aquatic creatures preserved in ten thousand ingenious ways against the swift and relentless decay that befalls protein-rich tissues in the tropics.

It is a circus of the senses, the setting for a Somerset Maugham story. Only the charbroiled backpackers in hot pants and spaghetti tops, naïve in their immodesty, and the souvenir shops flogging skull motifs on t-shirts, mugs, and baby bibs (Sarawak—Land of Headhunters!), occasionally jerk you back into the 21st century.

If James Brooke came back for a visit today, he would feel right at home. The man's essence is hard to escape in Kuching's historic district. There is even a James Brooke Café, which seduces with a breezy river view and handmade chocolate tarts; its name salutes the Englishman whose story is fused into Sarawak's history unlike that of any other European.

* * * * * *

Had the tale of the White Rajah dynasty been conceived as a period novel, publishers would have laughed the manuscript out the door for its overwrought drama and impossible details. Elevator pitch: a British army veteran launches a royal dynasty that will reign for more than a century over a private kingdom almost as large as the soldier's homeland. This adventurer's exploits are of such swashbuckling caliber that Mr. Swashbuckler himself, Errol Flynn, will later pen a biopic script about the man's life and beg Hollywood producers to let him play the lead. It is an unlikely tale, yet too unlikely to be false.

James Brooke, born near Calcutta in April 1803, was the son of an English judge. James spent his childhood in India before, at age 12, as was customary in the days of the Empire, being sent to the motherland where he was to receive further education, which he soon cut short by running away from school. After enduring a brief period of home schooling, he returned to India as an ensign in the British East India Company's Bengal Army. During the First Anglo-Burmese War, he fought in Assam until 1825, when he was wounded and sent back to England for recovery. After unsuccessfully attempting to trade in the Far East, in 1833 he inherited £30,000 (the equivalent of around £3,600,000 or approximately US$4.4 million at the time of writing) and purchased a 142-ton schooner.

Royalist, armed with "6 six-pounders, a number of swivels, and small arms in abundance", was a private warship, and Brooke put it to good use. Setting sail for the East five years later, he arrived in Kuching on August 15, 1839. At the time, Sarawak was a loosely governed territory under the control of the Sultanate of Brunei. Brooke found the rulers facing an uprising by local tribes. After meeting and being impressed by Rajah Muda Hashim, a relative of the sultan sent to govern and restore order in Sarawak, Brooke agreed to assist in crushing the rebellion. This move earned him the gratitude of the sultan, who in 1841 handed him the governorship of Sarawak in return for his help. James Brooke recalled, "I was declared rajah [Malay for "king"] and governor of Sarawak amidst the roar of cannon, and a general display of flags and banners from the shore and river."

Thus began the era of the White Rajahs of the Kingdom of Sarawak. It was not part of the British Empire, and instead of adhering to the imperial White Man's Burden doctrine, the Brookes favored a style of government that scored them points with many natives. While the Dutch ruled southern Borneo with an iron fist, the Brookes expected comparatively little of their subjects and interfered less with local customs than it was usual in those days. One of the exceptions was headhunting, a widespread ritual mostly practiced by young men who presented heads to their love interests to prove themselves as marrying material. The heads were also thought to bring the strength of their former owners to the head-taker's longhouse and help protect it. The Brooke government outlawed headhunting, but would reinstate it temporarily during punitive military expeditions, for tactical reasons; while on the warpath, participating natives were allowed to decapitate their foes to their hearts' content. It was the ultimate incentive; no amount of money, goods, or status had such pull. Headhunting has not been practiced for a long time now, but longhouse dwellers still proudly show off the old trophies. I would later see many such heads in Borneo, some in museums, others suspended from longhouse veranda ceilings, where they leer at the living through smoke-blackened eye sockets.

Dried seafood shop

The Brooke dynasty ended in 1946 when Charles Vyner Brooke, the third White Rajah, ceded the state to the British, who ruled it as a crown colony until independence in 1963. According to Wikipedia, the

> period of Brooke rule is generally looked upon favourably in Sarawak, and in recent times the government has accepted the importance of their legacy for its social, cultural, and touristic value. The Brooke family still maintains strong ties to the state and its people and are represented by the Brooke Trust … at many state functions and supporting heritage projects.

*　*　*　*　*　*

The far end of the Waterfront was a food lover's fantasy. A long row of spice shops, sandbagged like machine-gun nests with large, open sacks of every imaginable curry ingredient, turned the air into a fragrance fiesta. Across the street by the riverside stood the foodie temple: the wet market. An uninitiated set of Western sensory organs will experience a traditional Southeast Asian wet market as a solid wall of unfamiliar smells, colors, and textures; descriptors like "fascinating," "wondersome," "bizarre," "revolting," and "WTF, dude?" may spring to mind. Long rows of tables almost founder under mountains of alien fruits and vegetables; one speculates whether they're even known to science, let alone have English names. The butcher corner features a delirium of snout-to-tail products that leave nothing to the imagination, right next to armies of chickens plucked, gutted, singed, chopped, and ready for the kitchen. The floors are slippery with blood and guts, and it gets worse in the seafood zone. But you will instantly forget about the stench and the skating-rink tiles, for the denizens from the deep decorating the tables in the fish section will command your full attention. Right next to those teacup-sized sea slugs trying to creep out of their bin is a pile of 5-foot blue drive belts. Eventually you realize that they are fish, but while you're still struggling with the fact that you probably won't find this species even in the best-stocked oceanariums, a petite grandmother approaches, starts pushing and prodding the fish, examines eyes and gills for freshness, and finally points at one and asks the proprietor to wrap it up. No matter how wacky this animal seems to you, it will now become part of a family dinner, expertly steamed with ginger, chilis, and cilantro. Crustaceans are out in force, from tiny, dried krill to mean-looking mantis shrimp you wouldn't want to meet in a dark alley (their claws pack a punch that shatters aquarium glass with the speed and power of a rifle bullet). Cephalopods, the pigs of the oceans—cuttlefish and octopi are as smart as they are tasty—are represented by dozens of species, some already dissected, others still alive in nets and hatching escape plans. Sea cucumbers, pooh-poohed by Sir Hugh Low as "a dirty looking animal, which forms one of the many strange articles of luxury of the Chinese nation," seashells, seaweed, sea urchins—if its name starts with "sea," it's probably for sale here.

The zoologist and anthropologist Charles Hose noted in his *Field Book of a Jungle-Wallah*, an account of his decades spent in Sarawak as a colonial administrator, that "in the East, the faculty of wonder soon dies from overwork—especially in matters of diet." This is as true now as it was in Hose's day. As I have noted elsewhere, in regard to food obsession, Asians "make the French look like a bunch of dyspeptic Spartans,"[8] and this market is proof. There is a man processing coconuts into coconut cream. An old lady is selling giant leaves for wrapping steamed rice. Next to her, *gula apong* is on offer: dark brown nipah palm sugar with a distinct smoky bouquet. One stall is run by a very large Tamil with a bashful smile and fists almost as big as the pastel lumps of ambrosial curry pastes he offers. Tell him the type and weight of the meat you plan to put in your stew ("for one kilo of lamb, please"), and with a small knife that almost disappears in his bulging paw he will delicately scrape small bits from the various blobs, knead them all into a rainbow-hued ball, and add a few sprigs of curry leaves. "One ringgit, boss!"

My walk had brought me to the end of the Waterfront promenade where the visitor is greeted with the incongruous sight of a white medieval castle which the tropical sun appears to have shrunk to playground size. This, the Square Tower, was built in 1879 to guard the river against marauders. Since then, the structure—still with the Brooke-era coat of arms on its façade—has served, among other things, as a prison, a

8 Hans Breuer, *A Cobra Hijacked My Camera Bag!—Snakes and Stories from Taiwan*; Coachwhip Press; ISBN 13-978-1-61646-129-4.

[Left] Curry paste
[Right] Old Courthouse, Kuching
(photo, Marcus Kloft)

dance hall, and an art center. I imagined jailers in armor and prisoners in windowless cells, all of them wilting in the merciless heat and humidity. Across the street sits the Old Courthouse complex, a showpiece of tropical Empire architecture with low-slung ironwood awnings held up by white columns lining polished hardwood walkways. This cluster of buildings was constructed in 1871 to house the Sarawak government. Today I found cafés, restaurants, and spaces for live music, conferences, reading, and general recreation.

It was in these storied halls the Nepenthes Summit was to be held. A few locals squatted in the shade, smoking clove cigarettes and offering friendly greetings to tourists. I smiled back and found my way to the main hall where the public part of the summit would take place. There would be competition-level plant displays from local and foreign nurseries; information booths by carnivorous plant societies, general nature clubs, and Sarawak's Forestry Department; and even an art exhibition with a pitcher plant theme. The door was locked, so I put my face right up to the glass and squinted hard for a glimpse of the treasures. Hard as I squinted, though, it was too dark inside to make out anything at all. Suddenly the door opened inward, and the three men who had been blocking the light smiled at me. I recognized one of them from internet photos. Raven-haired, with a rock climber's physique, and gifted with the unfair good looks of an Italian runway model, this could only be Chien Lee. I'm not good at meeting celebrities, and after I had nervously introduced myself to the trio as the face behind Twoton, my forum handle, I thought it a nice icebreaker to let Chien know how much I admired his work, and to thank him for organizing the summit. I knew he was from California, but his name suggested strong family ties to the Middle Kingdom. I took a deep breath and began, in Mandarin, to sing his praise and express my gratitude. Halfway through my speech I noticed that the other two men had now replaced their neutral smiles with expressions of high amusement. This gave me pause, and Chien grasped the opportunity to get a word in: "Uh, very sorry, man, I don't speak Chinese. But would you like to join us? We were just about to grab some lunch."

The offer helped to suppress the tall wave of embarrassment building up in me, and I recovered sufficiently to thank him for the invitation and apologize for the awkward moment. Chien was visibly entertained by the episode and explained that while his father had indeed emigrated to the U.S. from southern China, the family language had always been English. Inside the Courthouse complex was a Lebanese open-air restaurant, and they had decided to eat here. One of Chien's companions was Rob Cantley, an Englishman based in Sri Lanka, where he ran one of the world's largest commercial *Nepenthes* nurseries. The third fellow, another lanky Englishman, named Will Taylor, worked in Kuching as an artist and field guide illustrator, and shared Rob's acerbic strain of British humor. Lunch was a jolly affair, with the two Brits exchanging witty nuggets about topics ranging from Rob's membership in the Colombo Hash House Harriers ("We're a drinking club with a running problem") to the dangerous tropical disease Will had once contracted while cleaning a fish in the jungle ("I was quite surprised to learn that a fly hook can kill you"). Chien patiently answered all my questions about anything and everything that came to my overloaded mind—plant cultivation, photography, Borneo in general, and its botanical riches in particular. Lucky for me, he spent twice as much time on his lunch as the others. Not a minute after he had polished off his first lamb burger, a towering structure flanked by massive side dishes, another set arrived for him from the kitchen. As he demolished the second monster burger with undiminished appetite, I cautiously inquired if he wasn't worried about weight issues. "Oh, I am," Chien replied. "But not the way you might think. Between all those expeditions, climbing, surfing, and martial arts training, I have to watch out that I don't get too thin." Will Taylor would tell me later that Chien always brought an additional knapsack on excursions, filled to the brim with extra comestibles.

I was highly impressed. Matthew Jebb's comparing Chien to Alfred Russel Wallace now made perfect sense. This was no suburban greenhouse putterer; this was a field biologist of Explorers Club caliber who deliberately put himself through great hardships to discover, study, and document the world's most fascinating life forms, and still found time for hairy-chested sports between trips. In short, the perfect person to make you loathe your flabby desk-jockey existence, and for a split second I wondered whether I had taken a wrong turn somewhere along my life's path. But my bout of self-pity was cut short by the arrival of dessert, and one authoritative piece of coconut-flavored sticky-rice cake later, my world was back on its hinges.

* * * * * *

My phone shrieked at me at the crack of the next dawn. My wristwatch overrode my subjective sensations by insisting that it was already 8:50 a.m.

"Good morning, Hans—welcome to Borneo!" the caller warbled in a voice disgustingly cheery for this early hour. "We're on our way to pick you up; see you in ten minutes!" I fought hard to resist the pull of sleep's quicksand and pawed through my mental fog for a clue about today's appointment. No joy. I sensed upcoming panic and opened the curtains.

Even this early, the sun could only be described as striking rather than shining, but the onslaught of heat and light kickstarted my memory. Coming to welcome me were Georges Schneider and Robert Jong, two Kuching-based members of my favorite *Nepenthes* forum; we had arranged this date online a long time ago. They wanted to show me wild pitcher plants in the bush, and now they were almost here. With a Herculean effort, I managed to get ready and arrive at the curb before my hosts did.

Robert, born and bred in Kuching, is a hobby photographer with a special affinity for pitcher plants, and his talent has earned him a membership in Britain's Royal Photographic Society. Frenchman Georges Schneider had spent most of his life abroad and eventually settled in Kuching after a long career working for Shell Co. in Sarawak. This would be the first time for us to meet in person, and I was excited. Robert and Georges loved nature and were constantly crisscrossing the island in search of wild things and places. I scanned the traffic for my ride, eyes squeezed half-shut against the bright morning. I figured that Georges and Robert, both outdoors nuts, would most likely show up in a badass four-wheel drive tricked out with snorkel, winch and monster tires for the conquest of Borneo's boonies. My clichéd assumptions quietly imploded when a sleek Mercedes-Benz sedan pulled up, a tinted window purred down, and the same voice that had yanked me out of my dreams earlier invited me to hop in the back.

Georges and Robert were accompanied by Georges' Kuching-born wife Jacinta, and after introductions they informed me that we would stop for breakfast on the way. In Sarawak, the morning meal is easily the most sociable. During breakfast time on weekends and the many public holidays, every food court is packed to the rafters with families and groups of friends fueling up for their subsequent activities, be they jungle trekking, mountain biking, shopping, or just slowly digesting in front of the TV while waiting for lunch. Robert had selected a food court that served Sarawak *laksa*, the state's signature dish. Anthony Bourdain famously termed it "breakfast of the gods," and for Sarawakians, this deceptively unassuming dish of rice noodles in broth is the object of impassioned affection. Much like devotees of Po' Boys in New Orleans or *döner kebab* in Berlin, everyone has their favorite eatery and will defend its merits with the zealotry of a Latin American soccer fan.

Sarawak laksa—breakfast of the gods

Foreigners are not immune to the phenomenon. After the first spoonful, I knew Sarawak laksa was going to be among the three food items I would bring to a desert island. The ingredients are from Scheherazade's recipe collection, and their very names seduce the mind even before their essence stuns the palate into awed reverence: among the fundamentals are shallots, garlic, galangal, lemongrass, chilies, candlenuts, sesame, cumin, star anise, cloves, nutmeg, cardamom, and tamarind. Generous amounts of coconut milk are added to the brew, and the final soup is poured over rice vermicelli. You will also find shredded chicken, omelet strips, mung bean sprouts, and large prawns frolicking in your stew. Topped with sprigs of fresh coriander and served with a lime wedge and a side of spicy *sambal* sauce, this is, as Bourdain has it, "the kind of broth that makes the world seem a whole lot better than it really is."

But even the most sublime breakfast must come to an end, and after I had licked my bowl to a sparkle and my friends had gently but resolutely discouraged me from ordering two more, we were back on the road. Within minutes we were crossing the Sarawak River on the Datuk Patinggi Haji Abdul Rahman Bridge (Malaysians like to bestow long-winded titles onto their luminaries and then name public structures after them; many roads and bridges can be driven much faster than spelled). Life on and by the river was a tapestry of mellowness. A white pleasure boat edged by a gravel barge, and anglers in decrepit dories snored beneath their sombreros. Other fishermen sat cross-legged on the sidewalk by the bridge railing, trying to spot their bobbers far below in the brown flow. Their cars and mopeds, parked in the outer lane with cheerful impudence, slowed down the traffic, but nobody seemed to mind.

The bridge provided a satisfying view of Mount Serapi, part of the Matang Range rising from the plains west of Kuching. This chain of small mountains is home to Kubah National Park, one of the last places in southwestern Sarawak with largely unlogged primary rainforest. It was one of those Borneo summer days that assault one's concept of reality with hypervivid cloudlessness, as if some extraterrestrial cruiser had vacuumed every last moisture molecule from the troposphere to fuel its hydrogen drives. The only imperfection in the perfect blue sky was a large cumulonimbus formation hovering above the entire length of the mountain and eclipsing the nearly 3,000-foot summit. It took me a moment to realize that the mountain was generating its own weather. Rainforest humidity evaporates from the leaves in the hot morning sun then rises to form dense clouds, and in the afternoon it all comes back down again in a brief but fierce torrent. The developed land around the mountain had also once been primary rainforest; in fact, not so long ago, most of Borneo had been seamlessly swathed in trees that produced the massive rainfall so crucial for the ecological balance of the entire region. I knew about the impact of deforestation on local and regional weather patterns, but had never seen the reality for myself, and with such frightening clarity. Compared to the surrounding vastness, the mountain and its dark cloud were inconsequential. The flat area around Mt. Serapi was now dominated by cropland, villages, and housing developments. A few parts had eroded into sun-parched badlands where the owners had abandoned old oil palm plantations or never developed anything at all after removing the primary forest for timber.

In the wet tropics, the oppressive heat in cities, villages, and open spaces in general directly results from the loss of rain-producing trees. When you step outside your cabin in the early morning in Mulu National Park, one of largest remaining chunks of virgin rainforest in Sarawak, chances are that you'll consider putting on a light sweater. Mulu's large size means copious precipitation that keeps temperatures at a tolerable level even in the open areas around the park. In contrast, wherever sizable forest clearing has taken place, the sky now sucks the life from the land. Sun and rain are two giants locked in an eternal battle for control over their equatorial world. Victory for either of those would spell doom—rain would inundate the land unless the sun were to create evaporation, and sun without rain would turn the land into a desert.

In this battle, lack of rainforest favors the sun's chances, and now we were headed to an area where the sun had triumphed—the badlands bordering Mount Serapi's green glory. As we drove toward it, the houses grew smaller and the gardens bigger, and then we were beyond civilization on the Autobahn to Nowhere. This four-lane highway leads through sparsely developed outback for a few lazy miles, then abruptly terminates in the middle of a coastal swamp. Rumor has it that this road was once meant to serve a new airport that was later scrapped. Whatever its original objective, traffic on it today amounted to little more than the odd moped heading for a plantation, and a peloton of gaily spandexed bicyclists racing to lunch in Lundu, 40 miles of oil palms and bushland further west. I was told that the Kuching Super Car Club drag-raced their vehicles here on Saturday mornings, as this was the only road around Kuching smooth and safe enough for the 5-inch ground clearance of their Aventadors and Carreras. At the terminus of the highway, the old coastal road with its one-lane bridges (too little traffic to warrant the expense for two lanes) took over, and this was our destination.

The scrubland here called to mind an aborted terraforming attempt on Mars. Like angry lacerations, slashes of naked red earth starkly contrasted with the lush background of Mount Serapi's rainforest. Much of the forest cover here had long been cleared for oil palm plantations and small-scale farming. But as low soil fertility is a characteristic of the red laterite[9] typical of this area, many of these projects failed to yield crops and were abandoned. Rain and sun, the warring titans, took turns in battering the unprotected earth into an alien planetscape with erosional features so extreme that in some places they would deny passage to even a battle tank. Pockets of boggy woodland, holding their ground against the daily assault from the skies, were surrounded by a sea of tough shrubbery that had evolved to claw out a living in this impoverished kingdom. Stunted trees with leathery leaves pointing up to prevent sunburn, stood amidst extensive stands of tall bracken ferns and other heat-resistant plants. Blackwater creeks slowly meandered through the landscape. Their acidic water had been dyed by tannin-rich leaf litter to the color of a good single malt. The Iban call this depauperated ecosystem *kerangas*, which loosely translates as "land where no rice grows". Natural kerangas, also known as Sundaland heath forest, is endemic to Borneo, and occurs on acidic sandy soils with a severe lack of nutrients. Kerangas vegetation also takes over wherever human activity has exposed the laterite, and if the land is left alone long enough it will show many of the attributes of natural heath forest.

All carnivorous plants thrive on nitrogen-poor soils because they receive nitrogen from their prey. Pitcher plants with their ultralight, wind-dispersed seeds are always among the first colonizing wave, and they were the reason we were out here.

The late morning heat was now palpable even from within the air-conditioned sedan. Two blue-throated bee-eaters in pastel plumage sat on a power line grooming their harlequin costumes. A young, but already sizable water monitor lizard[10] swaggered across the road with that saurian pimp roll so typical of its kind. Far up in the sky a changeable hawk-eagle[11] cruised, like the Red Baron ever ready to attack out of the sun, blissfully ignorant of the silly name humans had given it.

Georges pulled the car over, and everyone piled out.

"Hans, step over the ditch here and check this out!" Robert commanded with pride in his voice. I didn't see anything worth checking out, unless one counted that great welding torch in the sky which now began to sauté my brain despite my fancy Tilley Endurables Airflo hat which I had specially purchased for this trip, and which was now proving utterly useless. I ignored the rivers of sweat already cascading down my body and crossed the ditch as instructed. Robert directed me into a cluster of ferns until

---

9 earth-like decayed rock, often rich in iron oxide and aluminum

10 *Varanus salvator*

11 *Nisaetus cirrhatus*

Blackwater creek

I stood face to trunk with a 12-foot tree concealed by a dense tangle of vines. I gave Robert a puzzled look—what exactly was I supposed to see here?

He smiled gently, in that kindly manner people usually reserve for slow children, and pointed at a spot right before my eyes. I looked again, and my knees almost buckled. A beige, trombone-shaped *Nepenthes* pitcher the size of a small bugle hung in my face. A fat ant in dignified silky gray[12] wandered around the rim, and a quick look inside the pitcher revealed scores of its fallen comrades rotting in their wet grave. My botanical expertise immediately identified the structure as the upper pitcher of a *Nepenthes rafflesiana*. But all theory is gray, as a famous compatriot said a long time ago, and none of my plenteous yet dry knowledge had prepared me for the thrills that were about to throw me a surprise party. A zoomed-out scan of the tree disclosed the entire mess of vines as *Nepenthes* plants. Great numbers of their enormous pitchers hung like baubles on a Christmas tree decorated by an over-enthusiastic child. The thick vines also held many nearby trees in bondage, and long-stemmed *Nepenthes* inflorescences, pink and purple bottlebrushes made from tiny flowers, projected from canopy and undergrowth.

I was wonderstruck. Years of obsessing about tropical pitcher plants; wall-to-wall bookshelves overflowing with pertinent materials; all my free time dedicated to the genus—and none of it had readied me for *Nepenthes* in their natural habitat. These creatures here before me were not timid little greenhouse plants, housebroken and well-mannered. These were timber wolves, tremendous brutes that took over the neighborhood with savage intention, strangling, smothering, entombing everything in their path, and digesting along the way every critter that fell for their tricks. Here in the wild, their existence was a constant struggle for survival and dominance over their unsparing surroundings. Compared to their meek, potted cousins in my greenhouse, these plants were overlords from another galaxy. An intense longing took hold of me for a second, a craving to share their home with them, to admire them at any time of my choosing. But I repressed it quickly; that was just crazy thinking.

I took a few photos of the pitcher-wrapped trees and rejoined my companions, now hunched beneath flowery parasols and busy with their cameras. They showed me a patch of red earth adorned with long strands of *Nepenthes gracilis* spread out on the ground. Purple pitchers resembling finger-sized Greek amphoras stood in the sand in the hundreds, reminding me of an aerial view of a busy town square. A flowerpecker bird with a crimson skull cap flick-flacked through a nearby bush dappled with white blossoms. The air oscillated with heat and insects, and in the harsh light even the vegetation seemed animated. My face was prickly with sweat, and my shirt had turned into a sopping washrag. How divine it would be to live here and experience all this any time I wanted! Silly thought, of course.

---

12 *Polyrhachis pruinosa*

Nepenthes gracilis, *aerial pitchers*

[Left] Nepenthes rafflesiana, *inflorescence*

[Right] Nepenthes rafflesiana, *aerial pitchers*

Nepenthes rafflesiana, *ground pitchers*

Back in the car, Georges announced they were now going to show me "something very special." I wondered what could possibly top what I had just seen. Georges nosed the Benz into a narrow array of deep ruts unworthy of the term "road," and after a few minutes of apprehension about the car's underbody and our lumbar regions we arrived at a small clump of trees. These surrounded a mossy clearing covered with pitchers squatting on the ground, mouths agape. Camouflaged in green and red speckles, and roughly the size of fragmentation grenades, they resembled small, militarized versions of Winnie-the-Pooh's honey jar. They were *Nepenthes ampullaria,* the flask-shaped pitcher plant, the only carnivorous plant known to science that has adopted a semi-vegetarian lifestyle. While the plant is still able to process insect prey, it has evolved to digest and metabolize plant matter as its chief food source. It grows in rosette-shaped colonies beneath trees and consumes leaf litter that falls into the pitchers whose vestigial lids are completely open. *N. ampullaria* is a common and widespread species, but the sheer square footage of this cammo-clad pitcher army was an incredible spectacle. The anemic versions I grew in my greenhouse weren't even worthy of comparison. The longing to move here, however unrealistic, had now become an irritating itch.

On the way back to Kuching we stopped at a bus shelter, but before I could worry what grave social misstep I had taken to anger my gracious hosts into throwing me out

Nepenthes ampullaria *var. Hot Lips*

and to the mercy of public transport, I saw a huge *Nepenthes mirabilis*, a species with long, light green pitchers, creeping up the shelter right behind the bench. The two senior citizens on the bench seemed alarmed by the four sweaty people piling out of a swank automobile to no other end than to take pictures of a weed as if it were some rare orchid.

When I lay in bed that night, listening to the sounds of the Waterfront, I found myself returning to that irrational thought. With every visit it lost a little of its irrationality while increasing in attraction. This was a place where exotic, insect-catching-and-eating pitcher plants grew at *bus stops*. "Heaven" was too insipid a word. And who said I couldn't live here? All quaintness aside, Kuching was by no means a desolate hicktown. They would have schools for our boys, and there was high-speed internet for me to run my business. I had seen shopping malls and hospitals and cinemas, and even a Toyota Prius. In theory, it was possible for us to live here. But was it *sane*?

⁂ ⁂ ⁂ ⁂ ⁂ ⁂

The densely packed impressions of my third day in-country afforded me no leisure to further contemplate the thought. I took a tambang to see Fort Margherita, a very small, very English stronghold hidden behind a copse of trees on the other side of the river. Brooke had built the fort in 1879 to protect Kuching from pirate attacks. I followed hand-painted signs through a kampung and eventually reached an open space framed with neatly parked police jeeps and anti-riot vehicles. I assumed this was the local law enforcement carpool, but the idea was quickly dismissed by the apparent maturity of some of the cars. One of the Land Rovers dated back to the 1950s, and most of the others had lived through the Vietnam conflict, if not the Korean War. I was starting to worry about the mobility of Kuching's cops, when I spotted a helpful sign informing me that I was standing in the outdoor section of the Sarawak Police Museum. The car collection used to greet the visitor inside Fort Margherita, but the fort had been repurposed and was now a general historical museum. I did not bother with the displays inside the fort. Instead, I went straight into the court and onto the fort wall, where I sought to relive Rajah Brooke's experience through his eyes, gazing down the river from the bulwark and scanning the horizon for black flags and war canoes. My anticipation was kneecapped by the same copse of tall, wide trees that had half-concealed the fort from the other side; over the last 140 years, they had also swallowed the view from up here. I refocused my attention on the little rampart watch-tower next to me. A sign hung on the door, a simple drawing of a smirking skull. The room behind it was too low and too narrow for me to stand in, but it held an item that brought the mid-19th century to life with stark immediacy and brutal effect. It was an iron cage, suspended from the ceiling by a rusty chain, and it contained, at eye level and arm's length, four human skulls, grinning at me as only skulls can. Nothing else existed in the room, no explanatory signs, plaques, or texts. Even the museum guard was clueless. "They've always been there. No one knows where they came from."[13] I have rarely seen a museum exhibit that conveyed the spirit of its era in such a vivid way. (There was another iron cage with real skulls in the fake longhouse at the Sarawak Museum, but the fake electric fire beneath it contaminated its authenticity.)

At dinner time, Michael, another pitcher plant fan from Kuching, picked me up at the hotel. We were going to dine at the Kuching Festival, an annual gourmet event at a downtown park where local restaurants showcase their signature dishes in hundreds of small tents. Along the way, we picked up some of Michael's friends, a group of German freshwater aquarium enthusiasts, and after almost wrecking the suspension in Michael's ancient car by severely overloading it with Teutonic flesh, we arrived at the fairgrounds just in time to secure the last few portions of grilled skate with sambal and lime, served on a banana leaf. Sarawak is a food paradise with local pockets of intense alcoholic culture, and I remember little of the evening. I do recall our table being full of Tiger Beer empties, and that I popped the entire filling of a large durian cream puff onto my shirt. There were also numerous trips to numerous tents where I had spotted yet another dish I just *had* to try. I also recall lying in bed that night, thinking I probably would not starve if I lived here.

ﹶ　ﹶ　ﹶ　ﹶ　ﹶ　ﹶ

Day Four kicked off the Nepenthes Summit in earnest, with the plant show at the Old Courthouse opening for the public. I maneuvered my corpulence through the throngs of smartly uniformed schoolkids and tourists in bush hats, marveled at the botanical wonders and inspiring art pieces, and felt as blissful as a pig in slop. The exhibitors had made every effort to impress. A few booths sold *Nepenthes*-themed carvings, pottery, and paintings. Live plants and botanical books were also on sale, and workshops introduced the fine art of growing *Nepenthes*.

The crowd was diverse. *Nepenthes* gardeners mingled with curious tourists, and scientists could be seen giving impromptu lectures about vegetative carnivory to gape-mouthed fourth graders. A reporter from a local Chinese-language radio station overheard me converse in Mandarin with somebody, and insisted I join her in the studio the next day at oh-six-hundred for tea and scones. Her sole reason for the invitation was that she had never heard a European speak her language, and she wanted to share the oddity with the whole town. (I accepted gracefully but overslept most ungracefully the next morning. Fair radio lady, if you read this, please find it in your heart to forgive me!)

Meanwhile, the conference got under way in the auditorium next door. Malaysians are serious fanciers of pomp and pageantry, and since the Nepenthes Summit was co-

---

13 I learned later that the skulls had probably been brought to the fort by Iban police during the Brookes' reign, to appease the spirits and bring harmony to the building, just as they would in a traditional Iban longhouse.

sponsored by various government bodies most of the morning program was filled with stiff formalities. From the official timetable:

09:00	Arrival of invited guests and members of media
09:30	Arrival of Head of Departments and local dignitaries
09:40	Arrival of Assistant Ministers and Ministers
10:00	Arrival of YAB the Chief Minister of Sarawak
10:00	Welcome address by Chairman of Organizing Committee, Mr. Chien Lee
10:10	Keynote address by YAB the Chief Minister of Sarawak
10:30	Official Opening of 2007 Sarawak Nepenthes Summit
10:40	Presentation of memento and proceedings to YAB
10:45	Tour of Pitcher Plant Exhibition
11:00	Tea break

Happily, Malaysians take their tea breaks just as seriously as they do their VIPs. I had expected a few bags of Lipton's drowning in a plastic dispenser. Instead, I found a buffet table of sufficient size for a Viking funeral, groaning under silver platters laden with enough kinds of pastries to satisfy Lucullus, plus huge bowls with rice (fried and steamed), noodles (fried and boiled), soups, and more curry dishes than you could shake a pestle at. Just the kind of hearty repast you need after being subjected to a load of stuffy speeches.

After rites and bacchanals, science finally took over. Taxonomists, field botanists, hobbyists, and commercial growers presented papers and gave talks on widely varying aspects of the genus *Nepenthes* to a sold-out room. We heard deliberations on Phylogeny and Biogeography of the Genus *Nepenthes*; enjoyed A Review of the Nutrient Sequestration Strategies of Some Bornean *Nepenthes*; were introduced to An Inventory of *Nepenthes* Species (Nepenthaceae) in Tangkahan Forest, Gunung Leuser National Park, Langkat Regency, North Sumatra, Indonesia; and listened to A Preliminary Conservation Assessment of *Nepenthes clipeata*, a Critically Endangered Species, in West Kalimantan, Indonesia.

Just as enthralling as the presentations were the conference attendees. The summit was history's first conference on the subject, and although the world of pitcher plant buffs is small, a significant number of us had found our way to Kuching. I kept bumping into titans of taxonomy and heroes of horticulture. There was Dr. Shigeo Kurata from Japan, one of the first research pioneers, whose 1976 book *Nepenthes of Mount Kinabalu* had inspired an entire generation of botanists. Among these botanists was his daughter, who had accompanied him to Kuching to act as his assistant and translator. Slight of build and soft of speech, Kurata-san was embarrassed by the attention lavished upon him by the many fans who asked for his autograph or just wanted to shake his hand. Another giant of the field was Dr. Charles Clarke, an Australian who had made a name for himself through numerous descriptions of new *Nepenthes* species and was fabled for his outback sense of humor. Sharing his findings from a recent expedition into Borneo's interior, he showed a photo of a gallery forest and asked the audience what they thought they were looking at. The predictable answers ranged from "trees" to "forest," but Dr. Clarke dismissed them all. "You're wrong," he replied sternly. "You're not looking at a forest. You're looking at a hundred million leeches disguised as a forest."

At half past one, a lunch break was announced for those whose locust genetics permitted still more food intake, even after the morning's Roman orgy. At 4 p.m., another opulent tea blowout was served; the organizers had evidently suffered visions of conventioneers succumbing to starvation. At 6 p.m. sharp, the conference ended. Just in time for dinner.

On the second day, I gave a talk, introducing A New Grex Registry for *Nepenthes* Breeders. To this day, I do not fully fathom what exactly I introduced then. A Hawaiian nurseryman had created the presentation but had ultimately been unable to attend the conference and had asked me to give the speech in his stead. I did not do a good job. I was intimidated by the famous people in the room. I talked too fast and in hushed monotones, while toweling the sweat off my tortured brow every few seconds, all of which gave a strong impression of social awkwardness. I also overran my half-hour time limit by almost ten minutes, but that at least prohibited the planned Q&A session which would have further betrayed my ignorance of the matter.

My shameful debacle was quickly forgotten when the chairman of the Japanese Carnivorous Plant Association took the stage and gave the most memorable performance of the entire conference, with a vocabulary of not more than five words. Mr. Naoki Tanabe was not only a raving pitcher plant nut but also a magician by trade, and a gifted comic. His presentation was skeletal: a string of photos showing plants grown by members of the JCPA. Tanabe-san had selected the subjects with true Japanese perfectionism, and the images were of heart-stopping beauty. The fact that Mr. Tanabe's English was virtually non-existent was of little consequence since he hadn't planned on talking a great deal anyway. Instead, he reacted to each image with a marvelous repertoire of ludicrous facial and bodily expressions, underscored with various orgasmic shouts, grunts, and squeaks. By the end of his 30 minutes, he had said little more than hello, thank you, and the occasional "*Byootifurru des ne!!,*" but the entire room was rolling in the aisles and howling with mirth.

✦ ✦ ✦ ✦ ✦ ✦

Early next morning, the summit participants met in front of the Grand Margherita Hotel, next to one of Kuching's many cat statues. Kuching means cat, and while nobody seems to remember how the city acquired the strange name, the town fathers make sure you won't forget it. There is a cat museum of dubious educational and aesthetic value, and on prominent display all over town are large plaster cats in various degrees of hideousness.

The ghastly concrete felines on the traffic island failed to dampen our high spirits, though, because today we would visit Bako National Park and see pitcher plants in the wild! The attendees were well-prepared for our excursion into Borneo's wilderness. Everyone was decked out in the latest outdoor gear and gadgets. Moisture-wicking and insect-repelling space-age fabrics, upscale safari headgear, and Gore-Tex footwear was the dress code throughout, and some of the lenses around the photographers' necks put the Hubble telescope to shame. We were still waiting for our tour leader, Chien Lee, and curious what sort of equipment he would bring to the trip. Sixteen years of exploring Borneo's rugged terrain surely had equipped him with substantial knowledge about survival gear, and we were eager to find out how a true rainforest wanderer would prepare for a day in the bush. Chien finally arrived in an olive U.S. Army t-shirt, running shorts, and plastic flip-flops. His only concession to contemporary outdoors technology was a pair of high-end Swarovski binoculars that, in his own words, had been with him "to hell and back many times over" and very much looked the part. I was almost ashamed of our collective hi-tech deification and caught myself scanning the surroundings for a homeless person to whom I could pass my pricey German hiking boots and that stupid Tilley Airflo hat.

But the street was hobo-free, and a good thing for me it was, because we were soon to learn that Bako National Park provides little shade, and that sturdy shoes are strongly recommended, at least for the average milquetoast tourist. The park covers an entire peninsula and is only accessible by boat. A fleet of sleek and speedy skiffs transport visitors and supplies. The boats depart from Kampung Bako, a tiny fishing village a few miles down the coast from the park headquarters. The ride can be wet, but it is one of the highlights of a visit to Bako. The boats hug the coast and allow marvelous views of mangrove forests and bizarrely eroded sandstone bluffs sweeping up to a mesa-like plateau that covers almost the entire park area. As the tide was too low to disembark at the park jetty, the boatman unloaded us on the beach near the headquarters and we waded ashore through the surf.

Mangrove forest frames the beach on one side, while the other side is walled in by striated cliffs. More cliffs, bearded with vegetation, provide the backdrop. As we put our socks and shoes back on, we were treated to the spectacle of a white-bellied sea eagle[14] swooping into the surf. It came up with a decent-sized fish in its talons and glided toward the forest with the arrogant ease of an Imperial Star Destroyer. After a short briefing

---

14 *Haliaeetus leucogaster*

One of Kuching's many cat statues
(photo, Christoph Lepschy)

Jetty, Kampong Bako
(photo, Kevin Caldwell)

[Left] Sandstone cliffs, Bako

[Right] Water monitor lizard

Mangrove boardwalk, Bako

at Park HQ, we set out for the tableland, which is famous for its pitcher plants. From a boardwalk through the mangroves, we observed thousands of male scarlet fiddler crabs waving their grotesquely oversized right claws to attract crabettes. Smaller crabs in bright baby blue—a color oddly in conflict with their gray mud world—scampered between the lovelorn fiddlers, dodging mudskippers with iridescent bodies and grumpy faces. These amphibious fish are fully terrestrial for a portion of their daily cycle, and use their pectoral and pelvic fins to walk on land. The American nature philosopher Loren Eiseley observed:

> The world is fixed, we say: fish in the sea, birds in the air. But in the mangrove swamps … fish climb trees and ogle uneasy naturalists who try unsuccessfully to chase them back to the water. There are still things coming ashore.[15]

15 *The Immense Journey, 1959*

And what things they were. I was only familiar with the finger-sized species common in Taiwan, but the giant mudskippers[16] here were nearly a foot long and looked plenty capable of making life miserable for any cat, snake, or egret out for a meal. Before we entered the forest to start the ascent to the mesa, we watched a young water monitor lizard cross a channel in the mudflats. As the reptile entered the rivulet, it folded its legs back against its body, assuming the shape of a snake, and propelled itself across the water with serpentine tail undulations that had an almost hypnotic effect.

Soon we reached the relative coolness of the forest. I say "relative" because Bako is infamous for its infernal temperatures. The sandstone stores heat like a gigantic brick, the ocean reflects the sunlight toward the shore, and most trees are shorter and thinner than in proper rainforests, allowing more sunlight to enter. The trails did not help with the comfort level. There were often so many roots crisscrossing the path that they became the path. On some stretches we walked on nothing but roots, never touching the soil. Much of the hike took us over steep segments where rough ladders bridged impassable parts. On other sections of the trail, we monkeyed over, under, and between mossy boulders. Balance was maintained by holding on to yet more roots, fantastic tentacles that looked at us with great disdain from wrinkly wooden eyes. Gravity counts double in tropical climes, and at times I was swearing even more profusely than I was sweating. But the natural sensations along the way soon made me forget all the hardships (or what I perceived as hardships—my Victorian heroes certainly did not have air-conditioned buses waiting to take them to their air-conditioned hotels at the end of the day). Chien Lee introduced us to many phenomena typical of Bornean forests. Here, the rattan vines I only knew as garden furniture were covered in 2-inch barbs. The barbs at the tapered ends of the vines were so small they were almost invisible, and they spent their days lazily angling hats off people's heads and tearing holes in their high-tech shirts. We encountered a termite procession marching in four neat lines, each insect carrying a piece of lichen. The soldiers of this species[17] do not possess pincers, but instead use nozzles on their foreheads to spray noxious chemicals at enemies. The column contained so many individuals that by the time they had all paraded by it would probably be close to our dinner time.

Another insectoid highlight was the stingless bees which, as the name indicates, lack the classic weapon other bee species pack. They nest in hollow trees and construct wax tubes that stick out from the entrances as platforms to head off predators before they can enter the nest. The tubes range in shape from long, pencil-thin straws to designs akin to fishtail exhaust pipes on custom Harleys. Stingless bees are also known as sweat bees, by dint of their penchant for the mineral-rich liquid that the sizzling air

---

16 *Periophtalmodon schlosseri*

17 *Hospitalitermes sp.*

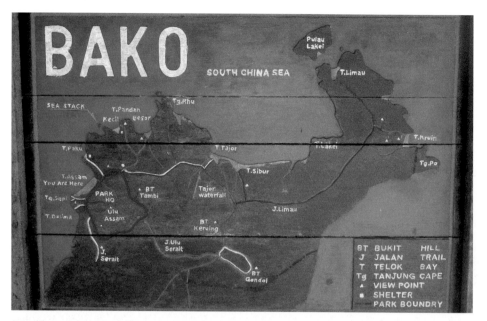

Wooden park map, Bako

extracted from us by the gallon. Their fondness for salty drinks sometimes leads them into places where no animal should ever go. After sneezing out a particularly adventurous band of bees from my sinus cavities, I was ready to move on to less irritating things of interest.

On the plateau we found a world quite different from the forest. In fact, it is a world quite different from any other place outside Borneo. The entire area is natural kerangas, original Borneo heath forest. Similarities with the badlands around Mount Serapi were immediately obvious. The same stunted vegetation eked out a living on hard-baked, leached sandstone. Bako is Sarawak's oldest national park and has been under protection since 1957, so the usual signs of human interference—the logging roads, the backhoes, the scream of the chainsaw—were happily absent.

Most of the scrawny trees were festooned with epiphytic ant plants of the genus *Myrmecodia*. An ant plant looks like a warty, dried-up elephant testicle with a few large leaves sprouting from a short stem, yet despite their ugliness, ant plants count among the world's great botanical marvels. They live in mutualism with colonies of ants that reside inside the plants' bulbous main parts. The bulb is, in effect, a prefab home with a complex system of chambers and tunnels; some rooms are created as nurseries, others for disposal of waste and dead bodies. To collect rent, the walls of the storage rooms absorb the nutrients from the excreta and the cadavers. The tunnels interconnect the chambers and provide passage to the outside. The ants are

Plateau Trail, Bako

fiercely protective of their digs; a gentle knock on one of the bulbs will bring them out in brigade strength, ready to whup anyone who disturbs their peace.

Along the trail were many puddles, remainders of the daily deluge. The air above them was abuzz with neon-red flashes, each half an inch long, darting hither and thither on barely visible wings. These were scarlet dwarves,[18] the world's smallest dragonflies. They shared their main food source, minuscule airborne insects, with the carmine sundews[19] that surrounded the puddles in the hope of luring some of those insects onto their glue drops.

Still, all these natural miracles paled in comparison with the plateau's main attraction—the pitcher plants. They were sensational, and they were everywhere. An elevated boardwalk took us across an expanse of low bushes and short trees choked with *Nepenthes*. The trees I had seen in the badlands, struggling against massive carnivorous vines like Laocoön and his sons trying to fight off the snakes, were mirrored a thousandfold up here. Everyone brought out the cameras. People shouted to each other about the pitchers they were finding, and the mighty heat and the lack of shade were all but forgotten. "This could be heaven or this could be hell," the Eagles sang … we decided it was heaven.

After filling our hearts and minds and memory cards with all sorts of unforgettable impressions, we moved on toward the forest edge where Chien showed us a few *Nepenthes hirsuta*, a woodland species known for the hairs growing on almost every part of the plant. When it was my turn to stoop over the little things and stand in awe of their hirsuteness, a 6-foot palm frond crashed down on my head. It had broken off its tree quite a while before and come to rest horizontally in another tree right beneath. Over time, plant matter and other bio-debris from above had collected and decayed on the frond, and just as I had stuck my noggin underneath it to examine the pitcher plant, the accumulated weight finally sent the frond down and buried me in a cloud of mold, dust, and monkey dung. My diary would later read:

> The sensation is like a sack full of sawdust and garden clippings opening right above you and emptying its contents all over your sweaty body. It feels like you'll never get rid of the stuff again, even with an infinite number of showers.

In other words, I looked like a wet clay golem caught in a woodchipper explosion, an assessment reflected in my fellow hikers' expressions of shock, pity, and feebly contained hilarity. But everyone quickly regained control of their emotions, and the Indonesian group members were particularly sweet about it. Apparently fearing I would grab a

---

18 *Nannophya pygmaea*

19 *Drosera spatulata* var. *bakoensis*

Ant plant (Myrmecodia *sp.*)
(photo, Kevin Caldwell)

Sundew (Drosera spatulata var. bakoensis)

parang machete[20] and go medieval on the surrounding—protected!—flora, one of the older Indonesian ladies rushed over to me and proclaimed with a disarming, motherly smile, "How wonderful! This is a sign of good luck! It means the forest is welcoming you!" Friend of the Forest became my nickname for the rest of the trip.

By lunch time we were back at sea level where another titanic buffet awaited us. As we filed into the dining cabin, someone caught sight of a fat Bornean keeled pit viper[21] 15 feet above us in a tree next to the building. It was resting on a shady branch, and only visible from the ground if you knew exactly where to look. It took a while and much squinting before everyone had located it ("Straight up there, see that fork? That green, rolled-up sausage on it, that's the snake. See it now? NO, not that fork, Hans!

---

20 Parangs are usually hand-forged from recycled truck leaf springs or chainsaw blades and serve as multi-purpose tools. Apart from clearing jungle trails, they are useful for building impromptu shelters and for opening durians and coconuts. They are great for camp food preparation; and, if that's your thing, they're also perfect for lopping off human heads.

21 *Tropidolaemus subannulatus*

Bornean keeled pit vipers mating (the small green one is the male)

OVER HERE, RIGHT ABOVE ME!") I had never seen a venomous snake in the wild and reacted with corresponding stupidity. Fear and adrenaline, spiked with a dollop of hysteria, flushed my system as for the first time in my life I faced an animal that could possibly end me in one single bite. All rational thoughts were on lockdown, reason was denied access. Manacled to the wall deep in my cranial dungeons, my remaining common sense tried to signal me that a snake shorter than a man's forearm has no interest in preying on a human hundreds of times its size. Reason tried to shoulder its way through my doors of perception, yelling, "Even in the highly unlikely event that the snake falls down, it will immediately race for shelter rather than unsheathe its fangs and kill everyone in sight!" It was also hollering something about the considerable distance between me and the beast, and my ability to outrun it even at my level of physical unfitness.

Meanwhile, the viper had not moved a muscle, and there was no evidence that it would do so anytime soon. In its jungle, I was just another asshole, as Christopher Walken would have explained it. Nonetheless, I chose to ignore it all. The exquisite horror of staring the Grim Reaper in the face—uninterested as Mr. Reaper appeared to be in coming to get us—was a grand emotion too delicious to extinguish with cold logic.

The others in the group were showing a broad range of reactions. The drama queens and kings stayed as far away from the snake as they could while still keeping it in sight, fanning themselves and twittering nervously. On the other end of the spectrum were the hardened jungle veterans who had seen, ignored, and stepped over more vipers than they could remember. They knew the sluggish serpent did not present any danger, and they were getting bored and hungry. "Guys, if you really need to photograph it, no worries. It'll still there when we've finished lunch. Let's eat already!"

But snakes, notably the venomous types, exercise a powerful fascination on humans. The one thing snake lovers and snake haters can agree on is this very allure. The admirers love the sinuous, elegant movements, the colors, and the patterns, while for the haters it is the trance-inducing effect of a train wreck in slow motion. I was caught somewhere in between. As a nature lover I realized my privilege of witnessing a rarely seen creature in its natural habitat. The ignoramus in me was soaking up the sensationalist drama that the term "venomous snake" usually conjures up for the uneducated. After marinating in sweet doomsday thoughts for a while longer, I finally entered the dining room with heavenly goosebumps on my arms, internally celebrating my new lease of life. After all, hadn't I barely dodged almost certain annihilation just now?

Little did I know that less than four months later I would develop an infatuation with snakes that surpassed my pitcher plant obsession by several orders of magnitude. I had no inkling that in the years ahead my herpetological knowledge would surge from "illiterate" to "snake nerd." My future self would become a fire-and-brimstone

Class photo after a successful snake talk

protector of this much-maligned family of animals, spend every free night searching for and photographing snakes, create a bilingual information website about them, and introduce the world of serpents to thousands of schoolchildren. And finally, I would write a book about it all.

But I'm getting ahead of the story.

* * * * * *

Shortly after sunrise the following day, we were on the road again. Our first stop was the old goldmining district of Bau where 800-foot limestone hills, draped in jungle up to the summit, jut from the plains like mossy dragon teeth. The green on their sheer sides is disrupted by chalky cliff faces running skyward at abrupt angles. A dense network of caves perforates the hills, and we stopped at the Fairy Cave, where five flights of stairs take the visitor up into the main chamber. The cave can comfortably accommodate a medium high-rise, while its vast mouth provides a commanding view over the surrounding land.

But spelunking was not on our agenda today. We parked next to the cave, opposite an immense limestone wall where a few climbers, basted with sweat, chalk, and lime dust, were trying to conquer the routes bolted into the white rock. Chien directed our attention toward a tufa formation extending from an overhang like a giant stone teat. I could make out dense vegetation but no details, so I borrowed a pair of binoculars from one of the better-prepared group members. The entire teat was overgrown with large specimens of *Nepenthes northiana*. This is a showy, colorful species with hefty pitchers, and mainly known from a few hills in the Bau area. Specimens from the wild were in great demand in enthusiast circles, not just for their beauty and endemism but also because their affinity for limestone impedes production of sufficient supply in cultivation. The only reason why this vertical field of big, healthy plants on the tufa teat and further up on the rock face had never been picked over by poachers was its inaccessibility. From the ground below, the plants were only reachable by jetpack; on the wall above them the dense jungle prohibited access by rappelling. These beauties had been enjoying a safe environment since the first seed had landed on the mountainside eons ago.

A few miles on, we trooped after Chien into the sweltering roadside bush. After much scrambling and swearing we stood before two impressive *northianas*. Their large, pinkish pitchers wore star-shaped collars with red and yellow sunburst patterns and stood out from the gray limestone like Andromedan Easter eggs. The plants grew on the ground and were perfectly accessible for admiration and photography. They were also perfectly accessible for poachers: all that remained of a third plant was one leaf and a dried pitcher. Footprints and the state of the remaining vegetation suggested the plant might have been ripped out as late as this morning. It was fortunate for posterity that so many of us took digital memories home, for three days later the two remaining *northiana* would also fall victim to extralegal harvesting (Malaysian law lists all *Nepenthes* species as Protected, some even as Totally Protected). Only trampled leaves and two holes in the ground hinted darkly at the glory that had once graced the site.

Next came a foray into a pathless patch of peat swamp forest. We were solidly brined in sweat but had long since stopped complaining. Chien picked an insect from his calf and put it on his arm for our perusal. "This is *Camponotus gigas*,[22] the giant forest ant, one of the biggest ants in existence. Very common, though." Long, slow seconds passed before my brain finally accepted that the beast before me was not a plastic novelty item for freaking out bug haters, but an actual, living ant. Giant forest ants (they're about an inch long, and mischievous children will tell you they're called eleph-ants, or gi-ants) are active day and night in every forest on Borneo, virgin or disturbed. In later years I would have many opportunities to point out these ants to first-time visitors, and the chain of reactions was always the same. First came incredulity ("This must be a prank, there are no beetle-sized ants in this world!"), followed by percolating comprehension ("Holy schlamoly, this IS an ant! No, no, no, wait. But it … it IS! My word, what a HUGE ANT!"). Finally, after surprise and confusion had worn off, raw fear ("Do they bite? Actually, I don't want to know. Let's keep walking, shall we?")

We arrived at the spot Chien had scouted out for us. Here, plants resembling enormous pineapple tops dominated the scene. Sword-blade leaves rose from the ground and bent down again 3 feet away under the weight of pitchers fat and red as ripe mangoes. One group member tried to photograph the interior of a pitcher with his cell phone, but the device slipped from his hand and sank into the slimy deep (We strained to maintain expressions of deep sorrow and sympathy, while unhinged glee tore our insides asunder.) The traps sat on the ground like misplaced drawstring pouches. A pair of long, curved barbs poked down from each pitcher lid, giving the appearance of a viper's maw poised to strike. This was *Nepenthes bicalcarata*, the fanged pitcher plant. When my Taiwanese friend had gifted me the *bicalcarata* cutting from his collection, I was dazzled by the proportions of the mother plant. But the plants here in the clearing were twice as big.

Chien pointed at the tendril connecting the pitcher with the end of the lancet leaf. Near the base of the pitcher was a swollen section. "Inside this thick part, that's where the ants live," he explained. Insects living inside insect-eating plants may sound like nonsense, but it is much more common than you might imagine. Many carnivorous plants live in symbiosis with a wide range of animals. Most *Nepenthes* infauna, as it is termed, is small. Spiders, crabs, flies, and midges make up the bulk. However, some bats also roost in the traps, and *Nepenthes hemsleyana* has even modified its pitchers

---

22 Later renamed *Dinomyrmex gigas*, Giant Terror Ant. In my opinion a much cooler name.

*Fanged pitcher plant (*Nepenthes bicalcarata*)*

to attract the flying mammals; a sound-reflecting structure at the rear of the inside wall mimics the surface of a cave wall and via the bats' echolocation advertises the pitcher as a suitable family home.

The fanged pitcher plants in this peat swamp accommodated ants. *Nepenthes bicalcarata* is not as efficient a hunter as other *Nepenthes* species; its pitchers lack the slippery walls, and its digestive trap fluid is much less effective. The plant resolves these shortcomings by housing colonies of the ant *Camponotus schmitzi* in the inflated tendril segment. Not only do the ants not perish in the digestive fluid, but they also find nourishment in it by scavenging less fortunate insects. They take only prey too large for the plant to digest, making sure the remains will not rot in the pitcher. The plant provides further sustenance in the form of nectar secreted on the pitcher rims. The ants repay the kindnesses: they attack pests, clean the pitcher rim to keep it nice and slick, and leave fecal matter as fertilizer.

Like every good *Nepenthes* geek, I knew about these symbioses. For me, they were the most fascinating aspect of a plant genus rich in fascinating aspects. As I could not recreate these collaborations in my greenhouse, they had been at the top of my to-see list for this trip. Now that I had seen one example I wanted to see more, and not just on short vacation trips.

✻　✻　✻　✻　✻　✻

Back at the hotel, I inquired with the receptionist about evening entertainment and was told, "Right here, mate, in the Sadau, our rooftop bar. Best drinking experience in town!" By the time I crashed into bed in the wee hours, I heartily agreed with that assessment. I didn't know what competing establishments might hold in store, but I was already convinced that none of them could possibly offer the full-on Bornean atmosphere I had experienced at the Sadau. That atmosphere started outside the bar, where a large sign asked you to take off your shoes before entering (although the mounds of footwear to both sides of the doormat rendered the sign rather gratuitous). The bar room was kept in traditional materials; wall-to-wall bamboo mats, palm-thatched low ceilings, strategically placed jungle plants, and low-hanging basket lamps made from rattan fish traps created a "longhouse away from the longhouse" ambience. They also diverted the attention from the Western pub fixtures of eight-ball table, foosball machine, and well-abused dartboard. The place was already pulsing with people, the bar beleaguered two rows deep. The Iban bartender, a strapping young lad, was currently distracted by a gaggle of inelegantly wasted Danish females hell-bent on seducing him ("Show us your crotch tats, baby!"). I secured a frosty can of Tiger Beer by wildly gesticulating at the bartender from the center of the room, and then retreated to a far corner of the bar to take stock of the patrons.

Tourists and locals alike sported abundant body art, Burning Man Nation meeting Rainforest Vintage. Tattooing has been an important part of Borneo's tribal life since time immemorial. The influence of Christian missionary work led to a sharp decline in the tradition during the 1950s, but in recent decades tattooing has enjoyed a strong revival. Tattoo shops abound, and even staid Chinese businessmen rock koi carps on their calves or headhunter whorls on the trapezius. Many ancient practices are alive again, and available even to outsiders. After signing a stack of waivers and disclaimers absolving all involved parties from any culpability attached to possible health mishaps such as food poisoning by live sago worms, drowning in whitewater rapids, and heart attacks induced by torturesome preindustrial skin art techniques, tourists with suitably-sized wallets can arrange for a lengthy trip into the *ulu* (remote upriver areas in Sarawak) via speedboat, longboat, then 4×4 Camel Trophy tracks, and lastly a sweaty trek to the target longhouse. There the client will be subjected to body embellishment customs unaltered for centuries. These often involve an artistic arrangement of nails protruding from a wooden board. The nails are dipped in black ink and pounded into the skin with a mallet. The excruciating pain will forever be, well, hammered into the tattooee's memory, and is just as indelible a part of the authentic experience as the design itself.

As I slowly sipped my sweating Tiger, an art competition unfolded by the pool table. A soused Liverpudlian hipster in Buddy Holly glasses had torn off shirt and pants to compare, amidst much noisy self-advertising, his collection of tattoos with those on the upper body of an equally drunk local kid. The local contender considered lowering his own britches for additional effect, but the rambunctious crowd had already picked him as their champion when he ditched his shirt, and his full-body jungle art brought the room to a brief but intense silence punctuated only by an occasional small gasp.

I spied a potted *Nepenthes* with orange pitchers sitting on the bar a few beermats down, in front of a middle-aged gentleman who was scrutinizing it closely. He had a blast of blond hair and a faintly tweedy look about him, as though he would favor an elbow-patched shooting jacket and knickerbockers over t-shirt and shorts any old day, even in equatorial proximity. I tried to identify the plant from a distance, and soon became aware that this attractive specimen—pitchers, tendrils, pot and all—was a plastic model.

This called for investigation, and I walked over and introduced myself. "Hello there! I'm Hans. You here for the Nepenthes Summit?"

He nodded and peered at me kindly through his wire-rimmed bifocals. "Nice to meet you, Hans. I'm Matthew."

"That's a good-looking little plant," I observed. "What do you reckon it's supposed to be?" At close range, the creature didn't even remotely pass for any pitcher plant I knew, and without waiting for Matthew's answer I voiced my suspicions: "I have over 350 *Nepenthes* in my greenhouse, but this thing looks nothing like any of them." Might as well ladle it on thick, I thought, let my fellow conference attendees know they weren't dealing with a greenhorn.

Matthew straightened on his barstool, picked up the plastic pot with its plastic inhabitant, and pronounced with an air of staged solemnity, "Without a shadow of a doubt, this is a species new to science, and will be described shortly by Jebb and Cheek."

I breathed in sharply, rerouting into my windpipe the beer I had just tried to swallow. After a brief but violent interlude of throat spasms that caused the brew to resurface through my nostrils, I recovered enough to apologize for the drama, and, more importantly, for not recognizing the man earlier. For here, in the very flesh, sat the estimable Matthew Hilary Peter Jebb, Ph.D., eminent botanist and taxonomist, Director of the National Botanic Gardens of Ireland—and, together with Martin Cheek, descriptor of half a greenhouse worth of *Nepenthes* species. Not really the person to brag to about a bunch of potted plants on your garage roof.

Matthew showed Old World class by ignoring my cloddish entrance and guiding the topic to firmer ground. We chatted about the summit and the exciting outings for a while, but when an equatorial downpour began to jackhammer the corrugated iron roof, drowning out any chance of civilized conversation, the good doctor made an early exit.

To my other side, a middle-aged gent with a sage-green uniform and sad eyes was staring a hole in the mirror across the bar. A name tag identified him as a Sarawak

Forestry employee. He was intently working on a small river of scotch, and he did so with knit brows and a grim sense of purpose. *Why would a government operator in full company regalia engage in solo bingeing in a public bar?* I mused, and decided to say hello.

This turned out to be a literally sobering decision. The man—let's call him Mr. B.—had already reached that depressive stage some people enter once there's more air than whisky in the bottle, and now he freely shared his grievances. He had grown up in Sarawak's forests and was passionate about the island's natural treasures. A career as steward of these treasures seemed logical, so Mr. B. had joined the Forestry Department. Now his 20th anniversary with the organization was coming up, and he looked back with bitter disillusion. He complained about rampant corruption and illegal logging, and fumed that the handful of the department's frontline officers stationed in Sarawak's remote hinterland that stretches along 1,200 miles of virtually unguardable border with Indonesia were as insignificant as "ticks on a dragon."

"My main job is to visit logging camps and see to it that they don't fell more trees than their assigned quota," he said. "These concessions are legal, but their methods are anything but. A few days before I arrive at a logging camp, the manager will meet me in a nearby town to give me a pre-inspection report over dinner. Between dessert and coffee, he'll put a thick envelope on the table and tell me, 'We've prepared this for you. The more issues your inspection turns up, the thinner this will become.' The envelope contains more money than I make in a year. For the logging companies, that's just chump change, they are rich beyond imagination—seen all those Ferraris here in Kuching? I have two daughters, and of course I want them to get the best education I can afford. So, what do I do? Nothing. I will not be a traitor to the environment. I push the envelope back across the table and say thank you but no thank you, while I silently boil with rage, knowing that many of my colleagues will pounce on the opportunity and in return close their eyes to tree harvesting at a rate that is far beyond unsustainable. It's a tragedy, plain and simple. You know, you can replant a tree, but you can't replant a rainforest."

I blinked in self-protective disbelief. I had read much about the mindless overharvesting of the rainforests, but this was the first time I'd met someone personally involved on the front line. While the removal of rainforest anywhere in the world is a calamity, the situation was especially dire in Sarawak. Borneo's rainforest had existed as long as 140 million years ago, and here on the north coast the Pleistocene ice ages had been of little impact. The climate had therefore been relatively stable for at least 23 million years, with wet rainforest refugia from climate change effects existing for 40 million years. The result is an unchanging environment where constant high humidity and high temperatures plus a relative absence of earthquakes provide nearly unlimited evolutionary possibilities.

Poor soils and lack of sunshine beneath the dense canopy created intense competition which in turn led to bountiful speciation, and all these factors produce a richness of biodiversity almost unparalleled on Earth. Incredibly, on just 6 percent of the globe's surface, rainforests contain at least 50 (some estimate 90) percent of all animal and plant species. In 2006, *The Times* of London reported that an average of three new species of animals and/or plants had been discovered in Borneo every month of the preceding decade—and this in a part of the world where forests had been reduced by 25 percent since the mid-1980s. Lambir Hills, a small national park in northern Sarawak, is blessed with 1,200 tree species on a 53-hectare research plot— that's less than 0.2 square miles. (For scale, fewer than 1,000 kinds of trees are found on the entire North American continent.) The impact of rainforests on global well-being is just as astonishing: they affect local weather conditions by creating rainfall and moderating temperatures; they stabilize the world's climate by absorbing carbon dioxide from the atmosphere; and they are a major part of Earth's oxygen factory, responsible for 90 percent of all land-based photosynthesis on the planet.

Borneo is one of the most imperiled ecosystems on Earth. In the early 1900s it was still under dense tree cover from coast to coast, including vast expanses of rainforest. The advent of the chainsaw and the bulldozer rapidly altered the landscape. *The Economist* wrote in 2012 that Sarawak had lost more than 90 percent of its primary forests to logging and has the fastest rate of deforestation in Asia. Only 0.5 percent of the world's tropical forest are found in Sarawak, but in 2010 the state exported 25 percent of the world's tropical logs. And at the time of this writing, Sarawak still has the world's highest rate of tropical forest loss, according to data from Global Forest Watch.

Mr. B. ordered another double and added, "And that's only the legal operations. The illegal ones, we don't even know where most of them are."

For a brief moment I was sorely tempted to join him in his quest for boozy oblivion, but then felt too sick. I thought of a passage Alfred Russel Wallace had written in 1869 about the Bau district half an hour from Kuching: "For hundreds of miles in every direction a magnificent forest extended over plain and mountain, rock and morass."[23] There is something immeasurably sad about realizing something precious and unique is irretrievably gone, sadder even if the causes for its extinction are avarice, shortsightedness, and stupidity. I bought Mr. B. another drink, thanked him for his confession, and went to bed in a homicidal funk—happily unaware that in the future I would frequently bear personal witness to the eco-horrors blighting the island.

Mr. B.'s story had shocked me back into reality—the kind of reality I'd been afraid to face all along, and the reason why for so many years I had longed for and dreaded a visit to Borneo in equal measure. And yet it did not extinguish my wish to move to the island. If anything, that wish kept preying on my mind with increasing intensity. The ants in the *bicalcarata* had been the final straw. They had made me realize with

---

23 Alfred Russel Wallace, *The Malay Archipelago*

great clarity that I would not get out of moving here. Anything else just wouldn't do. I needed to spend my life among Borneo's natural magic, able to see and touch all of it whenever I felt like it, and damn Mr. B.'s torpedoes! And with that mix of rapture and helplessness you feel when the rollercoaster is about to slink over the big drop-off, I accepted the fact that I would come back for good. On the last day of the Nepenthes Summit, during an outing to the small but neat Orchid and Pitcher Plant Garden in Padawan District, I gathered all my courage and confessed to Chien that I would move to Kuching as soon as circumstances allowed it. I half-expected him to fall off his chair in paroxysms of laughter. But he just smiled and said, "That's excellent! I'm sure you'll love it here. Let me know if I can be of assistance!"

*　*　*　*　*　*

Time always flies fastest during the last days of a vacation. I shopped for souvenirs (sarongs for my wife, headhunter shirts for the boys, *Nepenthes* posters for me) and visited the Sarawak Museum. I attended a farewell dinner at a high-end food court on the roof of a downtown high-rise, where across a mountain of pepper crabs and wasabi shrimp I bade beer-sodden adieus to newfound friends. Some of these people I would probably never meet again. Some would become my neighbors.

During the final days in Kuching, I battled a storm of incompatible emotions. Impossible highs predicting smooth going and a rosy, sun-and-plant-filled future in Sarawak were heckled by nagging reality checks. Would they have the right schools for our boys? How would the family cope with the heat, the rain, the languages? What about long-term visas? Would we able to register a car? How was the quality of local health care?

Tom Harrisson, legendary curator of the Sarawak Museum and an intense character not known for flights of indecision, cautioned: "The trouble with anything in Borneo is knowing where to begin." When I boarded my flight back home, I still didn't have the foggiest idea what exactly I was going to do, or how to go about doing it. I only knew that I was going to do it.

3 "YOU'RE MOVING WHERE?"

It feels good to be lost in the right direction.

Unknown

The steps of the iron staircase clanged like badly tuned gongs as I climbed toward the garage roof. I had just dropped the boys off at school in their new headhunter t-shirts they had insisted on wearing ("Teacher's so gonna freak out over the skulls!"), and now looked forward to reuniting with my other 350 babies in the greenhouse. Since my return to Taiwan the previous day, I had kept mum about moving to Borneo. I needed a winning plan of action first, a proposal that my wife and children would at least consider considering. All I had at the moment was a strong urge and a lot of confusion. Sharing some quality time with my precious plants would hopefully relax me enough to germinate a solution.

I fumbled impatiently with the padlock, then pushed the greenhouse door wide open to the familiar smell of mulch, wet moss, and stagnant water. I drew a deep breath and closed my eyes, savoring the homecoming moment. When I opened them again, something felt off. I peered at the plants. Nothing significant had changed during my absence. A few new pitchers had grown, some old ones were drying out. Nothing out of the ordinary. But something essential was amiss. I could sense, but not name it.

Then it hit me like the string-slathered refrain from a corny pop ballad: the love was gone. The passion for my caged jungle, center of my universe and backbone of my sanity, was no more. Gone, sailed, and sunk. Less than two weeks ago, I had worshipped the dirt these plants grew in, and now I found them about as sexy as a pile of unwashed socks. In deep shock, I staggered back outside, tripping over a sack of shredded bark, and leaned heavily on the railing. Out here, the universe appeared to be on track. In the distance, the East China Sea bashed its white heads against the shore. A crested serpent eagle shrieked at the clouds somewhere above me. Our mutts were engaged in a barking frenzy with the neighbor's mutts. But on the inside, I was completely derailed. My mind felt like confetti in a blender, incapable of a single straight thought. The proverbial rug being pulled from under my proverbial feet was too weak an analogy. I felt more like Wile E. Coyote, my legs spinning helplessly in the air after running off a cliff. I locked up the greenhouse and took the van to the car wash. Right now, the last thing I wanted to think about was plants.

Years later, I would write to a friend:

> The main reason why my first visit to Borneo completely killed my affection for my plants at home was the commensals, the infauna, and the interaction of the plants with their natural surroundings in the wild. There was an unmitigated, raw, and powerful life force present, manifested in a million things, from ants making their home inside *bicalcarata* pitchers, to giant *rafflesianas* climbing and choking entire trees, and I realized that I would never be able to achieve even a puny fraction of that in my greenhouse. Words can't describe what I feel when I see these things. They bring back the ability to marvel in wonder, an ability most people lose as they approach adulthood. And the more I think about this life force, the more questions I have, and very few of them have anything to do with those I asked back when all the *Nepenthes* I knew were sitting in plastic pots on top of my garage.

"*Alea iacta est*," my high school Latin teacher would declaim with a wolfish grin before handing out our test results. The die had been cast, critical mass reached. Over the next days, I resigned myself to my fate and started to craft a strategy. First, the mission objective: I needed wild *Nepenthes* on my doorstep, lest I never be whole again. Check. Therefore I would move to Sarawak. Check. Next, I needed an official reason for the endeavor. The Scottish thinker Thomas Carlyle believed that "a person usually has two reasons for doing something: a good reason and the real reason." I was 43 years old and possessed all the paraphernalia of what mainstream society calls a respectable existence: a loving spouse, two great kids, a modestly successful business, and a little house with garage and garden. After an early life studded with radical politics and anti-establishment hijinks, I had now reached the age of compromise and understood that it could work to my advantage if the neighbors did not regard me as a howling lunatic.

Ergo, I couldn't very well answer inquiries about my Borneo trip with "It was *awesome*, Mrs. Chen! Did you know there are bats on that island that use pitcher plants as nurseries? And spiders that bungee-jump into the stomach juices of these plants to catch trapped insects? It's such an incredibly fantastically insanely splendiferous place, we'll move the whole kit and caboodle there as soon as we can! Speaking of which, would you like to buy our van?"

The battle for the home front would be even tougher. Lisa suffered from first-world ignorance about Borneo, and her superhuman tolerance for my eccentricities would grind to a screeching halt at the thought of moving to some Conradian hell where her children would live in permanent danger from malaria, homicidal reptiles, and poisoned blowpipe darts from tribal drive-bys. I was convinced that, as with most social issues, education would be the answer, and set out to put my wife's mind at ease. I made a list of all the ingredients for happiness we would need in Kuching—from comfy, affordable housing and fast internet service to cinemas and grocery requirements—and started researching. I learned that the city not only boasted numerous traditional wet markets, but also a few upscale supermarkets carrying Löwenbräu beer and Gorgonzola. Those even had "air-flown" Australian mangoes for US$7 per pound, in case the free ones growing everywhere around town were too crude for your refined tastes. There were private hospitals and movie theaters, the latter with state-of-the-art sound systems. The cost of living in Sarawak was lower than in Taipei (if you stayed away from those "air-flown" mangoes); and compared to tiny, land-starved Taiwan the overabundance of real estate in this huge state made for laughably cheap rent.

Lisa and I had become increasingly concerned about the future of our children's education. Kids in East Asia are generally pampered during elementary school, but after that their life turns into one long grind of tedious rote learning, barbaric homework loads, and late-night cram schools, all to be endured without complaint in the name of the university exams lying in wait at the end of the ordeal. Your exam results will decide which college you attend, and likely define your social status for the rest of your life. Few Taiwanese people have fond memories of their high school years; all they remember is the inhuman pace and the old-school teaching style.

We did not relish the prospect of our boys going through this absurd system, and had been weighing alternatives for years. There weren't many. Short of emigrating to a more suitable country, our only options were Taipei's expatriate schools, namely the American School and the European Campus, which housed the British School, L'École Française, and the Deutsche Schule Taipei. All these world-class institutions offered education that complied with the highest standards of their respective homelands. They were also frightfully expensive; a minimum of US$1,000 per month and per child, plus a considerable non-refundable sum charged upon enrollment as contribution to the schools' advancement, put them far out of reach for us. Their fees were calculated for management-level employees of international corporations, whose contracts provided housing in the swankiest part of town, live-in maids, and of course, schooling for their children at motherland standards. Neither flattery nor begging would sway any of the school boards toward discounting their tuition for self-employed foreigners. Then again, they had no reason to show mercy—perk-loaded "real" expats were arriving in Taiwan every day.

Imagine my jubilation when I discovered a school in Kuching that offered a British curriculum from kindergarten to A-levels at a fraction of the Taipei rates. This was the breakthrough I needed. By various twists of fate, our boys only spoke Mandarin, plus a few scraps of Minnanyu, the local Taiwanese idiom, and were receiving only very rudimentary English lessons in school. But Taiwanese parents put a premium on quality English learning for their brood, and nothing says quality like going to school in an Anglophone country. So Lisa fell in love with the idea of our boys attending an international school abroad hook, line, and fishing boat. The Lodge International School Kuching instantly neutralized all the cannibal natives, the blood-lusting leeches, and the horrific diseases my wife might have presented as counterarguments. Now she was on cloud nine because our kids would get to enjoy a humane and affordable secondary education, taught in English, and in a place where English was among the prevalent languages. That this would require moving to Borneo had become a peripheral issue, as trivial as how many sun hats to pack for the trip.

Now that I had established my good reason, the rest was mere details. To ensure the boys had solid Chinese reading and writing chops before we left Taiwan, we decided to delay the move until after their primary school graduation. For Hans Jr., our eldest, that would be in two years; Karl had four more years to go. Also, we would not move them to Borneo at the same time. If Karl started at Lodge together with Hans, he would lose the last two years of Chinese primary education. But if we waited until Karl's graduation in six years, Hans would be 14, and we had been advised that switching to a new language environment after the age of 12 can keep the child from reaching native levels. So it was decreed that I would move to Borneo with Hans in 2011, and Lisa would follow with Karl two years later. During the separation period, we would visit each other during the summer and over Chinese New Year. It would be a challenge on many levels, but also bring about new adventures, experiences, and opportunities for both halves of the family. After the reunion in 2013, we would all live in Kuching, at least until Karl graduated from high school in 2021. Whatever lay beyond that date would be subject to further negotiations.

Our social circle greeted our resettlement plans with mixed enthusiasm. As expected, my fellow plant nerds celebrated my decision with no little envy and vouched to live my life on the wild side vicariously on Facebook. Our more strait-laced Taiwanese friends and family all approved of the educational angle but did not hold back with their stern warnings about the absence of culture, civilization, and proper Chinese food in our future home. A typical lecture would run: "You're moving *where*? Please tell me you're kidding. My friend/cousin/army buddy worked for a year at his company's branch in Kuching, and there is nothing to do—*nothing*, I'm telling you! And it's unbelievably hot and humid, and the locals are backward, and even the Chinese there, *they are not like us*!! Aiyaaah! Why don't you put them in a school in KL? That's a modern metropolis with all necessary amenities for a good life—big shopping malls and Chinese supermarkets and even Taiwanese restaurants!"

Before long, I learned that no argument—especially not *my* argument—would change their belief that standard of living defined quality of life. I was tempted to throw *The Man of La Mancha* in their faces: "Too much sanity may be madness. And maddest of all, to see life as it is and not as it should be." But I kept my own counsel; they all meant well and only wanted to keep me from committing my personal version of *Almayer's Folly*. My parents, relentlessly supportive as usual, were delighted at the prospect of their only child setting up shop where the wild things are: "Such a fabulous place! They have the world's largest snakes and crocodiles! I'm sure our grandchildren will have the time of their lives there!" My old friends back in Germany who had shaken their heads at my emigration to Taiwan two decades earlier now shook them some more.

Falling out of love with my potted darlings put the Grand Greenhouse Sale next on the agenda, and Lisa was really looking forward to this part. Compared to certain orchids, prices for rare *Nepenthes* will not land you in the poorhouse if you just indulge yourself in a new plant or two once in a while. But *morbus collector*, that creeping, debilitating disease, had corrupted my good financial senses and made me pour tragic amounts of money into that bottomless hole I called a greenhouse. Like any dependency, collector's madness also frays ties with your loved ones. I had first realized this when Lisa, during the celebrations for the arrival of my 50th plant, told me in a tone of pity and foreboding, "You know, the more plants you have, the more they look the same." She had seen me slide into too many obsessions, and had detected that manic glint in my eyes long before I recognized my own affliction. Trying to bring her to reason, I had grabbed a few random plants and explained the many obvious differences between them. To Lisa and most other inhabitants of the real world, however, those differences presented themselves in another form: as irrelevant details, perceptible only to fanatics. Guitarists can spend an entire Eric Clapton concert quarreling over the tonal distinctions between pre-CBS and post-CBS Fender Stratocasters ("What are you, man, *deaf*? It's *plain* as *day!*"). To the rest of humanity, for whom music is simply a distraction on the way to work, both instruments sound pretty much the damn same. My pitcher plants had always had a comparable effect on Lisa, but I was merrily oblivious to it. All I could reply was "I'm sure you'll see the light once I have a larger variety!"

Those dark times were over now. I had invested scary sums of cash in the greenhouse, but its inmates had grown in size and monetary value, and I was going to make a sizable profit. My plants had gained certain repute and were sold out ten days after the sales list went online. As the last happy customer drove into the sunset, pitchers swinging out the rear window, I stood in the empty greenhouse and felt like Scrooge McDuck—eyes bright with dollar signs, and not a shred of remorse in my heart.

Now, what to do with all that freshly freed-up time? Six-year-old Karl soon solved the problem when he snuck into my office and decided to give Dad's point-and-shoot camera a thorough examination. This resulted in a fried circuit board, a livid father, and a river of tears. After the smoke had cleared, I came to view the death of my little camera as an opportunity. I had always liked nature photography and took my camera everywhere but had never taken the craft seriously. Now I would finally upgrade to a DSLR and study the art of creating presentable photos. Flush with funds from the plant sale, I went to Taipei's Camera Street and returned with the latest Pentax flagship and a bunch of lenses. Ever a keen learner, I joined a shutterbug club, and it was there that I met my next fixation.

Among the members of the Taipei Society for Nature Photography was Professor Gauss Hsiang, a herpetologist who often regaled us with unbelievable shots of local snakes. Snakes had never really been on my radar, not for lack of interest but for lack of chances to really observe them in the wild. The three or four snakes I had come across in 18 years of hiking in Taiwan had been barely glimpsed apparitions that flowed across the trail and then evaporated into the vegetation. When I asked Hsiang how he had managed to find, let alone photograph, his quarry, he gave a shy smile and invited me on the next night hike he had planned for his students. That outing not only taught me elemental snake-hunting techniques, but also a new word, herping, which is defined as "looking for reptiles and amphibians in the wild for purposes of photography, or just sheer enjoyment." Most importantly, I learned that snakes were much easier to find, watch, and photograph than I had imagined. And before I could say "many-banded krait," snakes poured into my obsession slot left vacant by the pitcher plants.

During our remaining years in Taiwan, I threw myself into the noble sport of herping with the same gusto I had applied to growing *Nepenthes*. Unlike the collection of exotic greenery, snake stalking is a cheap and wholesome hobby. It did wonders for my figure, as it involved long hours of walking up hill and down dale in search of my new friends. There were almost no costs involved, save replacement batteries for my headlamp and the occasional purchase of a new snake hook when I had (again) bent the old one out of shape by running my car over it. And owing to the circadian rhythm of most snakes, I did most of my herping at night, which freed the days for work.

A friend introduced me to fieldherpforum.com, a website for fellow field herpetology nuts. There I posted pictures of scaly things I had found in the Taiwanese woods and accompanied them with short reports. There was no useful online information on the snakes of Taiwan, so I felt obliged to design and run, together with a fellow herper, the website snakesoftaiwan.com.

Our sons attended a tiny country school populated by children from fishing and farming communities, and most of the parents subscribed to the motto "the only good snake is a dead snake." This prompted me to create a presentation about snakes, geared specifically to elementary schoolers. I wanted to teach them the value and beauty of this much-slandered family of animals before the adults could ruin it for them. During those talks I showed photos and let the kids touch and examine skins, empty snake eggs, and live, harmless snakes, presenting it all with a liberal dose of silliness, fine-tuned to the sensitivities of anarchic third graders. Seeing myself as the champion of

all creatures scaly and misunderstood, I offered the talks for free. Not that I could have amassed riches anyway—schools are always short on cash, and lectures about yucky and probably deadly animals are almost never on their list of expenses. But schools are also thankful for gratis stuff to spiff up their curricula, and by the time we left Taiwan I had introduced the biology, ecology, and general coolness of snakes to thousands of Taiwanese kids.

And to frost the whole snake cake, I spent the last winter before our move to Borneo writing a book about my adventures as a bumbling herpetologist on *la Ilha Formosa*.[24]

Four years after the Grand Greenhouse Sale, pitcher plants, caged or wild, had become a thing of my past. But I was more thrilled than ever about our upcoming move to Borneo. No less than 167 recorded snake species awaited my arrival, among them one capable of swallowing an adult human being.

I was *stupid* with excitement.

---

24 Hans Breuer, *A Cobra Hijacked my Camera Bag—Snakes and Stories from Taiwan*; Coachwhip Press; ISBN 13-978-1-61646-129-4.

4 COMING INTO THE COUNTRY

Going up that river was like traveling back to the earliest beginnings of the world, when vegetation rioted on the earth and the big trees were kings.

Joseph Conrad, Heart of Darkness

Officer Singh eyed us with the impassive stare of an Egyptian temple guard—the 30-foot sandstone kind. Paddle-sized hands patiently folded behind his back, he towered over us like a smokestack. His smartly ironed uniform strained against the beefcake underneath, and not a hair was askew in his commanding mustache. The only thing missing was a discreet pin on his lapel advising "Action Figure Sold Separately." The silver badge on his navy-blue turban identified Officer Singh as a member of the Malaysian Immigration Department, and I was standing before his desk, hat in hand.

It was Tuesday, July 12, 2011, going on midnight. The Air Asia flight from Taipei had disgorged us at Kuala Lumpur International Airport ahead of schedule, and we had run into trouble straight away.

Earlier that day we had arrived at Taipei airport to emigrate to Borneo. We had brought our respective hopes, dreams, and expectations, plus 250 pounds[25] of baggage. There were six of us, as my nephew Yahsiu, 9, and niece Hsiaochih, 12, were coming along on the trip. They were Lisa's younger brother's children, and Karl and Hans Jr.'s best friends. They had never left Taiwan before, so we had invited them along for six weeks of fun, adventure, and moral support for our boys. At the end of August, Hans and I would remain in Kuching, while Lisa returned to Taiwan with the others.

Our moods varied. The kids were as animated as dogs on a road trip, metaphorical heads stuck out the figurative car window, tongues flapping in the wind. I, on the other hand, was on the verge of a stomach ulcer. After four years of intensive planning and checking my list way more than twice, I still had spent the previous 72 hours fretting

---

25 ~115 kg

nonstop about the most ridiculous stuff. Had we brought Yahsiu's eye drops? Had we really turned off the gas and locked all the windows? Would the airline let us check in the four giant plastic tote bags we had favored over regular suitcases because nothing else would hold all our clothes? There had been so much to prepare and do and check and pack that statistically we just had to have forgotten *something*.

Yet everything had gone without a hitch. The flight had been uneventful, even mildly amusing (my seat neighbor was an ancient Tamil lady nervously clutching a pamphlet titled "Our Lady of Fatima, save us from the evils of Communism!"), and by the time the cabin crew prepared for landing, the knot in my stomach was dissolving. At long last, things were looking up.

Until we reached the immigration counter. Four of us had already passed through, and now the officer flipped through Hans Jr.'s German passport. His face clouded over: "Where's the exit stamp from Taipei?"

Hans took out his Taiwanese passport and showed him.

"Very sorry, but I cannot put an entry stamp in a passport different from the one stamped at your last point of departure."

Our boys hold double nationality, and for no apparently sane reason I had thought it a clever idea for Hans to leave Taiwan on his Taiwanese travel document and enter Malaysia with his German passport. The latter, because at that time Taiwanese nationals without a prearranged visa could only stay in Malaysia for two weeks, while Germans were granted 90 days on arrival, and Hans, starting at the Lodge School in January—six months from now—would not receive his long-term student visa until after Christmas. So, making use of the 90 days' allowance, I had planned a swift visa run to Singapore with him in September, when both our Malaysian visas expired, to renew them for another three months.

That scenario was now being clubbed to death before my eyes. For Hans Jr. entering Malaysia on his Taiwanese passport would require him to leave again after only two weeks to apply for a proper three-month visa at a Malaysian embassy abroad—Indonesia, perhaps, or Singapore—and only then would he be allowed to rejoin us in Sarawak. That would be a logistical nightmare for us and throw a massive wrench in our plans.

I stepped in: "Uh, sir, my son and I aren't coming to Malaysia for a vacation—we're *moving* here. He will attend high school in Kuching in half a year, you see, and we're coming early to prepare our life there, you know, find a house, buy a car, settle into our new lives, and so forth. Are you really sure there's no way around this?"

I only realized my unfortunate choice of words after they had left my mouth. I had no intention of bribing our way through. I had heard rumors that local law enforcement occasionally responded kindly to supplementary income, but I did not believe in the practice. I was not keen, either, to test the young officer's views on the subject, knowing that Malaysian penitentiaries were not exactly the kind of tropical getaways I would want to explore further.

After the official had declined my request twice, and with unwavering politeness, a deep despair came over me. There had to be some way to get his entry visa stamped into his German passport without resorting to illegal devices.

"Sir, may I please speak to your superior?" My voice started to rasp.

To my surprise, the man put up a Counter Closed sign, locked his station, and motioned us to follow him through a door labeled IMIGRESEN. We walked through a long hallway lined with strongly perfumed prostitutes from China. They were most likely facing deportation for overstaying their visas, but they were having the time of their lives nevertheless, comparing handbags, shoes, and nail polish, and filling the narrow corridor with blasts of shrill laughter and jolly expletives. The kids were bewildered by this vigorous display of streetwalker culture, but before they could start with the awkward questions, we were ushered into an office. A policewoman working on a typewriter gestured with a friendly smile at a row of seats along the wall. We had barely sat down, when her boss emerged from a door behind her, his turban narrowly missing the door frame.

Officer Singh's body language made it plain that he did not need anybody's counsel before making decisions. Should he also refuse to put an entry stamp in Hans' passport, we would be out of options. It was do-or-die now. Unnerved and desperate, I stood up, held my baseball cap in both hands and, without waiting for the man to speak, started to blurt out our entire story. Why we had come. Where we wanted to go. What our plans were. Why we really, *really* needed that entry stamp in the German passport.

During my entire speech, Officer Singh neither spoke nor moved his gaze from my eyes. When I was done, he met my plea with no sign of acknowledgment whatsoever. He stood silent, immobile, and as cryptic as a bronze image. I was filled with the direst dread, and worked the hat through my fingers like a madman speed-praying with a rosary. The man was teasing me, I thought. Like a mouse to a cat, I was just a bit of sadistic amusement to brighten his day. Under no circumstances would he break the rules. My panic strengthened into hysteria, and for want of any finer inspiration, I blurted out the entire story a second time, like a broken record, hat still in hand.

After the second telling, the officer was still looking at me wordlessly, giving no indication that he had even heard me speak, let alone registered any of it. By now I was a nervous wreck and had abandoned any kind of hope. Just when I was about to lose it—burst into tears, perhaps, or set the room on fire—Officer Singh turned to the lady at the typewriter and barked something in Malay at her. He swiveled his massive self on the heels of his mirror-polished shoes, and without so much as a by-your-leave, left the room the way he had come, again putting his turban in grave danger. No sooner had the door closed behind him than the woman smiled at Hans and asked to see his German passport. Into this she then stamped an entry visa valid for 90 days, handed the document back to him with another warm smile, and said, "Welcome to Malaysia!"

In all likelihood, I will never find out what exactly went on in Officer Singh's mind that night. But in the years to come I would enjoy many more encounters with Malaysia's Finest and their tendency for practical, if sometimes unorthodox solutions. Like that one time when I reported my truck as stolen[26] in downtown Kuching. The old Iban bobby handling my case didn't have the best English, and asked me to help with the procedure. I will forever treasure the memory of sitting at a real police desk, in front of an actual police computer, and typing a real, actual theft report for my own car.

* * * * * *

Our connecting flight to Kuching did not depart until the next morning, so we spent the night in an airport hotel. The no-frills Tune chain ("5-star sleeping experience at a 1-star price!") is affiliated with the low-cost carrier Air Asia, and in those days operated by the same principles. Every service was readily available, but none of it was included in the starting price. The basic room rate, highly attractive on paper, lost its luster mighty fast once you added all the components essential to surviving an equatorial summer night inside a concrete bunker. Soap, shampoo, and towels must be booked ahead, ditto for the air conditioner, and you needed to specify the exact number of hours you wanted to stay cool. The rooms were so tiny they probably doubled as morgue drawers during times of low occupancy, so we had to leave most of our baggage at the reception overnight. The hotel did not serve any food, nor were there any restaurants in the neighborhood, and we found ourselves on the patio of a 7–11 the next morning, for a breakfast of boxed milk tea and Maggi instant noodles.

Our youngsters offered play-by-play comments on the people going about their business around us. Most of those were ethnic Malays, and their customs were strange.

"Look, they touch their own hearts after shaking hands. How cool is that?"

"The girls wear headscarves. That must be so hot in this weather!"

At checkout time we asked for a cab, and the receptionist pointed at the taxi stand outside.

"Did you see that?" Hans yelped on the way out. "He pointed with his *thumb!*"

I explained that in Malay culture pointing at anything, especially people, with any finger other than the thumb is considered rude. The children were so impressed by this considerate concept that for the next six weeks they would chide Lisa and me with great earnestness every time they caught us breaking this rule of thumb in public.

Now, at 1:20 p.m. on Wednesday, 13 July 2011, after almost four years, I was back in Borneo, and this time for good. As we walked out of Kuching airport into the blazing afternoon, the view of the hills around the city sent shivers down my spine. Oh, the adventures we would have! The things we would discover! The life we would lead! It was a grand emotional moment, and for a second I expected the heavens to part

---

26 It wasn't stolen. I had just forgotten where I had parked it.

and cherub choirs and trumpeters bathe the world in a bombastic score of the sort Hollywood last used in *The Ten Commandments*.

Before my ecstatic visions could rouse me to kiss random strangers or otherwise make a complete fool of myself, my family tore me away from my moment of rapture. Lisa wanted to organize two taxis, and asked me for the address of our hotel. Hsiaochih needed to visit the girls' room. Karl and Hans Jr. claimed the puny inflight lunch had left them in a state of severe malnourishment and they wanted money for McDonald's. And little Yahsiu had frozen in his tracks, aghast at the sight of eight young Middle Eastern tourists, the men boisterous in beach shorts and pimp shades, their women silent in black burqas.

We arrived at Tracks Bed & Breakfast by the Waterfront in the late afternoon. A few wild-looking backpackers shuffled about the lobby. Most wore elephant-print harem pants, likely bought in different locations along Southeast Asia's Banana Pancake Trail. Although the nearly identical garments would all have come from nearly identical Chinese sweatshops, the wearers seemed to view them as expressions of their respective individualities.

Robin, the Iban proprietor, greeted us in person. He was an energetic sort with retro spectacles and a ponytail, who ran a second guesthouse next door and also worked in his own tattoo studio across the street. For the most part, Taiwanese society holds conservative views on body art, and in those days, tattoos were seen as the domain of gangsters and convicts. Robin's striking collection of traditional Iban motifs on his bare upper body therefore drew intense stares from the children. With great pride and patience, Robin explained every single image and its backstory to us. The front of his shoulder was emblazoned with the *bungai terung,* the eggplant flower. This is the first tattoo an Iban receives. It marks the Iban tradition known as *bejalai,* when a man leaves his longhouse on a journey seeking knowledge and wisdom. The spiral at the center of the flower is called the Rope of Life and symbolizes the beginning of a new life. All of Robin's tattoos came with captivating tales, but it was the *pantang rekong* that enthralled us the most. It looked like a hybrid between a cockroach and a crossbow, crept up the entire throat, and was meant to strengthen the skin. Not in a moisturizing-revitalizing, *Estée Lauder* sort of way, mind you, but to protect from decapitation by rival headhunting tribes. The kids were floored. This was *awesome* stuff.

Robin had cleared the furniture from the biggest guest room and laid mattresses wall to wall, creating a camping atmosphere. Soon our little clan was spread out on the floor, telling stories after lights out, and sharing the excitement about the strange new world outside. We all slept very well that night.

The next day Robin showed us the breakfast corner with free tea, toast, and marmalade, but we were in the mood for more exotic fare and tried our luck outside. Half a block away we found a magical place. It was a typical hole-in-the-wall *kopitiam*

Food court

(coffee shop, in the Chinese Hokkien dialect): tables in the middle, drinks counter in the back, a Chinese-style buffet along one wall, and a stall selling *roti canai* (Malay pancakes) across from it. We ate at this kopitiam for the next seven mornings, and tried everything on offer. Our preferred dish was *murtabak*, a stuffed, savory pancake large and hearty enough to get a hard-working rubber tapper through the sweaty morning. Among the ingredients are beef, chicken or mutton, green onions, eggs, and potatoes, all seasoned with shallots, garlic, ginger, cumin, coriander, and turmeric. And since boredom is immoral and must be avoided at all costs, murtabak is served with *dhal* (lentil stew), chicken curry – and, if it's your lucky day, a homemade sambal chili dip that tastes like concentrated sunshine and sends tears of joyful pain down your cheeks.

Fueled up with chicken, carbs and *kopi-o kosong* (lit. coffee, black, with zero), we set out to conquer Borneo, starting with a leisurely stroll about Kuching. The Waterfront, the city, Mount Serapi in the distance; they all felt quite different compared to my last visit. They were *mine* now. To varying degrees, a visitor's experiences are all tainted by impermanence. But this time I had come to make the island my home. On the last night of my previous visit, a harried-looking expat searching for a friend in the alleys of the bar district had asked me, "Are you a local?" "No," I had replied, "but I wish I were." And now I was. Not a seasoned one yet, but that would come in due course.

Borneo's natural richness was omnipresent even in these urban environs. A water monitor crossed the river with lazy tail strokes, sparking hyperventilation in the four kids until I educated them about the difference between crocodiles and giant lizards. Almost every tree hosted epiphytic orchids. Some had naturally landed there as seeds;

city planners had introduced the rest. The dominant birds were Javan mynas,[27] members of the starling family. In Borneo they mainly exist in the Kuching area, where they were introduced a few decades ago, supposedly by a bird fancier who forgot to lock a cage door. Their black and brown plumage is contrasted by yellow legs and a matching beak. Like rats, they are clever, adaptable, and omnivorous, and they impress with courage that borders on foolhardiness. Whole packs patrol food courts and snatch crumbs from between the patrons' sandals with impunity. With a goofy, bouncing gait they run onto busy highways to yank edible trash off the asphalt. Attempts at shooing them off rarely amount to more than an impertinent "you want a piece of me?" glower from their yellow eyes, followed by an even bolder try to get at the scraps under your chair.

We walked to the river taxi jetty to secure passage to Fort Margherita. Some of the captains were taking breaks in their boats, eating Malaysia's national dish, *nasi lemak* (lit. fat rice = rice cooked in coconut milk), from plastic bags, while their naked toes held fishing lines running into the latte-hued water. The tranquility was sporadically disturbed by a thrashing 6-inch prawn being pulled from the depths. This caused the other pilots to briefly come alive with nods and grunts of respect, before calm and quiet took over the scene again.

The children had discovered a kiosk that sold chicken wieners, lychee soda, and sprayable candy with melon flavor, and they dragged me there under the pretense of needing provisions for the Great River Crossing (which takes all of four minutes). On the pavement in front of the shop lay what looked like a bumblebee created in preschool by little Darth Vader. It was the size of a small stag beetle, and every detail was kept in a mean, metallic black: the huge spherical eyes, the wide neck plate, the broad protective bands around the body. The menacing livery was countered by short, stubby wings and a comically bulbous body shape. The whole design reminded me of the Messerschmitt Komet, a cartoonish, rocket-powered fighter plane used by the German Luftwaffe in World War II. The insect before me was not as famed for its record-breaking airspeed, but was still a formidable creature. It was a tropical carpenter bee,[28] one of the world's largest bees. It lives a solitary life, chewing deep holes into dead wood to create nests, and the low drone of its wings brings to mind war machines from the golden age of propeller flight.

As we squatted down to get a better look at the lifeless beast, I wondered what had killed it. It was still in good shape; there were no signs of violent death. When I picked it up for closer inspection, I learned the reason for its excellent condition: it was still alive.

Without the slightest warning, the giant bee drove its giant stinger into my thumb. A galaxy of supernovae erupted behind my eyes, and I flung the thing far away from

---

27 *Acridotheres javanicus*

28 *Xylocopa latipes*

me. I howled like a banshee and clutched my thumb, which now looked twice its original size, and felt ten times bigger. Luckily, the agony didn't last long. Pain and swelling subsided soon, and I got back on my feet. My cries had attracted a dozen passers-by, and I thanked them for their concern. The crowd dispersed quickly after realizing that all the crazy hollering had been a false alarm. Nobody had lost a leg in a crocodile attack. Not even a finger. It had just been a wimpy tourist overreacting to some bug.

*   *   *   *   *   *

The family enjoyed the city's attractions and its cultural diversity just as much as I had four years earlier, and we were all in full adventure holiday mode. But we were also on a mission to build a new life in Sarawak, and our first objective was permanent accommodation. Every morning we bought every local English and Chinese newspaper, and over breakfast combed the classifieds for rental properties. We also searched online, but our efforts remained fruitless. The meager choices on offer were either too far from the Lodge School or did not inspire confidence. We were mystified, since we had seen so many For Rent signs. The town's real estate culture seemed to be stuck in the 19th century, when deals happened not through media exposure but through personal recommendations, mouth-to-ear, or a hand-scrawled notice nailed to the gate. There were agents—but none of them dealt in rentals. Our acquaintances in Kuching had promised to look out for suitable dwellings. So far, no word from anyone.

The transport situation compounded our annoyance with the housing situation. Kuching's rate of car ownership is remarkably high; the result is an anemic bus system. There are very few buses, and the nonexistence of signage on many of them and at most bus stops exacerbates the problems for out-of-towners without wheels. There was also no online information about bus routes—*any* bus routes. Before we took delivery of our car three weeks into our stay, taxis were our only option for transport, and they came at a premium. We were soon frittering away a fortune on cabs because hoofing it all over town in the debilitating sun was taking the starch out of us.

On our seventh day in Sarawak, the gods decided to relent. First, we met with the principal at the Lodge School and left with a favorable impression of staff and school. Later that morning, I managed to open a bank account, and the scene in the bank reinforced my good opinion about the flexibility and friendliness of the Malaysian people.

"Good morning. I would like to open an account."

"Good morning, sir. Do you have a work visa?"

"No, I don't."

"I'm deeply sorry, sir. Foreigners are not allowed to open an account without a work visa."

"My son will attend the Lodge School, starting next January. I'm here to live with him. I therefore need a bank account. Here are his admission documents. Would those help somehow?"

"One moment, sir. Let me call headquarters and see what we can do."

Twenty minutes and a flurry of signatures later, I was the proud owner of two accounts at RHB Bank, Tabuan Jaya Branch. One was for Malaysian ringgit, the other for foreign currency. I also had an RHB debit card now. Since I owned no collateral in the country, they had drawn the line at issuing a credit card, but I was happy and felt warm and fuzzy about Malaysia. Like Officer Singh, these people had bent the system out of sheer kindness, to help strangers. (I will admit that the prospect of profit probably played a small role in the matter of the bank account. But surely a negligible one.)

We were celebrating with some fresh coconut water in a kopitiam when my phone rang. It was Amos, the Taiwanese ex-soldier with the orchid nursery. "We found a house you might like. Where are you now? Tabuan Jaya? I'll pick you up in a bit."

Half an hour later, we were in his off-road pickup heading to see the house. In best Chinese networking fashion, Amos had found the place through a friend who lived next door to the cousin of the guy that groomed the landlord's dog, or something equally Byzantine. The architecture (tropical colonial) was identical to all other houses in the quiet, palm-lined neighborhood. It was a fully furnished, semi-detached, two-story home with a small garden out back, a front yard with space for two cars, and, as is often the custom in Malaysia, encircled by an intimidating fence. My wife, the choosiest woman on the planet when it comes to living quarters, took one quick look in every room and asked the landlord when we could move in.

The answer was tomorrow morning, and that was when we returned in a small armada of taxis carrying our 250 pounds of baggage. We spent the next few days installing ourselves in the house and surveying the neighborhood. It had everything we needed. The Lodge School was just over a mile away, and the town's biggest wet market was en route to the school. A large medical center sat across from the market, and there was a supermarket in walking distance. In Borneo, of course, "walking distance" means "across the road." Due to the climate, nobody actually walks anywhere if they can help it; everybody drives, even if the destination is just around the corner. We had ordered a car the day after moving out of the guesthouse, but wouldn't take delivery for another two weeks. During this time, the neighbors observed our daily hikes to the supermarket and the food courts with suspicion: "Why don't these people drive? Don't they know how unhealthy it is to walk?"

Every morning, birdsong woke us from the trees and bushes in our little garden. The mynas were there; and sparrows that seemed to follow the mynas the way hyenas trail lions. Yellow-vented bulbuls, quarrelsome birds with lemon derrieres and chocolate mohawks, battled with Asian glossy starlings over the feeding rights to our trees. The starlings' gleaming, bluish-black plumage paired with their blood-red eyes gave them the look of evil seabirds just rescued from an oil slick. The impression was completed by their eerie, high-pitched warbling, like a human voice recording played at 20 times the original speed. White egrets stood on the power lines, often playing wingmen to a collared kingfisher in dress shirt and blue jacket, all of them scanning the open drains for frogs, snakes, and other delights. Other common birds around our home were pink-necked green pigeons that roped in your attention with their bright orange breasts, and zebra doves—absurdly small pigeons that didn't seem to know they had wings. They spent most of their time hurrying around the street with that head-banging pigeon trot, and foraged with an absent-minded intensity that led to many an end beneath a car tire.

Close to our house was a small, neglected park with a bunch of sad trees and a waterlogged soccer pitch. The shallow runnels along the jogging paths were hopelessly overtaxed by their task of draining the place from the daily torrent. On our first evening walk through the swampy park an orchestra of amorous amphibians greeted us. Asian painted frogs[29] were prominent in the ditches, distinguished by mahogany backs, off-white bellies, and an orange racing stripe along each side. Without a distinct head to go with their ovoid bodies, they looked like miniature rugby balls inflated close to the burst limit. Nephew Yahsiu remarked, "As if somebody hid Easter eggs in the ditches and then forgot to invite the kids."

A group of teenagers sat in and under a tree, listening to Malay hip hop. We asked them what kind of animals lived in this park, beyond frogs. "Monitor lizards," they said in unison. "They eat the rats in the drains. There are some pythons, too, but you never really see them." My mouth fell open. Only two python species are known from Borneo: the chubby Borneo short python,[30] a reptile not known to favor suburban surroundings, and the reticulated python,[31] the world's longest snake, with specimens recorded at lengths of 32 feet. The retic, as snake lovers call this fantastic beast, thrives in fields and forests, but also wherever trash attracts rats, and where people keep chicken coops. This includes urban centers.[32] I was thrilled beyond description. If I bought a live chicken and tethered it to our gate, I calculated, maybe I would get to watch a wild retic from the comfort of my kitchen window! But I dismissed the idea. Should I actually commit such animal abuse, my family would first rescue the chicken and then feed me to the snake. I contented myself with the knowledge that I was now neighbors with one of the largest serpents ever to slither the Earth.

---

29 *Kaloula pulchra*

30 *Python breitensteini*

31 *Malayopython reticulatus*

32 From the *New York Times*, (11/30, 2017): "'There's no way we could survive if there were more fires than snakes.' — Prayul Krongyos, deputy director of the Bangkok Fire and Rescue Department, which has responded to more than 31,000 calls about snakes this year. Some pythons have even slithered up through toilets."

Asian painted frog

The teenagers also informed us that there were owls in these trees at night. They grinned and rubbed their bellies, which was odd. They couldn't possibly eat owls, could they? Maybe we had misunderstood, and they just meant birds? There sure were a lot of pigeons around, a favorite fowl in many world cuisines. I hesitated to inquire further, fearing an embarrassing rebuke ("You *trippin'*, man? Why would we eat *owls*? Do *you* eat owls?"). But my curiosity got the best of me, and I asked. Their English was halting, but with the help of some full-body charades and wild mugging, they described how they caught the birds in cages and then barbecued them. We were shocked, but cloaked our disgust and indignation.

According to the Rainforest Action Network, "an average of 137 species of life forms are driven into extinction every day in the world's tropical rainforests." Large-scale habitat loss is the usual culprit, but in many places the locals hasten the process by killing and eating everything they can catch. In Borneo, the menu contains among other things monkeys, civets, bats, snakes, pangolins, and birds of any feather. Even leopard cats end up on the grill. The reason is neither poverty nor protein shortage; hunting is no longer necessary to survive in Malaysian Borneo. But it is still wildly popular as entertainment. Borneo's indigenous tribes have maintained their hunting traditions through the centuries, but along the way many either failed to notice the shrinking forests and the ballooning human population or chose not to care. The effect on the wildlife is serious, and steadily worsening.

The atmosphere was subdued on the way home. But Borneo came to the rescue by presenting me with my first self-found wild snake, and it could not have been a prettier species. The painted bronzeback[33] sat on the path just inside the park entrance, and what a beauty it was. It was as long as three pencils laid end to end, and not much thicker. A checked pattern in dark blue and black raced down its back, and its huge eyes revealed it as a diurnal hunter. I was over the moon. My first snake in Borneo, and such a gorgeous animal to boot! It mattered little that the snake had been dead for days and was as flat and papery as a discarded straw wrapper. It was my first snake in Borneo, and while the family soon stifled yawns and eventually headed home, I stayed well past midnight, taking pictures from all angles.

*   *   *   *   *   *

Now that we had nailed down the prerequisites for an orderly life, we finally had time to see the Borneo we had come for. According to some travelers at the Tracks guesthouse, public transport outside Kuching was even more infuriating than in town, so we decided to wait for our own car before exploring the natural treasures further away. In the meantime, our daily jungle fix came from a place conveniently located near our house, a small recreational woodland euphoniously named Taman Rimba Sama Jaya (Sama Jaya Forest Park). East Kuching had once been forest, but over the years, much of it had been converted to residential zones. Just before the last 93 acres fell prey to the bulldozers, some compassionate soul in the government saw sense in keeping a green lung for the city, put a fence around the land, and pronounced it a nature reserve. I came to call it Rainforest Lite, because it is the ideal entry-level introduction to Borneo's wildness. The experience with its wildlife (and often its visitors) could be rich and unfiltered, and it began right in the parking lot.

Our first visit to Sama Jaya was also our first proper expedition into Wild Borneo, and the kids came prepared with seaweed-flavored Pringles and two six-packs of 100Plus, Malaysia's carbonated answer to Gatorade. Admission to the park was pleasantly cheap—one ringgit a pop, about US$0.30 at the time. We had to register our names, nationalities, and ID numbers; should we get lost in the grounds, this information would give search parties an idea who to search for. This seemed unduly patronizing. Sama Jaya isn't exactly Yellowstone backcountry; you can see the surrounding civilization from almost anywhere inside the forest. But the estate is run by Sarawak Forestry, the governing agency for the state's nature reserves, and therefore subject to the same strict rules as Mulu National Park with its unending jungle.

As we filled out the forms at the ticket hut, we were distracted by a large troop of

---

33 *Dendrelaphis pictus*

Long-tailed macaques
(photo, Christoph Lepschy)

long-tailed macaques[34] moving in the skinny palm trees that fringed the parking lot. In Malay, these monkeys are called *kera*, a name that supposedly mimics their alarm call. Dark red fruit hung from the palm tops in heavy bead curtains, and the monkeys were cramming them into their cheek pouches to grotesque effect. (One could be forgiven for thinking of a goiter epidemic.) Some of the younger macaques on the ground were misbehaving in ways typical for most adolescent primates. Every so often, their mothers or older siblings would remember their roles as mentors and guardians, and a loving slap would send the kid cartwheeling into the next hibiscus bush. Our four youngsters got in on the act and started making silly faces at their furry cousins. Apes and monkeys are highly intelligent, and recent studies suggest that in consequence they possess a sense of humor. But baring your teeth at them is never considered a laughing matter—in their eyes, it is an act of aggression. While I explained this to the children, the macaques helped with visual teaching aids. They slowly advanced toward the kids, snorting, cackling, and maintaining eye contact, and keeping their fanged dentures in full sight. This left a far deeper impression than my dry lecture, and the children felt it was time to skedaddle. We slowly backed away from the monkey mob and regrouped at a lily pond on the far side of the parking lot.

Though barely larger than a standard bathtub, the pond was a herpetological hotspot. A fat sun skink[35] had appropriated one of the rocks by the pond as a tanning bed, and the scales on the lizard's back reflected the light like hammered copper. As soon as our shadows touched it, it zipped underneath its sunning deck. Two red-eared frogs,[36] squatting on lily pads like clichés, were made of sterner stuff. They only fled their floating command posts when our younger son waded, Godzilla-like, into the pond to chase a small snake that had shot into the water from beneath a rock. After Karl had returned empty-handed, we sat on the rocks for a while and waited for his shoes to dry, then set forth toward the forest. Lisa stood up, turned onto the path, and almost tripped over a lizard the length of a small alligator. The young water monitor had been inching across the trail in stop-and-go motion while its bifurcated blue tongue read the air. Monitor lizards of all species are said to possess near-mammalian intelligence, and they are among the wariest animals I have ever met. This fellow, though, ignored the point-blank presence of six humans, and tried to waltz right past them. Either it was the ballsiest sauropsid since *Velociraptor*, or dumber than a bag of hammers. Whatever the cause, it shot my wife a peeved look and hustled behind the next palm tree. Believing it would just hide behind the trunk, we followed it in the hope for a photo opportunity. But behind the tree was only the empty lawn. We were perplexed. This was not possible. We knew the lizard had not run past the tree; we would have

---

34 *Macaca fasciularis*

35 *Eutropis multifasciata*

36 *Hylarana erythraea*

Dawn in Sama Jaya

seen it move across the grass. Nor was there a hole in the ground into which it might have disappeared. And of course, I judged without hesitation, it was not on the tree; it was much too large and heavy to scale the smooth, concrete-like palm bark.

In the end, Lisa solved the case. Unlike me, she is what I call with benign ridicule, a civilian—a person not too conversant in the intricacies of the natural sciences. Also unlike me, she's not disposed to half-baked preconceptions and rash assumptions, and instead meets her daily challenges with common sense. And now, for all the above reasons, Lisa looked up the tree. Sixteen feet above us, the granite-colored lizard held fast to the trunk with its grappling-hook claws and flicked its bright blue tongue at us, as if to say "who's dumb now, suckers?"

The forest started right behind the palm trees, and we entered on a wide cement trail. A Chinese lady of carefully concealed age jogged past us in a mauve tracksuit while berating her stockbroker on a rhinestone-encrusted iPhone. Ten joggers later it became clear that this was Sama Jaya's main demographic: middle-aged ethnic Chinese who came to exercise in the relative cool of the forest. Most people ran or power-walked, but some practiced more traditional arts like tai chi, qi gong, and tree slapping.[37] A few Malays and Bidayuh were also present, but in a different function: most wore the olive uniforms of park wardens.

37 In the Chinese world, tree slapping is a commonly seen "energizing exercise that brings the palms and arms to life."

[Left] Niece Hsiaochih with Macaranga gigantea *leaves*

[Right] Termite nest

Inside the forest, the first thing that caught our eye was the leaf litter. In some places it was deep enough to hide a fully-grown python, and some of the leaves were of cyclopean dimensions. The largest kind looked roughly like a maple leaf but was 4 feet long and had a stem as thick as a bullwhip.[38] Another leaf, only slightly less gigantic, prompted the children to shouts of *"Dinosaur feet!"* These leaves were shaped like the footprints a three-toed theropod might have left as it walked the Earth 60 million years ago. The children lost themselves in the magical leaf carpet, and only my hyperbolic descriptions of venomous creepy-crawlies possibly lurking underneath finally convinced them to return to the trail. But they did not leave without souvenirs; for the rest of the day, Hsiaochih used one of the ginormous leaves as a parasol.

Curiously enough, the trees from which those giant leaves had fallen were not giants at all. Sama Jaya is not a primary rainforest where trees that are as wide as a man is tall support a crown 250 feet above. It is a peat swamp forest with trees of modest height and girth; yet some of these modest trees produce those freakish leaves. The trees of Borneo are never boring, not even in this little patch of forest where stilt roots seize the ground like skeletal fingers, and buttress roots hold up shallow-rooted trees. Between some of the buttresses lumps of poured concrete had hardened against the trunk: the

38 *Macaranga gigantea*

Stilt roots

nests of a certain termite species. There were also termites here that built homes which hung like petrified goat udders from rocks and fallen tree trunks. Another species favored distinctly phallic nests that rose from the ground to knee height and made the kids snicker whenever they found them.

Not all trees had outsized leaves or showy roots, but those that didn't made up for the lack of personal achievement with external ornaments: vines and epiphytes. The *Encyclopedia Britannica* defines epiphytes as plants that grow on other plants or objects for physical support and elaborates that these plants "are found in moist tropical areas, where their ability to grow above ground level provides access to sunlight in dense shaded forests." Kuching's 85 percent average humidity nicely fits the description "moist," and in Sama Jaya epiphytes flourished in astounding shapes and numbers.

Epiphytes are common among mosses, orchids, ferns, and many other groups of the plant kingdom. About one third of all ferns is epiphytic, and so are two thirds of all orchids, the second-largest family of flowering plants.[39] In this forest park, epiphytes came in all sizes. They accessorized tree trunks with dainty ferns like popsicles, and with orchid blossoms smaller than a thumbtack. In many tree crowns, bird's nest ferns[40] as large as truck wheels perched like lookouts on windjammers. Vines crept up and down the trees, some ascending from the ground, some descending from the canopy. One vine had large, heart-shaped leaves so densely covered in hairs that they felt like coarse fur. As the vines journey toward the sun, stem and leaves fasten themselves to the host trunk with short, root-like fibers. These connections are surprisingly tough and make the vines difficult to remove. We admired spiky rattan lianas of such lengths they seemed to have neither beginning nor end, and our favorite was a delicate little thing we called the seagull vine.[41] The shape of each leaf echoed the silhouette of a boomerang-winged bird in flight, attached to the vine by the beak. The leaves were arranged in single file, and from afar you saw an infinite string of green seagulls soaring up the tree.

In urban areas, even small undomesticated habitats like Sama Jaya attract animals from miles around, including many birds. As is common in tropical forests, we heard more birds than we saw, but from time to time one or two would come into sight, darting across the trail, or feeding in trailside trees and bushes rich in fruit or bug life. The most conspicuous bird was small and brown, with a white shirtfront and scowling white "eyebrows." It twirled through the underbrush like a dervish, hopping and skipping and flitting without pause. As it danced its frantic fandango, it kept spreading and closing its broad tail in rapid succession. An image came to my mind of a cantankerous crone at the Yellow Emperor's court, flashing her paper fan into a servant's face for bringing the

---

39 According to a checklist published by Zotz (2013), there are 27,135 known orchid species (2,500 to 3,000 in Borneo), of which 18,814 grow epiphytic.

40 *Asplenium* sp.

41 *Adenia cordifolia*

Bird's nest ferns

Crested fireback, Sama Jaya

wrong tea. The bird was a pied fantail,[42] and there was a method to its mad gymnastics. By fanning its tail, the fantail scares insects from their hiding places, and then picks them out of the air. The Malays know the little mad-bird as *murai gila* (crazy thrush).

A plump, pheasant-like thing strolled from the undergrowth. Instead of reacting to us humans like a sensible gamebird, namely hurrying back into cover as fast as its short wings allowed, it made a beeline for Lisa. Next to the flashy males of her species, the female Bornean crested fireback[43] looks rather frumpy: mousy-brown back, mottled white front, and a little centurion's crest. But she scores with the broad, powder-blue face wattles that ring her ruby eyes. The bird waddled around Lisa's feet, excitedly peeping and chirping in the most ridiculous way. Hans Jr.'s penny dropped first: "I think she wants food. Maybe someone who looks like Mom comes here to feed her." He tossed a seaweed-flavored Pringle on the ground. The fireback promptly devoured the potato chip and resumed the pathetic peeping. After treating her to another chip, Hans suggested we keep walking. We shouldn't really contribute to the habituation of wild animals, he cautioned with precocious wisdom. Besides, we had only brought one tube of Pringles. (My son's evaluation proved to be accurate months later, when we met the elderly Malay lady who regularly visited the park to feed the fireback with raw rice. She had the same stature as my wife, and even wore a similar sunhat.)

---

42 *Rhipidura javanica*

43 *Lophura ignita*

Cup fungi
(photo, Marcus Kloft)

We rested in a small *pondok,* an open shelter with concrete pillars designed to look like tree trunks. Paper wasp nests stuck to the underside of the roof like garlic bulbs, and the floor was crusty with dried bat droppings. A sign advised us to Beware of Falling Branches, and a massive bough on the ground next to it intimated the consequences of ignoring the message. A clutch of most delightful cup fungi[44] grew on the rotting wood. Imagine a kumquat at full sun-kissed ripeness, top third cut off, hollowed out, then tipped slightly to the side. The opening curled inward along the lip, and silky, translucent hairs grew on the inside and outside. Sunlight shone through the orange walls, and at the right angle the whole strange structure gave off a beautiful glow. I remarked to my family, "This is probably what alien abduction traps look like," but they only smiled back thinly in embarrassment.

A row of small terrestrial orchids grew like scaled-down streetlamps beside the fallen branch, and a little invertebrate, shorter than a ballpoint pen, was bulldozing its way through them. It looked like the track of a toy tank that had snapped off and taken on a life of its own. Closer scrutiny showed dozens of tiny legs, two pairs on each individual armor plate. The creature belonged to a family of bugs aptly called tractor millipedes. (My friend Phil Brabbs calls them "hundred-wheel drives".)

Tractor millipedes are blind and rely on touch and smell to find decomposing organic matter to recycle. Unlike the venomous, flesh-hunting centipedes, which they

---

44 *Cookeina tricholoma*

Tractor millipede
(photo, Marcus Kloft)

superficially resemble, millipedes are harmless. Well, sort of harmless. For better viewing, Karl placed the little crawler on his hand, where it curled up to protect its soft underbelly. After Karl had released it again, he found a drop of reddish-brown slime on his palm—the animal's secret weapon. Many millipedes defend themselves with chemical warfare by secreting a variety of harmful chemicals, including hydrogen cyanide that smells like almonds. These substances act as deterrents to anyone fancying a millipede meal. Karl was duly impressed and immediately scrubbed the stuff off his hand with a clump of leaves, but not before thoroughly checking them for more toxic avengers.

The children were running ahead, deeper into the forest, and we still heard their laughter long after they were lost from view. Suddenly they went quiet. When Lisa and I caught up with them, they were looking at a clump of grass growing beside the trail. The blades were stiff and sharp-edged, but otherwise unremarkable, if you ignored the fact that they were almost 20 feet tall.[45] As we all gawked at the colossal growth that would have required a frigate-sized lawn mower to trim, bizarre noises rained down from further up in the treetops. It started with short siren bursts from a police cruiser, followed by gibbons howling inside an echo chamber, and escalated into a free-for-all screeching jam. After craning our necks for a while, we caught sight of the hell raisers in the tip of a dying tree: two common hill mynas.[46] Their feathers were a lustrous

---

45 Actually, the leaves of *Benstonea affinis*, a plant from the Pandanus family

46 *Gracula religiosa*

black, with a flash of yellow around the eyes, and the birds looked much bigger than the pet I remembered from my childhood in Germany. My parents had owned a toy shop, where they kept a caged common hill myna. Early on a snowy Sunday morning, my father was in his office doing paperwork when he heard two cars colliding outside. He rushed out to look at the street but saw nothing out of the ordinary. Nothing was happening in the white silence outside. There were no pedestrians, and the only cars he saw were parked and capped in fresh snow. Confused, Dad returned to his paperwork. A few minutes later there was another resounding crash. Again, Dad ran out and checked the street. Still nothing to see but wintry quietude. He was about to turn back to the office when the cars crashed a third time, and now it dawned on him where the accidents were happening—inside the myna cage. During the previous night, two cars had met head-on outside the shop. The bird had memorized the noise and was now repeating it over and over for its own amusement.

Captive common hill mynas have the extraordinary ability to imitate the sounds of nearly everything they hear, from footsteps to ringtones to the human voice across all its registers. This skill makes them popular cage birds and is slowly leading to their demise in the wild. In the 1990s, almost 20,000 wild-caught birds were brought into the pet trade each year. While the International Union for Conservation of Nature

Hill mynas

(IUCN) lists the common hill myna on its website as a Species of Least Concern, it also notes that the population trend is decreasing.

My niece needed to use the bathroom, and left to find one. As we waited for her return, a pair of male crimson sunbirds[47] entertained us with a king-hell brawl in the middle of the trail. Sunbirds are long-billed nectar eaters and the Old World's ecological analog to the New World's hummingbirds. This species was easily recognizable. To all appearances, the bird had dunked its upper body in a bucket of scarlet paint, leaving only a drab-olive butt and wingtips, and a sinister black forehead patch. It was unclear whether these two antagonists were fighting over territory or a damsel's honor. Either way, they tussled with such intensity that their vermilion feathers littered the trail by the time Hsiaochih returned, at which point the birds, still mad as thunder, took their argument into the understory.

Hsiaochih told us of a large praying mantis she had seen on the toilet wall. "And it looks like a bunch of dead leaves!" This was not to be missed. We hiked over to the little lavatory and—ignoring decorum for a minute—all crammed into the ladies' room. On top of the mirror sat a large insect with a body like a sloppily rolled cigar. The bug's flared shoulders invoked some particularly laughable orc armor from *World of Warcraft*, and the head was comprised mostly of two huge compound eyes with pseudopupils roving across the surface. The eyes, like the rest of the mantis, were the color of dried tobacco, which begat its common name, dead leaf mantis.[48]

Outside in the forest, none of us would have spotted it. Camouflage helps the wearer blend in with the surroundings and is crucial for hunters and prey alike. Together with mimicry, its mocking, hiding-in-plain-sight twin, camouflage is one of the great showpieces of the incredible diversity of life in Borneo. Spiders mimicking broken twigs, bugs that look like flowers, geckos with lichen-like skin—it's all too strange for fiction. There are even snakes, longer than a pickup truck, with deceptive markings that fool your eyes until you're about to step on the reptile. Over time, we would encounter some of the most astonishing practitioners of this art, including one of those snakes.

"In forests as rich as these, education never stops," ornithologist Bruce Beehler wrote in *Lost Worlds*. He was talking about the vast, trackless jungles of New Guinea, but the sentiment also applies to this little woodland in urban Kuching. In the short time it had taken us to explore every trail in Sama Jaya, we had witnessed a teeming profusion of life. I was awestruck that a few treed acres like these could harbor such a pageant of life forms. At the same time, I was angry and bitter that only these few acres had survived the greed for progress. But maybe I should have been more grateful for what was left standing; 93 acres would provide room for many more condos.

---

47 *Aethopyga siparaja*

48 *Deroplatys dessiccata*

* * * * * *

On the first day of August, we finally received our car. For the same reason that the bank had refused us a credit card—no collateral in Sarawak—we had to pay cash. Regrettably, Malaysia is one of the world's priciest countries to buy a car. Its automobile import policy protects local manufacturers, and its import taxes turn a Toyota Camry into a luxury ride. Decent used imports are also hideously expensive, so we decided to bite the bullet and buy a locally manufactured car, the brand choices being Proton or Perodua.

We had budgeted for a family sedan, and all that bought us was a Perodua MyVi. A compact car smaller than a Ford Fiesta, its 1,000cc engine is still comfortably in the motorcycle range, and the workmanship would have any German auto safety inspector reach for the smelling salts. My elfin wife could easily dent the bodywork with her thumb, and when I drove the car from the dealer's lot, bumping over the curb as I turned, a hubcap flew off. There is an engineering maxim, "Good, fast, cheap. Choose two—you can't have all three." The MyVi was none of the three. Its only redeeming feature was that despite its size it accommodated all six of us, if we contorted ourselves into the right, if awkward, positions. This gave every outing the air of a circus act ("Look, there's the clown mobile again! And the fat one's driving—how did he get behind that wheel?"). But there was a silver lining to the whole car farce. After suffering financial defeat for the privilege of owning a car in Malaysia, we found all other related expenses below bargain level. Compared to the U.S. or—heaven forbid—Europe, gas was practically free in this oil-producing nation, spare parts cost next to nothing, and talented, hard-working mechanics usually charged so little for their services that we always tipped generously out of sheer guilt.

Plunging headlong into Sarawak's traffic, we had to adjust to some local idiosyncrasies, such as driving on the left side of the road. This required a level of spatial intelligence that was beyond me. For the first weeks, every second behind the wheel was a harrowing ordeal for me, as my brain kept steering back to the side it was comfortable with. Even after a full year of driving in Borneo, I would still slip up on occasion. After stopping on an empty country road in the middle of the night to photograph a snake, I would get back in the car and drive off on the wrong side of the road. My sons would then gently draw my attention to this potentially fatal mistake: "Uh, Dad? Change lanes, please?" Lisa, on the other hand, took to left-side driving like a duck to water. "I really don't understand what your problem is, dear. It's just the other side of the road!"

Clown car or no, the MyVi greatly expanded our horizons. We visited Kuching's Sunday Market, a huge wet market held in the streets of Satok, a neighborhood by the Sarawak River. It was loud, smelly, chaotic, and a fire hazard—in short, wonderful. The high-impact colors and patterned arrangements of the fruits and vegetables drew swarms of amateur photographers. There was produce we had never seen before, and familiar groceries like bananas in at least a dozen different unknown varieties. One stubby little kind, which our children dubbed banoonies, was phenomenally sweet, terribly cute, and bore the local name Hotel Banana, because five-star inns worked them into fruit arrangements for buffets and lobbies. The largest type was a 2-foot colossus that could double as a war club and was used for the ubiquitous banana fritters sold in street stalls.

In a back street dwelled the dark side of the market, the pet section. Here you could find animal species you probably only knew from *National Geographic*, all of them incarcerated. There were birds of all feathers and squirrels of all stripes. A barred eagle-owl[49] with a Batman mask and feathery donkey ears flaring sideways trained its onyx eyes on us. Small mammals were jammed into filthy wire-mesh cages. Nocturnal creatures tried in vain to hide from the sunlight. All of them were wild-caught, and everything about their presence in the market was illegal. This we learned weeks later from two Sarawak Forestry posters displaying the animals that were Protected and Fully Protected under state law. That day, in the Satok Sunday Market, the law seemed far away.

A DVD shop lured costumers with music at ear-melting decibels. Most disks cost about US$1, older ones 50 cents. The new ones were so new that the films were still

Barred eagle-owl

49 *Bubo sumatranus*

playing in theaters. We bought a few and discovered the cause for the parallelism: the movies had been shaky-cammed—recorded at the cinema with hand-held devices. Audio and video quality were beyond dreadful. Some of the older DVDs were much better because they had been copied from original disks. Not one among the thousands of disks in that shop was legally produced, and we wondered about the legitimacy of the enterprise. Maybe it was another one of those Malaysian live-and-let-live things.

*　*　*　*　*　*

Three weeks after our arrival, we finally met that most emblematic of Borneo's ecosystems, the primary lowland rainforest. Tropical rainforests loom large in the collective human imagination. They raise in our minds images of primeval luxuriance, of breathtaking beauty existing alongside primordial strangeness, all of it in shocking variety. Rainforests are hundreds of millions of years old. They shape weather patterns across vast regions. They hold a wealth of medical and other scientific knowledge, possibly even a cure to cancer. They are so complex and rich that our knowledge of them hardly scratches the surface.

But many people choose to ignore these facts because rainforests are money-printing machines. Logging not only generates enormous cash revenue (a single tree of the right kind can net hundreds of thousands of dollars), but also creates space for palm oil plantations. The fruit of the oil palm yields over ten times more oil than soybeans and sunflower seeds; palm oil is therefore the planet's most consumed vegetable oil. After petroleum, it is the second-most important oil in modern consumer society. It is found in about half of all packaged supermarket products, from snacks to soaps, and is also used as biofuel. After Indonesia, Malaysia is the world's second-largest palm oil producer. In 2015, 15.8 percent of the nation's total land area and over 70 percent of the nation's agricultural land was carpeted with oil palm plantations. The World Wildlife Fund website informs us:

> [T]he uncontrolled clearing of [tropical rainforests] for palm oil plantations has led to widespread loss of these irreplaceable and biodiverse rich forests. Plantations have also been connected to the destruction of habitat of endangered species, including orangutans, tigers, elephants and rhinos.[50]

---

50 "In the past 10 years, the world's orangutan population has decreased by 50 percent as a result of habitat loss from forest clearing for palm plantations. There are only 6,300 Sumatran orangutans left. It is estimated that 1,000 orangutans are killed a year, a major factor in these deaths being forest clearing for palm production. In 2006, at least 1,500 orangutans were clubbed to death by palm workers." (Source: *http://www.onegreenplanet.org/animalsandnature/top-10-facts-you-need-to-know-about-palm-oil/*)

But we already knew all this when we arrived at Kubah National Park. Most schoolkids in developed countries know that rainforests are much more than a bunch of wet trees, and that these forests need saving. However, most developed countries are also worlds away from them, and few first-worlders have first-hand knowledge of what a tropical rainforest looks, smells, sounds, and feels like. Today, we would enjoy the privilege of finding out.

Kubah National Park is a tract of lowland rainforest on Gunung Serapi, the mountain next to the *Nepenthes* badlands I had visited four years earlier. On the way to the mountain, we already noticed the immense height of the trees, most of them dipterocarps. Dipterocarp means two-winged seed. The trees were given the name for the shape of their reproductive elements; think maple whirligigs of tropical

Kubah National Park

proportions. Dipterocarps are those classic Southeast Asian rainforest trees with spherical crowns; on aerial photos they look like densely planted broccoli fields gone wild. We left the car at the park entrance, bought our tickets, and registered our personal information, in case we got lost (unlike in Sama Jaya, this made sense here). Armed with a complimentary map, we walked up a narrow road to the entrance of the Waterfall Trail where we descended into the jungle on very steep and slippery concrete steps. The air was unmoving and heavy with moisture. Two flights of stairs down, the stillness became intense. It was less of a silence—birds and insects were making sure they wouldn't go unnoticed—than an almost complete absence of movement. Apart from the occasional falling leaf and a bird flicking about in the canopy, little seemed to stir. Where were all the animals battling for "the most competitive place on Earth," as David Attenborough called the Bornean rainforest in *Planet Earth II*? He was spot on about another thing, though: it did look like Eden. The plant life defied description. Some rainforest patches in Borneo hold more species of flora in less than 4 square miles than all of North America and Europe combined. Of the hundreds of palm species in Borneo, almost a quarter can be found in Kubah. On this biological treasure island, botany is a science of superlatives and never-ending surprises.

In the primary rainforest, the dense tree crowns ensure that only about 2 percent of the sunlight reaches the forest floor, and now the low light added to the atmosphere. Although it was going on noon, I regretted not bringing my camera flash. It has been said that on Charles Darwin's voyage on the *Beagle*, the tropical rainforests became the

Licuala orbicularis, *a palm endemic to Borneo*

"cathedral of his religion." Surely the lack of light and movement contributed heavily to this image. On the rainforest floor, everything fights for the few lux that have made it this far. This makes for comparatively little undergrowth between the generously spaced tree giants and further intensifies the cathedral mood.

When our eyes had become accustomed to the shady conditions, suddenly Sir David's statement about the intense competition in the rainforest made sense. Never mind the animals; it was the greenery that was waging an epic war here. Plants, fungi, lichens, they all occupy individual niches, and they utilize nifty devices to defend and expand their turf and stay supplied with those precious sunrays. Whenever one of the huge trees crashes to earth, it creates an open sunroof in the canopy. Young saplings spring up in these gaps with blinding speed, and spar for the suddenly available sunlight. Most trees here were monopolized by epiphytic plants, from the roots to the canopy 200 feet above us. Lianas thicker than a man's thigh coiled around trunks that three adults could not encircle with outstretched arms. Some climbing vines were braided in thick strands like mooring hawsers; others were flat, like gigantic wooden duct tape; and they hung from the sky in knotty Gordian messes that would make any machete cry uncle. Dense curtains of air roots descended from the distant green ceiling. A few plants that were more familiar to us in their terrestrial forms had more venturesome cousins here. There were climbing palms, aroids, and ferns, and even some begonias had developed lofty aspirations and were well on their way toward the sun. Creepers, the climbers' pedestrian kin, had not yet managed vertical progress and

Air roots, Kubah
(photo, Christoph Lepschy)

Cauliflory

instead slunk around the forest floor at invisible speeds. They often sprouted meaty pumpkin leaves with thick bristles, a feature supposed to harness the humidity. (I cannot fathom why this should be necessary in the almost drinkable air of a rainforest. Isn't that like showering underwater? But what do I know … ?)

Fern colonies reigned over many trees. Large clumps of bird's nest ferns wowed the visitor, but they were a mere sideshow to the dazzling staghorn ferns[51] jutting dramatically out of the crooks of trees. Their cabbage-like shield fronds reached the size of beanbag chairs and held root balls that securely anchored the ferns to their host trees. The multifurcated fronds hanging from these orbs looked like massive antlers, magicked into floppy green wigs by naughty forest sprites.

The plants had all learned how to deal with their unique surroundings. To stay upright in the shallow soil, some of the tallest trees were propped up by buttress roots that dwarfed people and were as solid as walls. Some leaves had long, thin drip tips; others had holes, great and small, all designed to keep mold at bay by allowing quick runoff of the daily rains. Cauliflory was another survivalist trick; it made flowers grow directly from the tree trunks. This takes advantage of the myriads of invertebrates— and a few vertebrates—moving up and down the trees. As they drag their bodies over the flowers, they unwittingly help with pollination.

---

51 *Platycerium* sp.

"To some men," the explorer William Beebe assessed, "the jungle is a tangled place of heat and danger. But, to the man who can see, its vines and plants form a beautiful and carefully ordered tapestry." And just in case someone still complained of monotony in this highly organized chaos, there were enough orchids present to drive even the most jaded collector crazy—if not at their beauty, then at their unobtainability. Apart from a few terrestrial species, they all grew high up in the trees.

No magic world is perfect without a few dark elements, and Kubah did not disappoint here either. Two twisty bends down the next trail section (this one a web of roots, but at least mercifully flat), an angry cackle splintered the quiet. Above us in a tree sat the biggest and prettiest squirrel[52] I had ever seen. It wore a lush black-and-tan coat offset with cream and examined us with bottomless obsidian eyes. It was almost as big as a dachshund and didn't hold back with its opinion about us being in its forest. Safe on its perch, it made no attempt at concealing itself and kept hurling squirrely invectives at us with the brazenness of the untouchable.

The novelty of getting cussed out by a supersized rodent eventually wore thin, and we turned our attention to the tree it sat on. Gandalf's remark "There are older and fouler things than Orcs in the deep places of the world" started blinking in my mind. This can't be a tree, I thought. This must be something created by H.R. Giger's unsound imagination during a quick peyote break on the *Alien* set. The technical term is strangler fig, and like those African eyeball-eating worms it is a creature that will severely erode your faith in a benign God.

The strangler's life cycle starts mundane enough, with a bird eating one of its figs and later discharging the seed. For the strangler to develop in the right way, the bird needs to do its business on a tree branch—the higher the better. The seed grows slowly at first, getting its nutrients from sun, rain, and fallen leaves. It sends out thin roots that snake down the trunk of the tree or hang from the branches. When the roots reach the ground, they dig in and start growing aggressively, competing with the host tree for water and nutrients. They also send out more roots that encircle the host and fuse together as a network. As the roots grow thicker, they squeeze into the trunk and cut off its flow of nutrients. This usually kills the host, and the strangler fig becomes a columnar tree with a hollow core. (Some believe the strangler fig can help the support tree survive storms, but I reckon that's wishful thinking. Just ask Gandalf.)

The monstroddity looming before us had long since suffocated its poor host. After the victim had turned to dust, the fig's tree-sized latticework of massive roots remained, with enough room inside to shelter both of our sons and their two cousins. There was ample space for the four children to play house. The residents, though—a bat colony and a few battalions of multi-legged things—weren't in the mood for company, and the kids beat a hasty retreat.

---

52 *Ratufa affinis*, cream-colored giant squirrel

Strangler fig

Ornate coraltails (Ceriagrion cerinorubellum)

More dodgy flights of steps zigzagged between the giant tree bodies to the bottom of the valley where a boardwalk led to a pretty bridge across a shallow, unhurried stream. The forest had been slow in revealing its deeper secrets, but down here it finally began to relent. Invertebrate damsels and dragons now flitted, now levitated, above the water, their glassy wings too fast to see, and common tree nymphs,[53] large white butterflies with black polka dots, did their graceful slow glide like flakes of soot. One puzzles why such languid mode of flying has not led to the nymphs' extinction. Even a slow bird could catch a tree nymph with one wing tied behind its back. But the caterpillars of this species eat poisonous plants, which turns them into highly unpalatable and often lethal insects. Just as the highly visible, colorful bands on a coral snake advertise the reptile's venom, the nymphs' slow flight advertises their distinctive pattern, which birds, through experience, associate with a very unpleasant meal.

Two elephant ear plants[54] grew nearby, each heart-shaped, thickly ribbed leaf the size of an umbrella. On the far side of the bridge beckoned a begonia stand half the size of a tennis court. As I marveled at this field of marmoreal hunting-green leaves, I wondered why I had always snubbed begonias as Grandma's windowsill weeds, unattractive and banal. Now I understood that wildness was the key. Granny's house begonias were to this expanse of jungle what her lonely, caged parakeet was to a flock

---

53 *Idea stolli*

54 *Alocasia robusta*

Boardwalk, Kubah
(photo, Christoph Lepschy)

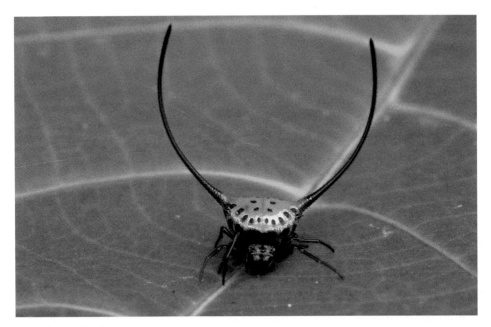

Long-horned orb weaver

of its wild peers screaming across the Australian desert. No wonder, crazy as I am about snakes, that I always feel that once confined to a terrarium they're even duller housemates than bricks.

Crossing the bridge, I ran my hand along the railing for support and almost crushed a long-horned orb weaver,[55] one of the freakiest arachnid designs in all creation. This spider's trapezoid body, smaller than a chickpea, is clad in shiny yellow armor with a line of black spots along the rim. Two short spikes point upward at the rear end, and a black head pokes out from under the casing. Pretty enough, but it all pales in comparison to the horns. On each side of the tiny body grows a black, inward-curving skewer that ends high above the body. For a similar head-to-antler ratio you would need to strap a set of oryx horns to a cat's skull. Common sense forbids seeing any logic in this body plan. How does this animal go about its daily business without its crazy horns getting tangled up in the vegetation? But like most things in nature, it all makes sense: the horns keep hungry predators away. Unless you're an expert sword swallower, this spider will stick in your craw. And the deterrent works so well that the spider has chosen to pay the small price of working around the handicaps it presents.

Hans Jr. shouted from the rear, "All hail the Queen of the Jungle!" His hands were in *namaste* position, palm-to-palm before his chest. His eyes were closed, and he affected

---

55 *Macracantha arcuata*

Hans Jr. with alien tiara

a facial expression that he doubtlessly considered a regal smile, although to everyone else he looked like a constipated Yoda. Stuck to his sweaty forehead was a kitschy ornament, the sort you would expect to see on an alien princess from a 1967 *Star Trek* episode. It was a crescent-shaped diaphanous sheet like a small rice-paper boomerang, and a brown, oval chip was embedded in its elbow. This was the world's largest flying seed, and an aerodynamic marvel. The Javan cucumber[56] is a scrambling vine from the pumpkin family that, upon reaching the upper stories of the canopy, grows basketball-sized seed pods. Every pod contains hundreds of these all-wing paper planes. As the seed ripens, the wing flaps curl upwards in a textbook example of modern aircraft design. When maturity is reached, the bottom cracks open, the seeds fall through, and their aerodynamics allow them to slowly glide away from the tree and travel huge distances. They move through the air like butterflies—they gain height, stall, dip and accelerate, once again producing lift, and their relative flight stability has inspired several pioneers of early aviation.

As the waterfall came within earshot, the humidity increased further, and so did the number of fungi. Heat and rain constantly leach the rainforest soil and leave it largely infertile. Most of the nutrients the plants receive come from recycled dead leaves and other vegetation. Fungi are among the most important recyclers, and here they showed amazing diverseness. Classic hat-style mushrooms in stylish deep carmine and hazmat-suit yellow grew alongside more offbeat structures. Pink bracket fungi clung to trunks like flying saucers docking at their motherships. Black mummified claws, commonly known as dead man's fingers,[57] reached for the living from their mulchy graves, and

---

56 *Alsomitra macrocarpa*

57 *Xylaria polymorpha*

Fried egg fungus with giant forest ant, and flip phone for scale

Waterfall, Kubah

a large stinkhorn[58] sent mixed messages by sabotaging the pristine aura of its white lacy bridal veil with an odor more commonly found in dumpsters. One fungus even pretended to be a fried egg—another great, if wholly unintentional, example of perfect mimicry. Assisting with the recycling efforts were 7-inch millipedes in varying liveries, from Ferrari red with bright white legs, to the colors of the German (and, incidentally, the Sarawakian) flag, all propelled forward by synchronized leg waves. One short, squat type, the pill millipede,[59] rolled up into a ball when picked up. In this position, the margins of its first and last dorsal plates fitted perfectly together to create a sealed sphere and the appearance of an exquisitely crafted nautilus.

After traversing over wet stone slabs that had now replaced the dirt trail, we arrived at a pond fed by the waterfall. The broad cascade rushed down three stories of layered black rock that looked like an ancient temple wall. The water was cold, the air filled with cool spray, and we did what every sane person would do after poaching in their own skin for two hours: we stripped and dipped. We floated on our backs in the crystal pool, humbled by the treetops surrounding the blue sky-hole half an infinity above us. We watched the air traffic—birds, butterflies, leaves, seeds—listened to unknown sounds, and breathed in scents telling of ancient rot and new growth. Our sense of time eroded; the time in the pond felt like immortality, untethered to any other reality than that of the forest. Meanwhile, little skin-eating fish were hard at work on our feet, giving us the mother of all exfoliation jobs. It was pure, unalloyed contentment, and a deeply refreshing experience in many different ways.

But the effects of the Cosmic Spa were not to last. Too soon after leaving the water, we were marinating again in our own juices, our efforts to dry off by basking in the sun stymied by the very attempt. As we put our sweaty clothes back onto our sweaty bodies, steeling ourselves for the climb out of the wet valley through the wet air, we were treated to a musical indulgence. For a moment, the arias of the bulbuls and the barbets, and the cicadas sawing their metalworking tunes, merged into a riotous biophony, and a large green stick insect with pink underwings dipped and flashed across the pond, as if conducting the piece from the air.

A metallic *meck!* pierced the afternoon, the unmistakable call of a Bornean horned frog,[60] a grouchy-looking amphibian that mimics dead foliage. The effect is achieved by fake mold spots and raised lines across the skin that imitate leaf veins. Spiky protrusions above the eyes that break up the frog's stocky outline perfect the illusion. The frog is haughtily aware of its superior camouflage. In ambush mode, it sits in the leaf litter waiting for dinner to march by—mostly insects, but it won't turn up its pointy nose at smaller frogs either. When disturbed, the Horned One will not,

---

58 *Phallus indusiatus*

59 Order Sphaerotheriida

60 *Megophrys nasuta*

Giant millipede

Bornean horned frog

Find the horned frog
(photo, Guek Hock
Ping (Kurt))

as lesser croakers might, vault off into space in high panic. Instead, it performs a short hop forward, and dares you to find it again on the leaf-strewn forest floor. To rephrase William Beebe's narrative about an encounter with a snake in similar disguise: while you are thinking frog and looking frog, your eyes insist on registering dead leaves, and it will be a while before you can honestly say "This is leaf; that is frog."

Bornean horned frogs are as legendary for their visual trickery as they are for their rain-predicting skills. Many frogs react to impending bad weather with increased calling, but this species is a highly effective early warning system. The brassy twang of their call travels long distances, and Chien Lee once suggested to me, "Run, don't walk, to the nearest shelter when you hear these guys." And now, true to Chien's warning, the world turned to water.

There was no shelter by the waterfall, and we took the full brunt of the biblical cloudburst. It came with shocking suddenness and the intensity of a car wash at full blast. Within seconds, we were as wet as if we had never left the pond. We started back up the valley, miserable and unsure how long the rain would last, or whether we would see the sun long enough again to dry out before sunset. Twenty minutes later, the rain was still bucketing down with unchanged strength, but strangely, the sky was clear. It took us a while to puzzle out that the heavy rain had now been replaced by heavy runoff from the leaves. At last, the shower stopped entirely, and the sun spit-roasted the world again. Sarawak receives 120 inches[61] of rainfall every year, and according to the locals, there are only two distinct seasons: a wet season and a very wet season. If this was the wet season, I was not looking forward to the other one. On the bright side, the forest had now changed for the magical. The green hues had intensified and multiplied into a million shades, and all was coated in a glistening, vivid sheen. The smells were more acute and pleasant, and even the ever-present musk of moldering vegetation now seemed to promise an abundance of life.

Borneo's rainforests may be fractured relics, but they are also an intact presence from an epoch long before we human apes started to remodel the planet. Kubah's incredible age and unimaginable number of biotic elements had filled me with awe and a heightened awareness of the life around us.

After meeting a wild silverback gorilla in Zaire, Douglas Adams wrote in "Last Chance to See" about his "inability to comprehend any of the life we had left behind in the forest" and proposed that "somewhere in the genetic history that we each carry with us in every cell of our body was a deep connection with this creature … always invisibly and unfathomably present."

In a similar vein, I was convinced that here in Kubah we had witnessed one of Earth's fundamental components.

We reached the parking lot in a semi-sundried state. I was fishing for the car key in my backpack when Karl started flailing his arms and bellowing like mad:

61 over 3,000 mm

"SNAKESNAKESNAKESNAKESNAKE! No, wait—it's a lizard! **Omigod, OMIGOD, IT'S A SNAKE EATING A LIZARD!"**

On the narrow strip of lawn that separated the parking lot from the jungle, a slender snake about 2 feet in length periscoped from the grass. Its head and neck, inflated for intimidation, was a gorgeous palette of bright red, blue, and yellow, while deep copper patches dominated the back. This beauty would have been a lucky find in and of itself, but we were indecently lucky. The beast carried in its maw a very agitated lizard with a fetching saw-tooth crest on the nape of its neck. Highly stressed about its predicament, the lizard had swapped its standard grass-green hue for a more appropriate black. The *Photographic Guide to Snakes & Other Reptiles of Borneo* that I kept in the glove compartment suggested we were watching a Kopstein's bronzeback[62] about to make a meal of a crested garden lizard.[63] Bronzebacks are a family of nonvenomous lizard eaters known for fast movements and needle-sharp teeth. If I wanted to take photos, I needed to lay out a meticulous plan to capture the snake swiftly and without bloodshed. I needed to be faster than the snake and smarter than the snake, and to stay away from those teeth.

"Focus!" I told myself, almost as stressed as the lizard now. "Stay in the present!" To calm and fortify myself for the imminent battle, I tried to recall inspirational quotes from Sun Tzu's *Art of War* ("In the midst of chaos, there is also opportunity!"). As always, the best-laid plans will be uprooted by teenage impatience, and without waiting for me to execute my grand stratagem, Karl snatched up the two reptiles in one hand and shoved them in my face with a scowl: "C'mon already, Dad, let's take some pictures!"

I always carry a small snake hook for such occasions and now used it to gently take the bronzeback and its prey to the center of the parking lot. Still perched on the hook, the snake prepared for defense by releasing the lizard. To avoid a crash landing, the lizard clamped its jaws on the snake's tail on the way down and now dangled in mid-air. Soon it realized how ludicrous it looked in this position and let go of the tail. Before it could hit the ground, the kids secured it for further inspection. In preparation for our photo session, I placed the snake on the ground and covered it with my bush hat to calm it down. Snakes are not the most perceptive of creatures; any dark place will do as a safe space. Covered with a hat, they mellow out in the dark and coil up after a few minutes. Once the hat is removed, you will get a few shots in before the snake gets wise to the scam and tries to run off again, restarting the cycle.

This works with most snakes, but apparently not, as we soon learned, with *Dendrelaphis kopsteini*. A fast and aggressive lizard chaser, it displayed copious vim and vigor. Instead of chilling under the hat like a good little snake, it sought escape with a vengeance, snapping at everything and everyone in its way, at one time even climbing my body in search of freedom, another time venting its righteous fury by emptying its bowels (a scare tactic widespread among snakes) onto my poor hat. My hopes for a few

---

62 *Dendrelaphis kopsteini*

63 *Bronchocela cristatella*

photographs worthy of the next *National Geographic Snake Special* were shat on by the snake's spirit of survival; the few shots that came out in focus despite the mayhem were all ruined by some undesirable visual element such as a finger, a shoe, or a child's face overjoyed with the insanity of it all.

*   *   *   *   *   *

Soon we mounted another expedition into the wilds of Borneo, this time to the wet market in Serian, a small town an hour southeast of Kuching. The drive took us along a well-kept, mostly four-lane highway and through a showcase of local agriculture. In front of a background of limestone karst cones were fields of eggplants and loofah gourds, neatly strung on long trellises, alternating with pepper vines scrambling up sturdy ironwood poles. We passed papaya and banana gardens, corn and tapioca patches, fishponds, and rice plots. Occasionally, a pig farm or a little settlement—two food courts, a bank, and a farmers' market—would break up the pastoral green. At the entrance to Serian Town, we were greeted by an 18-foot statue in the middle of a traffic roundabout. In the rest of the world, towns commemorate in statuary famous persons from their midst, often also historical events. But here, surrounded by artfully arranged palm trees, stood the concrete manifestation of a pale green fruit. Shaped like a rugby ball and covered in scary spikes, it bore likeness to a medieval weapon. Next to it was another one, cut open to show pillows of yellow flesh. Serian prides itself in producing the best durian fruits in Borneo, and the townspeople are so proud of this achievement that they commissioned not one but two durian statues. Long before social media became the battleground of choice for vicious partisan wars about anything people care to disagree about, people took to print to voice their feelings about the durian. It is one of those food items that smell like hell but taste like heaven; think Munster cheese or Taiwanese stinky tofu. US author John McPhee described durian as "a fruit that smells strongly fecal and tastes like tiramisu." Its scientific name, *Durio zibethinus*, from the Italian *zibetto* (civet cat), refers to the association of both creatures with foul odors. The durian gets to you before you get to it, and makes human nostrils quiver with either delight or disgust. There is no neutral ground on the subject, no demilitarized zone, but militant opinions exist aplenty on both sides of the Great Durian Divide. The hater faction usually resorts to descriptions like "pig-shit, turpentine and onions, garnished with a gym sock," or, if a generous mood prevails, "vanilla custard infused with rotten garlic." In 1869, Alfred Russel Wallace quoted in *The Malay Archipelago* a certain Dr. Paludanus, an early European visitor to Borneo, who offered one of the first and most on-the-nose descriptions of the unique smell and cultural status of durian:

> This fruit is of a hot and humid nature. To those not used to it, it seems
> at first to smell like unwashed genitals but immediately they have tasted

it they prefer it to all other food. The natives give it honorable titles, exalt it, and make verses on it, much as they treat the human phallus.

Wallace made no bones about his own feelings on the matter:

> Its consistence and flavour are indescribable. A rich butter-like custard highly flavoured with almonds gives the best general idea of it, but intermingled with it come wafts of flavour that call to mind cream-cheese, onion-sauce, brown sherry, and other incongruities. Then there is a rich glutinous smoothness in the pulp which nothing else possesses, but which adds to its delicacy. It is neither acid nor sweet, nor juicy, yet one feels the want of none of these qualities, for it is perfect as it is. It produces no nausea or other bad effect, and the more you eat of it the less you feel inclined to stop. In fact, to eat Durians is a new sensation, worth a voyage to the East to experience. I should certainly choose the Durian … as the king of fruits.

But why would God wreck what must surely be His favorite dessert by adding dozens of what scientists call "genetically turbocharged volatile sulfur compounds," the source of the smell? The answer is, predictably, survival. All fruit serve as bait for seed dispersers, but durian seeds are so big that the usual suspects like birds and squirrels cannot handle them. Larger mammals, such as orangutans, sun bears, deer, and tigers, are all able to open durians and swallow the seeds intact. Elephants are known to roll durians in leaves to protect their stomachs from the spikes, then swallow the bundle whole. Since large mammals roam large territories, the plant has evolved an odor that can be detected over long distances.

Durian statue, Serian

[Left] Durians at a roadside stall

[Right] Durian wholesalers, Padawan District

As luck would have it, a little old lady sold the real fruit from a folding table next to the statue. Sarawak's durian season runs from November to February, but a few individual trees will bear fruit in summer. During these mini seasons, which rarely last longer than three weeks, the short supply drives prices into the stratosphere. It was August now, and the durians on the lady's table weren't exactly bargains. But I freely admit to an almost unhealthy enthusiasm for the Sultan of Stink, and I will never let money stand between me and a good durian. Previously, I had only tried durians in Thailand and Taiwan (imported from Thailand), and was, despite my infatuation, ignorant about selecting a quality fruit.

The durian vendor, however, was an expert in her produce and in human nature. Seeing a bunch of gringos shyly approaching her stall, timidly touching the fruits, clearly craving them but also clearly clueless, she pounced on us like a leopard on a peg-legged monkey. Picking up a durian from the pile on the table, she proclaimed with conviction, "This is the best one. You should buy this!"

We were skeptical. The fruit had a fat, black bruise on one side, where some animal had tried to gnaw its way in. "Are you sure?" Lisa asked. "There's squirrel damage!"

"Oh, yes!" beamed the old lady. "That's how you know it's an excellent durian—the squirrels always know the best ones!"

And just as she had predicted, we bought both the fruit and her explanation. As fresh-off-the-boaters, who were we to doubt the wisdom of the people who had lived in these jungles for generations? All these years later, I am now positive that in at least one of the many native languages on Borneo there must be a phrase analogous to "I have a bridge to sell you," involving partially eaten durians and the street smarts of small mammals.

After we had eaten the (mediocre) durian right on the spot and under the amused eyes of the old lady, we drove into Serian to see the market. We took selfies in front of

[Above] Snakeskin fruit

[Right] Traditional rattan basket, woven with modern materials

the second durian sculpture, this one across from the entrance to the roofed market, and entered the building. Serian District has a population of about 90,000 scattered all over the surrounding countryside, chiefly consisting of indigenous people from the Bidayuh and Iban tribes. The market reflects this demographic. A broad roof, low ceiling, and weak bulbs created a subpar light, but the vivid colors of the produce, clothing, and handicrafts balanced out the dimness. Compared with the markets in Kuching, this one was "same-same, but different," as the Thais say. Same in the way it assaulted the senses, different in the products on sale. Here in the bush, many things were completely unknown to me. Bundles of edible fiddlehead ferns called *midin*[64] wrapped in large leaves sat next to trays with *salak*, snakeskin fruit, that grow at the bottom of a palm tree.[65] These resemble garlic cloves with hard brown scales, and taste like a crunchy cross between banana, pineapple, and industrial vinegar. Horse mangoes, from the wild, challenged us with a noxious smell immortalized by their scientific name, *Mangifera foetida*. Large stacks of thick green bamboo tubes were waiting to be stuffed with chicken, rice, and herbs, and cooked in an open fire. More upsetting for my inner horticulturist were the stubby, fist-sized *Nepenthes ampullaria* pitchers that had been repurposed as culinary treats. They had been cleaned out, filled with sticky rice, and steamed into tasty snacks. Among other plant parts used in ways unfamiliar to us were banana and ginger flowers that apparently could be sliced, fried and eaten.

The Serian market is also renowned for its native handicrafts, in particular woven rattan objects such as hats, bags, baskets, fish traps, and other useful and decorative

---

64 *Stenochlaena palustris*. Fun fact: After the end-Cretaceous mass extinction caused by an asteroid impact, a species of *Stenochlaena* was essentially the only common plant across North America for several thousand years.

65 *Salacca zalacca*

things. Finding good rattan in Borneo's overharvested forests has become difficult, and the artisans have resorted to an alternative source of material: post office packing bands. These plastic strips provide the same strength and toughness as the jungle vines, and unlike them, they come in more than one color, a bonus aspect that expands and enrichens the traditional art.

We bought a few faux-rattan pen holders and moved on to the meat section. It was mostly stocked with the usual cuts and chops from cattle and chickens, but there were also some articles whose consumption looked to be a matter of some courage. At the bottom of a shallow blue plastic basin, thumb-sized maggots with pincered black heads wobbled around, extending and contracting their bodies in a nauseating accordion motion. With their multiple bands and fat mid-sections, they looked like little Michelin men without heads and limbs. They were sago worms, the grubs of the red palm weevil,[66] a large snout beetle that lays its eggs on sago palm trees. After hatching, the larvae bore into the living tissues of the palms, where they feed until pupation. Sago worms are considered a major pest in palm plantations, but they are also a great source of fat and protein and, regardless of their sickening appearance, are considered a great prize around these parts. The writer Carl Hoffman, veteran of many sago worm barbecues among New Guinea's stone age tribes, compares their taste to "buttery, liquid pistachios." Others describe it as "about 60 percent prawn and 40 percent (fried) potato … or maybe peanut." The grubs can be roasted, sautéed, or fried, but most prefer to eat the little nasties alive. Sarawakian food blogger Poh Huai Bin describes how it is done:

Step 1: Pick a big, fat, and juicy worm. Care should be taken to not touch the sago worm's head since it has pincers that will bite you. The pincers are used to burrow into the sago palm trunk, so they're quite sharp.

Step 2: Look the sago worm in the eye. You're about to pull its head off and eat it so it's only polite to smile at it before doing so. Worms have feelings too.

Step 3: After the niceties have been done away with, it is time for heads to roll. Grip the squirming worm firmly with one hand and use the forefinger and thumb of your other hand to grasp the sago worm's head and rip it off.

Step 4: Insert the still wriggling worm into your mouth.

Step 5: Chew. Take the time to savor the taste of live sago worms. There is a burst of flavor when you first bite into the wriggling worm from the innards spilling out onto your palate. Delicious!

---

66 *Rhynchophorus ferrugineus*

I am sure that maggot guts exploding into your mouth are one of life's most divine treats, but for some inexplicable reason I decided against it and turned my back on the grub fest with a slight shudder.

Three stalls down, a bare-bellied man with a mullet haircut sat behind two sacks that seemed to contain large snakes. Through the cloth of one of the sacks I made out the distinct net pattern of a reticulated python. A look inside confirmed my observation, but alas, the snake had been chopped into dozens of thick slices ready for the grill. The snake in the other sack appeared at first glance to be an amputated, still twitching elephant's trunk. At the end of the trunk was a tiny head with two beady eyes on top. The mullet man gave me permission to lift the snake out of the sack. The snake's tiny, mud-colored scales were not flat and overlapping in that classic reptile style, but pyramid-shaped and granular to the touch. One reason for this odd feature is the snake's lifestyle: elephant trunk snakes, also called file snakes or wart snakes, are aquatic ambush predators that spend most of their lives at the bottom of rivers and estuaries. They catch fish by coiling their bodies around them, and their rough scales help secure the grip against the prey's mucus coating. The wart snake I was holding now[67] was 5 feet long and of extraordinary girth, another characteristic of these archaic creatures. It was also as docile as a kitten and made no attempt at escape. This made things easier, because despite the grippy granules, the snake was quite difficult to hold. The skin was astonishingly loose and felt almost disconnected from the underlying flesh, as if the snake had bought it three sizes too large, and I feared the reptile would slip from my embrace at the slightest movement. The way the creature looked at me broke my heart. Buying and releasing it would suggest more demand to the vendor and encourage him to procure more of these snakes. Calling the cops to deal with this flagrant violation of the Sarawak Wildlife Protection Ordinance would be useless at best. Most country folk in Borneo live in tight-knit groups that share not only kinship with local law enforcement, but also dietary preferences. The further you travel into the heart of Borneo, the more protected animals you find in the markets. In the frontier towns of the Kapit district, roughly one long day from Kuching, pangolins, mouse deer, civets, and other highly illegal items of fare are routinely sold in the presence of lawmen, sometimes even to them.

* * * * * *

Three days later we were at the Air Asia check-in counter at Kuching airport. Lisa, Karl, niece Hsiaochih, and nephew Yahsiu were going back to Taiwan. The next two years would be interesting, in good ways and bad. Karl would attend his final elementary school years in Taipei before joining his brother at the Lodge School in Kuching. Hans Jr. and I would spend the time on our Boys' Own adventure—alone in Borneo, without

---

67 *Acrochordus javanicus*

wife, mother, son, and brother. Hans would attend a new school and learn, think, and live in a new language; and for both of us it would be life in a new country. The family would convene twice a year for the school holidays—winters in Taiwan, summers in Sarawak. The rest of the time, the internet and real-time video communication would help ease the 2,000-mile separation.

But I was convinced it would all be worth it. After these short six weeks on the island, I could already predict with certainty that it wasn't just English that our sons were going to learn here. In their other school, Borneo's wilderness, they would learn life lessons about nature, ecology, and the grand scheme of things. And they would gain insight about our role on the planet, and our responsibilities as its stewards.

5   ALONE IN THE JUNGLE

Boredom is immoral. All a man has to do is see. All about us nature puts on the most thrilling adventure stories ever created, but we have to use our eyes.

William Beebe

The bickering geckos in the air conditioner woke me before the alarm clock could do its dirty deed. The Malay name for these pale little wall runners[68] was one of the first words I had learned in that language, and I kept hearing it in the house day and night. The males barked it out whenever the mood took them—"*Chichak chichak chichak!*"

I got up, hit the shower, and yelled "GET UP AND HIT THE SHOWER!" in the direction of my son's room. A while later, still blurry-eyed from our snake-hunting cruise the previous night, Hans Jr. and I climbed into the car and headed for our regular Sunday program. The two of us had been fending for ourselves in Borneo for over half a year now. Hans had adapted well to life at the Lodge School, his English was progressing rapidly, and we both had settled into a comfortable routine. On Sundays, this meant rock climbing at the Fairy Cave for him, and for me, exploration of the boondocks. At Hans' behest we had made contact with Kuching's rock-climbing scene, which I had seen in action during the 2007 Nepenthes Summit, and he had applied himself to the sport with unanticipated fervor. Our clown car was history now, replaced by a proper Borneo Macho Mobile, a black Mitsubishi Triton off-road pickup with added roof lights for our nocturnal snake drives. The truck bed held everything needed for a day on the walls: shoes, chalk bags, harnesses, 400 feet of rope, and a duffel bag bulging with carabiners, ATC belay devices, quickdraws, Grigris, and other esoteric geegaws with names and purposes not immediately comprehensible to non-climbers.

On this brilliant Sunday morning, we were once more on our way to the limestone walls in Bau. We stopped at a food court to pick up the *Borneo Post* and breakfast:

Rambutan fruit

steamed Chinese pork-and-egg buns, iced cocoa, and a large kopi-o kosong. Many food courts aren't big on takeaway drinks, and since I had forgotten my travel cup, the cocoa and coffee came in two little cellophane bags tied up with strings, straws sticking out from the knots. As rock climbing is a sport rich in camaraderie, we also relieved a fruit hawker of six durians and a few kilos of *rambutan* to share with our friends. Rambutan loosely translates into "hairy one", and denotes a plum-sized fruit covered in red feelers in dire need of a trim (think Animal, the Muppet Show drummer). Rambutans can be likened to lychees but taste much more binge-worthy. To many, they're the fruity equivalent of Pringles: "Once you pop, you can't stop!"

The vendor also had fresh mangosteens, the Queen of Fruits to King Durian. These deep purple orbs are the size of tangerines, and their half-inch thick shell protects a nest of fluffy white segments. The taste is impossible to describe. Various comparisons to strawberries, kiwis, and peaches have all been attempted and failed. The closest approximation I am aware of is found in the diary entry of a "traveler to the East" only known as "T.W.K.", who noted on February 5, 1878:

> The pulp melts away in your mouth after the manner of a ripe peach or strawberry; it has a taste which nobody can describe any more than he can tell how a canary sings or a violet smells; and I know of nothing more forcible than the statement of a Yankee skipper who pronounced the mangosteen the "bang-upest fruit" he had ever seen.

The mangosteen's manna-like appeal conceals a darker side. The fruit is banned from many hotels in South East Asia, because the purple sap from the skin is incredibly difficult to remove from linens and towels. Hans Jr. was worried that his precious gear and garb would suffer indelible stains from unwashed after-snack hands, but I promised to bring out the mangosteens only at the end of the climbing day, after everything had been safely wrapped and stashed.

I had to keep my eyes on the road and my hands on the steering wheel, so my son fed me pork buns while he read the *Borneo Post* headlines to us. Apart from the usual Saturday night fare—drug busts, alcohol-induced vehicular crashes, and a spot or two of domestic violence—the news showcased how closely the lives of Sarawakians are intertwined with nature, some of it severely red in tooth and claw. We learned that the Sarawak Forestry Department had culled two 12-foot saltwater crocodiles[69] near Betong, where the beasts had been hanging around riverside huts in a suspicious manner. In other news, a villager was in the hospital after a cobra bite. The snake had crept onto the man's porch where he and some friends were guzzling *arak*, high-octane moonshine, which explained why the man had insisted on petting the venomous reptile. We also heard about the fate of an Indonesian dockhand. Instead of walking all the way from his workplace to the portable toilet, he had squatted in the boggy waters of Kuching Harbor and promptly got his behind snacked on by a juvenile croc. The victim had escaped without severe injuries, with the possible exception of a badly bruised ego (I'll bet his buddies will never let him hear the end of it). All levity aside, it was a textbook case of humanity's increasing encroachment on crocodile territory; the poor animal must have been half-starved to attack prey of that size.

The sun already ruled the sky when we arrived at the climbing site. The area beneath the white crags was strewn with mats, climbing equipment, and picnic trappings. About a dozen climbers plus entourage were on the ground. On the walls, a dozen people aged 7 to 57 monkeyed up the pre-bolted sport routes. Rock climbers are a free-spirited tribe, and the monikers given to the routes ranged from the descriptive (Chimney, Chichak) to the gnomic (Pickpocket, Bacon Burger, Bus Lychee). The walls also had names, but those reflected more concrete realities. At the top of the Tiger Wall grew a huge stand of tiger orchids, the world's tallest orchid;[70] and the reward for reaching the anchor on the Nepenthes Wall was a close view of an impressive *N. northiana* colony. With the expanse of primeval green on the hillsides, and the caves inside the limestone formations providing shelter for plants and animals of all sorts, Wild Borneo was on show here. Among the dense vegetation on the walls and slopes above the climbing routes were exquisite orchid varieties like Mr. Stone's lady's slipper,[71] and *Plocoglottis hirta*, locally known as the mouse trap orchid for the shape of its flower lip. In the air, cave-dwelling swiftlets performed aerobatic insect hunts,

---

69 *Crocodylus porosus*

70 *Grammatophyllum speciosum*

71 *Paphiopedilum stonei*

*Climbing at the
Fairy Cave*

and a greater coucal[72]—a chicken-sized cuckoo—hop-skipped around the access road in search of fresh roadkill. Egrets, herons, and various kingfishers populated the ponds and paddies across from the crags. A pair of owls nested next to one of the climbing routes. Lucky climbers who disturbed a flying snake[73] basking on a wall could observe it spread its ribs and glide off to the next tree in rippling movements like a kite tail in a breeze. As I am writing this, I glance from time to time at the 10-foot skin of a dog-toothed cat snake[74] on my office wall. The snake had shed it across the Rodeo route, 40 feet from the ground, and my sons had brought it back to me as a Father's Day present.

I parked the car under an overhang and helped Hans unload his stuff and the fruit haul. After some chitchat with the climbers, I sat under a large fig tree and organized my camera gear. I had planned a visit to an oil palm plantation a few kampungs down the road. I had heard that the fallen palm fronds were favorite nesting places for rats, which in turn attracted large snakes, which in turn attracted large German snake connoisseurs. When I zipped up my camera backpack, an animal launched itself off the fig's trunk, spread its wings, and landed on my knee. I knew right away what it was: my nemesis.

According to Melissa Mayntz' Bird Glossary,[75] in birding circles a nemesis bird is defined as follows:

> A bird that is highly sought after by an individual birder but despite repeated efforts to be seen, remains elusive and is not able to be added to

---

72 *Centropus sinensis*

73 *Chrysopelea* sp.

74 *Boiga cynodon*

75 https://web.archive.org/web/20161017172100/http://birding.about.com/od/Bird-Glossary-N-O/g/Nemesis-Bird.htm

the birder's life list. Nemesis birds are often regularly seen by other local birders and the birder missing each sighting can eventually come to see finding the bird as a quest or challenge to one's birding honor.

That speckled-gray thing on my leg was now flashing its yellow dewlap at me in an entertaining display of high testosterone. It was not a bird, though. It was a small, delicate lizard with spindly claws, a long, skinny tail, and a pair of wings folded against its sides. In hunting terms, a fat pheasant had just landed on my shotgun. I told my racing heart to be still, gently closed my hand around the scaly aviator lest it take to the air again, and had a proper look. The genus *Draco* contains more than 40 species of so-called flying dragons. Their day-to-day habits are nothing to write home about; they live on trees and spend their days lapping up ants that march up and down the bark. Their body structure, on the other hand, is the stuff of High Fantasy. These lizards have a set of elongated ribs they can extend and retract. Between the ribs are folds of often colorful skin, and both rest flat against the body when not in use. Once unfurled, ribs and skin form large, rounded wings that allow the reptile to ride on the wind like a hang glider, while its long tail does the steering. Like all gliding animals, *Dracos* are not capable of powered flight, but through skilled maneuvering they often obtain lift during their glides. Sorties of 200 feet over which the lizards lost less than 30 feet in height have been recorded. This is an exceptional feat, considering that these dragons are rarely longer than 7 inches, tail included.

The little dragon had dropped its silly posturing and was fixing me with a cocked stare. *Look at us,* I thought. *Two life forms from the same planet, locking eyes in mutual inscrutability.* We occupied the same spot and breathed the same air, yet we were poles apart in design and lifestyle. I allowed myself to luxuriate both in the company of this unbelievable creature and in my personal victory. *Draco sumatranus* is one of the most common species in Borneo, and found at forest edges, in open shrubland, plantations, and gardens. Found by everyone but me, that is. Since our arrival in Sarawak, I had been looking everywhere for this reptile, and while all my friends swore up and down that *Dracos* could indeed be found everywhere, I kept striking out. Fellow naturalists told me that the palm trees lining the parking lot at Sama Jaya Forest Park were practically infested with dragons. Well, not when I went there, they weren't, and not the next 20 times either. No sight. No sign. No nothing. Birders were the worst, driving me mad with their attempts at being helpful:

"Dracos? Oh, we see those all the time."

"Oh yeah? How come?"

"Well, we're birders; we look up into the trees, don't we?"

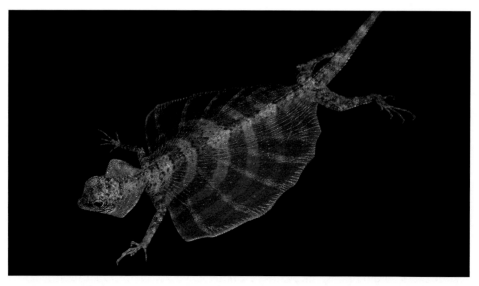

Draco quinquefasciatus
(photo, Björn Lardner)

At times it was difficult to stay composed when all I really wanted was to strangle someone with their binocular straps. In a just world I should have already racked up at least two dozen sightings. But in retrospect, maybe the *Draco* being served to me on a silver platter was the universe's reward for lasting eight dragonless months without murdering anybody.

I called Hans over and showed him the little flyboy, which excited him to no end. After taking a few photos I suggested releasing it by way of a flight show. From my open palm, I pitched the beast high in the air, where it unfolded its mighty wings and took off like Smaug leaving Lonely Mountain, sharply banking toward the next tree. To our amazement, it also gained considerable altitude and landed on the trunk a good 15 feet above the ground.

Flying snakes and lizards, frogs and geckos with parachute feet, wing-suited mammals—why are there so many species of gliding animals in Borneo while there are none in the Amazon region, and only a few in African forests? The reason might be that Borneo's rainforests are dominated by giant dipterocarp trees. These are not only spaced more widely apart than the trees in the other two regions, but they fruit infrequently and unpredictably. To survive, animals often need to travel far, and gliding from tree to tree saves time-consuming trips to the ground and energy-consuming climbs back up again.

A stone's throw from nowhere, not far from the Fairy Cave, lies the tiny hamlet of Serikin. Downtown Serikin is not very impressive: a few simply built houses, a chartreuse police station. At the end of the main drag sits a large parking lot. On most days it is empty, but on weekends it struggles to accommodate the flood of vehicles arriving for the Serikin Border Market. Traders from both sides of the Malaysian/Indonesian border hawk a mind-boggling variety of things here, with the useful competing for attention with the kooky. Sarongs, rattan furniture, and hand-woven mats are laid out next to dried crocodile penises and plastic ukuleles. The snack vendors are loyal to the gustatory credo of the American Deep South—"if it ain't fried, it ain't food"—but the wellness-minded visitor need not despair. There is plenty of fresh jungle produce from both Sarawak and Kalimantan, as the Indonesians call their part of Borneo (and, indeed, the entire island).

I left Hans Jr. with his climbing gang and drove to Serikin to stock up on fruit and fritters for my trip to the oil palm plantation. The parking lot was nearing capacity, and the market street jammed with shoppers. Weaving my way through the throng, I noticed a little man behind an empty folding table. He was very thin and very sunburnt, and he wore the traditional Borneo frontier costume—flip-flops, soccer shorts, and a *Fly Emirates* promo t-shirt.

As soon as his eye caught mine, he leaned across his little table and began to gibber at me in a throaty half-whisper: "Sir! Hey, sir! Turdleks? Ping-pong? TURDLEKS? PING-PONG?"

What on Earth was he jabbering about? An alien race that loved table tennis? Ambushed by this apparent nonsense, my mind failed to produce a better explanation. The man rolled his eyes at my flummoxed expression. After a furtive glance to the left

[Left] Serikin border market

[Right]Dried crocodile penises, Serikin border market

and right, he removed a shoe box from under the table and showed me the contents: dozens of little white spheres that looked like ping-pong balls until I realized what I was looking at.

Sea turtle eggs.

There are seven species of sea turtles in the world, all of them are endangered, and many at risk of extinction. A major cause for their predicament is poaching. Sea turtles are protected by law in most countries; regardless, they are hunted for their shells, meat, and eggs. Studies have found that regular consumption of turtle eggs is bad for you; they contain extreme levels of heavy metals, industrial pollutants, and cholesterol. They are also ridiculously easy pickings. A gravid turtle comes ashore and digs a hole in the sand, where she deposits between 50 and 200 eggs, depending on the species. She fills the hole with sand again and swims back out into the ocean, leaving the hatchlings to fend for themselves. A layer of sand is the only protection for the eggs. Any child can harvest them, and in doing so, it helps decimate an entire generation of a creature with a truly glacial reproduction rate—female sea turtles need at least 30 years to mature into reproductive adults, and they only lay eggs every two to four years. Bluntly put, cleaning out a sea turtle nest borders on genocide.

Malaysia considers sea turtles a national heritage. Turtle conservation is taken seriously at many levels, and local laws ban the harvesting, trade, and consumption of sea turtle eggs. But like in feudal Russia, in Borneo "God is high above, and the tsar is far away." Wildlife contraband was almost to be expected here in the sticks. But I was in no mood for forgiveness. I gave the egg poacher a cramped smile and went straight to the cop shop across the street to rat on the bastard.

The lobby of the police station was deserted, as was the area behind the counter. I waited a few minutes, then announced my presence with a loud *Selamat pagi!* even though the morning didn't seem so good to me anymore right now. My call was not answered. I called out a few more times. Nothing stirred in the building. I checked the station's parking lot and noted with some alarm that each space was occupied by a police car. If their cruisers were all here, where were the cops? For all I knew, they were lying in their own blood somewhere in the back, massacred by turtle egg poachers, or by a former headhunting tribe on a nostalgic mission to revive cherished customs.

I returned to the lobby, which was just as dead as it had been five minutes ago. This wasn't about turtle eggs anymore now. Very possibly, an atrocious crime against Sarawak's Finest had taken place here. I steeled myself against the horrors I was about to witness and ventured further into the bowels of the building, shouting, "Hello! Anybody here?" as I went along. The kitchen was abandoned, the men's prayer room vacant. After some inner negotiations, I plucked up the courage to peek into the women's *surau* and the officers' quarters. No body anywhere, alive or butchered. The place was as silent as a church on bingo night. I scanned every room in the station,

Wooden hornbill heads, Serikin border market

including the toilets, without finding anyone, and left through the back door. Behind the house, the only living being was a one-eyed calico cat whose arched back and raised hackles made it clear that it wasn't going to share its dumpster with me.

I was at a loss. Though glad I had proved my mass murder theory wrong, I was still outraged at Mister Ping-Pong's nerve to sell his ill-gotten loot in plain sight of a police station. I had a burning need to take him down but didn't feel like spending all Sunday waiting for the cops to return to duty from wherever. And what if they didn't come back at all? I looked at the hordes passing by outside the station. Did they know what was going on, and why? I didn't even dare speculate about the what and why, for fear of arriving at some very depressing results. To get over my foul mood, I told myself that I couldn't right all the wrongs I saw, and that I really should lighten up—hey, there were snakes waiting for me in that oil palm plantation! I bought a cup of freshly pressed sugarcane juice and 2 pounds of *langsat*,[76] grape-sized fruit with a tan, velvety skin and a grapefruit aroma that always had a cheering effect on me. Then I climbed into my truck and put Serikin in the rearview mirror in the hope the day would improve.

---

76 *Lanium parasiticum*

* * * * * *

The drive to the plantation zigged and zagged through cultivated and abandoned farmland, wild-looking scrub, and patches of secondary forest. The dominant green left little room for other colors; variation was mostly provided by the blue sky and the black bitumen. The pavement was hot enough to sear a steak, and I harbored little hope of seeing jaywalking animals of any kind.

I hadn't quite finished that thought when a small snake with four legs at the front end emerged from a row of tapioca plants and moved onto the road. I stomped hard on the brakes, almost fishtailing the truck into the tapioca. In full disregard of the heat (and my hair-raising stunt), the snake took its sweet time to cross the broiling asphalt, giving me a chance to study it. It was not a snake at all, but a little lizard striped in copper and green, with a slim body and a streamlined head that reminded me of a Japanese bullet train. Unlike the Shinkansen, though, the lizard had a tail, and this tail was more than three times longer than the rest of the animal. Borneo had delivered another superlative to me—the six-striped long-tailed lizard,[77] owner of the longest tail in all lizarddom.

When I slowed down to turn into the oil palm plantation, I noticed a 3-foot length of black rubber hose on the opposite lane. It was so black it was almost blue, and it had a highly polished shine to it. One end of the hose rose a few inches from the ground, trained its eyes on me, and flared a cobra hood. I had a mind to roll down the windows, turn the stereo to 11, and blast "Ordinary Man" from the movie *Tapeheads* ("Any ordinary man would have given it up by now!") to share my triumph with all of southern Sarawak. For behold! the shiny black tube was an equatorial spitting cobra,[78] another nemesis species I had coveted since we moved here. This one was not a well snake, though. Snakes seek cool places when it's hot, and warm places when it's cold. But even an equatorial species would never intentionally sit on a blacktop in the

Six-striped long-tailed lizard

---

77 *Takydromus sexlineatus*

78 *Naja sumatrana*

Equatorial spitting cobra

tropical sun at noontime unless something was fundamentally wrong with it. I pulled over, walked to the cobra, and carried it out of the murderous sun with my snake hook. Had it been attacked by a predator, or hit by a motorist? Impossible to say. I would have loved a thorough photo session with this beauty, but that would have amounted to animal cruelty. The snake was too weak to even hood up in protest now, let alone spit venom. I placed it in a moist spot under a fallen banana leaf, took a voucher shot with my phone, and hoped the cobra would regain its strength before nightfall, when the wild boars and other snake eaters started their rounds.

The dirt roads inside the plantation were an offroader's wet dream. They looked like the receiving end of a busy artillery range, and early morning rain had ramped up the muck factor. The deep ruts and potholes were filled with a mixture of muddy water and watery mud that caked my truck like brown plaster. I found the plantation manager, an ethnic Chinese by the name of Mr. Chong, placing offerings in a little Earth God shrine. The plus-sized *angmo*[79] in fatigues asking him in Taiwan-accented Mandarin for permission to search for snakes on his plantation threw Mr. Chong into a brief culture shock. But he quickly recaptured his composure and kindly agreed; even more kindly, he offered to give me the grand tour. I happily accepted his assistance, because palm oil plantations are perfect places to get good and properly lost. There are few landmarks

---

79 lit. red hair; Hokkien nickname for Caucasians

Oil palm plantation

apart from the dirt roads, and every palm tree is an exact clone of its neighbor. The effect is that of opposing mirrors and their infinite reflections. Mr. Chong told me proudly that the plantation was too big to walk across in one day. Tailoring the tour to my specific interests, he showed me a hole in the ground in which he suspected there lived a very big snake that came out at night and ate his chickens. He backed up my information that rats, attracted by the nutritious palm fruit, loved to build their nests under fallen palm fronds; and that their presence brought in hungry snakes. Pythons and rat snakes, he informed me, were sighted almost daily, and once in a while they would spot a king cobra[80] looking for its staple diet of pythons and rat snakes. I could not believe my luck. I hefted my snake hook and went to work on the nearest mound of palm fronds.

It didn't take me long to wise up to the folly of my undertaking. An oil palm frond is between 6 and 10 feet long and can weigh over 20 pounds.[81] Pulling apart a whole heap of them was exhausting work, and every pull threatened to deform my hollow aluminum snake hook, which had not been designed as a stump ripper. Sometimes a frond was stuck and required even harder pulling. In such cases, the frond would often

---

80 *Ophiophagus hannah. Ophiophagus* means snake eater.

81 1.8–2.0 meters and over 9 kg

break free, releasing all tension and sending me crashing on my butt. After a few of these mishaps I realized that should I also uncover an enraged snake in the process I would find myself in an awkward, if not downright dangerous, situation. I explained my defeat to Mr. Chong, who looked relieved that I had finally seen the madness of my ways. In his kindness he offered consolation: would I perhaps like to visit the workers' living quarters instead?

Riding shotgun in my truck, he directed me to a wide creek traversed by a tall, one-lane bridge. Wooden boards covered its roadway; on top of the boards two parallel lines of planks ran along the bridge. The distance between the planks matched a car's track width. They increased the stability of the bridge but required drivers to place their wheels exactly on top of them. I had driven across similar bridges before and skidded off those rails several times. Usually, sliding off was hardly more than an inconvenience; you just steered your vehicle back onto the tracks and kept going until the next slide-and-repeat. This bridge, however, had a terrifying handicap: it was barely wider than my car and had no guardrails. Drifting off the tracks might very well result in a 20-foot tumble into the shallow waters below. Mr. Chong was looking at me expectantly, unconcerned with the mortal danger we were facing. From the far side, a small dump truck piled high with palm fruit thundered onto the bridge without slowing down. In mid-crossing, the driver lit a cigarette. He cupped his left hand around the lighter in his right hand, leaving the steering wheel unattended. My stomach lurched. No way in hell was I going to partake in this lunacy. I announced to Mr. Chong that we were going to walk. I could sense that his opinion of my manliness had just nosedived, but, kind as he was, he kept his disappointment to himself and led me across the bridge to the workers' quarters.

Walking through the sea of identical palm trees, I remembered some facts about the biodiversity in these plantations. When forests are leveled for palm oil, all forest trees and plants, three quarters of forest birds and butterflies, and half of the other insect species are lost. According to a 2018 study published in the journal *Biological Conservation*, oil palm plantations host a much lower number of frog species than the forests in the same area. Moreover, these monocultures exhibit an edge effect which extends as far as 2 miles on all sides, resulting in a decline in the frog diversity in adjacent forests. Rats and their predators, like snakes and monitor lizards, are among the few animals that prosper in an oil palm plantation.

The effect of palm oil cultivation on forests and its inhabitants, including nomadic jungle tribes like Borneo's Penan, is well known. A less appreciated fact is the de facto slavery many plantation workers are subjected to. Mr. Chong took me to a small unpainted longhouse that served as the staff quarters. Apart from the stilts, the charmless structure seemed to be entirely made of thin plyboard—walls, roof, floor, ceiling, even the cooking platform at the far end of the main room. A laundry tub, a ripped-up plastic couch, and a pioneer-era vanity set all evidenced the room's

[Left] Plantation worker playing cards

[Right] Oil palm fruit

multifunctional character. Five young, bare-chested Indonesian men greeted us shyly. One lounged on the ratty couch, the others sat in a circle on the floor, playing cards. One of them had a small bottle of orange soda tied to his ear with a string. Mr. Chong helpfully explained, "They have no money to gamble, so whoever loses gets the bottle hung on his ear until another one loses."

While I watched the four men play, I asked Mr. Chong about their lives. His answers were surprisingly candid. All his plantation workers had crossed the border illegally on "mouse trails", jungle footpaths used for smuggling, and were now illegally staying and working in Sarawak. They toiled long, backbreaking days, cutting 50-pound palm nut clusters from the trees using sickles with 16-foot handles, and loading the clusters onto trucks by hand. Health insurance, occupational pensions, and labor unions were not in the picture. Their pay was below the state's minimum wage and partly paid in salt, which they took back to their families in Kalimantan during their annual leave. Lacking funds for airfares or even for long-distance buses, they hitchhiked wherever they could, and walked when luck ran out. Getting home could take up to ten days. Mr. Chong told me all this in a matter-of-fact tone, as if the five Indonesians before us were mere commodities. I made a vow to remember these guys and their brutal lives every time I went shopping for toothpaste, margarine, soap, ice cream, cosmetics, instant noodles, packaged bread, chocolate, Nutella, Doritos, and a gazillion other innocuous-looking supermarket products containing palm oil.

After taking Mr. Chong back to his office, I walked around aimlessly to clear my head, careful to stay on the roads and avoid any turns I wouldn't remember later. I found a well-stocked fishpond, built as a protein larder for the workers. There I rested under a shady tree and ate a few langsat. A little Eurasian kingfisher,[82] head and back a glamorous metallic-blue, its front a solid orange, perched on a low branch nearby and surveyed the water for prey. These birds have an extremely broad distribution, from Ireland to Japan. I had seen them in my youth in Germany, and later around the brooks outside our house in Taiwan (where they're called fish dogs). I turned to reach into my bag for more langsats, and when I looked to the kingfisher again, my heart almost stopped. The bird was still there, but it was stonking huge now and had changed its colors. The beak was crimson and large enough to kill a rat; head and front were beige; only the wings and tail had remained blue. I briefly entertained the notion that the Eurasian kingfisher might possess magic properties allowing it to change size and colors at will. Then I grasped what had happened. While I had rummaged in my bag, the smaller bird had flown off, and seconds later, a stork-billed kingfisher,[83] the biggest species in Borneo, had taken over its spot.

On my way out of the plantation I gave the dirt roads another chance to muddy the few remaining clean parts of the car they had missed on my way in. I took lunch in an eatery-cum-general-store in a nearby kampung. It was a dimly lit place with two tables and a no-nonsense menu scrawled on the wall: Fried rice. Fried noodles. Instant noodles with fried egg.

A brindled puppy was snoring in the corner, deaf to the two squabbling chickens circling it. The rice, fried in butter, was mixed with roast pork, fish balls, eggs, and leafy vegetables, and flavored with a mix of herbs and spices that made the desert bloom and the angels sing. The meal came with an aromatic and highly incendiary dipping sauce that made my tongue smile and my nose run like the Energizer Bunny. Every ingredient had been locally sourced within a mile of the village. Clearly, the culinary arts were being taken seriously here; after the second mouthful I wondered why the *Guide Michelin* inspectors kept ignoring Sarawak's backwoods.

Anthony Bourdain, of course, knew all about the treasures of the hinterland:

> As I have found in my travels, a certain degree of dirtiness, lack of refrigeration, and close proximity to livestock is often a near-guarantee of something really good to eat.[84]

Friends in Kuching had recommended an interesting two-hour trail nearby that connected two villages and ran through jungle, orchards, fields, and rubber plantations.

---

82 *Alcedo atthis*

83 *Pelargopsis capensis*

84 *The Nasty Bits*, 2006, Bloomsbury Publishing Inc.

I parked in the closest of the two villages and looked for someone to show me the trailhead. It was beastly hot, and the place was deserted. The village dogs lay under a stilt house, too listless to even flick their ears as I passed by. Half a dozen mopeds and two dusty pickups were melting in the sun, but none of the owners were around. In fact, nobody was around at all. I thought about aborting the mission and retrying it next weekend, when I noticed an old man in a rocking chair smiling at me from the deep shade of his porch. He wore only shorts, and his wrinkly, yet still athletic, body was decked out from chin to ankle in tribal tattoos. He waved and offered a dentally challenged grin. What a crying shame we couldn't communicate, I thought. This old-timer must have some fascinating stories. But I spoke neither Malay nor Bidayuh, his native language, and the idea of him conversing in English was wishful thinking. He had probably spent his whole life in this village, dropping out of school early to help his parents in the fields, learning only what life taught him.

He stood abruptly, widened his smile, and said with flawless British intonation, "Good day to you, sir! How are you this fine afternoon? I'll bet you're looking for the trail to the next village. I daresay you look the sort. Quite a few city folks fancy that trail. Come now, I'll show you!"

The trailhead was forgotten; all I could think now was *How in tarnation did he learn that?* My mouth was dry when I finally managed to stammer a response: "Ah, hello. Sir. Uhh, very kind of you, that. Yes. Uh. Hah! Nice to meet you. Say, your English is totally beyond awesome, man. Where did you learn it?"

His eyes lit up. He invited me onto his porch, pulled up a chair for me, poured me a glass of iced bark tea, and for the next half-hour educated me about the Good Old Times. He had been born during the Japanese occupation of British Borneo and had spent ten years with a road construction crew led by British engineers. With Sarawak's 1963 inclusion in the Malaysian Federation, Malay became the country's official language. But as a result of almost 120 years under British rulers and a deep-rooted independent streak, Sarawak is still today one of only two Malaysian states where English is the official language of the courts (Sabah is the other such state), and where a lot of the old kampung dwellers still speak it beautifully. Many of them still see West Malaysia's federal government as a hostile occupying force; although they will have learned Malay in school, they're not overly fond of using the language of what they regard as their oppressors.

The old man—I never learned his name—was in the middle of a tirade against the Malaysian government and its tragic incompetence, lamenting that everything had been so much better under the Brits, when I looked at my watch. He broke off his rant. "Oh, I am so sorry! Of course, you came to find the trail, not to listen to me whinge about politics! Really, terribly sorry! Come on, let's go!" I grabbed my pack and gulped down the last of my bark tea, but he was already striding across the village square, motioning me to follow him. At the trailhead he repeated his apology for wasting my

[Above] Drying tree bark to make tea

[Left] Rubber tree seed pods

time with his old geezer twaddle. I had found his story very enlightening and told him as much, but he insisted that he'd been an utter bore. After a few final pleasantries we shook hands and I started down the trail, still shaking my head in wonder.

The first leg of the trail was a line of wooden boards across fruit gardens and small cultivated plots. A bandy-legged man with a face like a walnut walked out of the tree line toward me. Lifting the shotgun in his fist in a friendly greeting, he stepped off the board into a pineapple patch to let me pass. The forest was secondary-growth, dense and relatively cool. Legions of cicadas shredded the sylvan serenity with their tinnitus songs. A 1936 *New York Times* article described North American cicadas as sounding like "a wood-working shop with every lathe and chisel and saw and band roaring full tilt." The Bornean species sure made their Yankee cousins proud. Every now and then, the cicada hymns were supported by reports from small-caliber pistols. The shooters were rubber-tree seed pods that had reached maturity and exploded to disperse their three grape-sized seeds.

The trail varied in quality; now wide, now narrow, now muddy, now desiccated. Intersections branched out into the forest. I reworked dead twigs into directional arrows and placed them on the ground, in the hope they would keep me from walking off the edge of the Earth on my return. Borneo veteran Tom Harrison warned in his biography, *World Within*: "Take two steps off the trail, get disoriented, and that's the last anyone sees of you." A Tasmanian friend once climbed a mountain in Mulu National Park without the legally required guide and took a wrong turn on the descent; 12 days later, and only through incredible serendipity, one of the search parties found him, hallucinating and close to death.

Before I took first-timers on forest walks I always held a short briefing. During the Q&A section, one question was guaranteed to come up: "What's the most dangerous animal in the jungle?" At that point I would pull out a small mirror and show it to them: "You're looking at it. The most dangerous animal in the jungle is *you*. If you're sloppy and don't look where you put your hands and feet, if you mess with unfamiliar plants and animals, or go off-trail for a closer look at something, that animal is very likely to cause you a world of grief." I spoke from experience. Within five months after our arrival, I had managed to get lost four times in various forests around Kuching; once even in full view of my car and with no idea how to cross or get around the field of 5-foot ferns between me and the parking lot.

Four boys aged six to ten appeared from a rubber-tree grove and silently watched me work on another life-saving arrow. The oldest wore a black Sid Vicious t-shirt (God Shave the Queen) and carried a short, thick piece of bamboo with a little crossbeam affixed to one end. Fastened to the crossbeam were two open bamboo pieces the size of shot glasses. One was filled with birdseed and the other with water, and three little green parrots were helping themselves to the food and drink. The blue dots atop of their heads identified them as male blue-crowned hanging parrots,[85] one of Borneo's five parrot species. Hanging parrots are unique among birds for their tendency to sleep upside down like bats. They are often caught in glue traps and kept or sold as pets; two villages from here, a man who openly trades in wild-caught birds always has a flock of hanging parrots in a UFO-shaped cage, fabricated from the wire grill of a ceiling fan. The kids spoke no English (or were too shy to) but they allowed me to take a group photo of them with their birds before moving on, innocent about their impact on the local wildlife.

---

85 *Loriculus galgulus*

Farmer's hut

The trail briefly left the woods to run through a hill rice field, then disappeared again into the welcome shade of a swamp forest. Thin trees on stilt roots and huge palm fronds with rudimentary trunks grew from the wet soil. There was little dry ground, but slim tree trunks, split in half, notched, and laid across the wet patches, kept me from sinking in. For Western naturalists, traversing these logs presents a special kind of danger, as Alfred Wallace reported in 1869:

> From the landing-place to the hill a Dyak road had been formed, which consisted solely of tree-trunks laid end to end. Along these the bare-footed natives walk and carry heavy burdens with the greatest ease, but to a booted European it is very slippery work, and when one's attention is constantly attracted by the various objects of interest around, a few tumbles into the bog are almost inevitable.

Traditional Borneo pole bridges spanned the creeks and deeper wet spots. One or two bouncy bamboo poles and a handrail is all it takes to set up one of these contraptions, and they are dreaded by anyone weighing more than a jockey. The handrails were as thin as my index finger, balanced on a pair of upright forks, stuck in the mud at each end of the bridge, and only offered support of the psychological variety. Ignoring all evidence to the contrary, my local friends kept trying to convince me that these bridges supported much more weight than the trivial 300 pounds on my 6'3" frame.[86] And indeed, I had often seen farmers shoulder heavy loads across these fragile structures. But I had already caused the demise of a few pole bridges; a British friend had even designed a commemorative t-shirt saying "German Bridge Buster" a not-so-subtle nod to our common history. Well, life is hard, but it's harder if you're stupid, and ultimately I learned from the experience and took to wading instead of taking the treacherous high roads. There were a lot of pole bridges in this swamp, but I bravely resisted temptation and always crossed the hard way. When I exited the swamp into a field of leafy mustard greens, I was thoroughly soaked up to my butt, but at least uninjured.

It was getting on to teatime now, but the thermometer was still stuck at Blast Furnace. In the white glare of the sun, a distant penciling of hills indicated the Indonesian border; behind it, tomorrow's bad weather was already mobilizing. At the edge of the field stood a lone *tapang,* or bee tree, still a youngster at barely 40 feet. *Koompassia excelsa* is an emergent rainforest species, which means it belongs to a very exclusive club of trees that tower over the canopy at up to 260 feet.[87] The tapang's white trunk is slippery and has no branches, making the tree's crown a prime choice for giant honey

---

86 21 stone/136 kg and 1.9 meters

87 12 meters and 80 meters

Tapang tree

bees[88] and their jackfruit-sized combs. The smooth, branchless trunk protects the bees from sun bears, and the presence of the bees protects the tree from lumberjacks, as the honey is valued more highly than the wood. Sarawak's laws prohibit logging tapangs; only the trees that have died from natural causes may be used for timber. The tapang before me demonstrated the high value of that honey. Short hardwood wedges had been hammered into the trunk to aid climbing. Blackened wood torches, used as bee smokers, littered the ground. I tried to imagine climbing up those terribly short and very unsafe-looking wedges, hand over hand, foot over foot, lighting the smoker upon arrival, and hoping I wouldn't get stung so badly that I lost control and fell to my death. I wasn't sure if they used ropes at all, but even roped up, it looked like a suicide mission. I had not been aware that wild honey was so valuable to the locals that they accepted such serious risks to obtain it.

I was so transfixed by the concept that I didn't see the tiny old lady until she stood right in front of me and giggled. A tall rattan basket hung from her back, held in place by a bark strap slung across the top of her head. She wore traditional Bidayuh headgear—a turbanlike creation the size of a big throw pillow—and a long, curved parang was strapped to her waist.

My startled look seemed to amuse the lady. She said something in Bidayuh which I took to mean "Hail fellow, well met!" and greeted her in English. That elicited a chortle and a vigorous headshake. While we small-talked past each other some more, I saw that her basket was full to the brim with *tampoi*,[89] small orange jungle fruit that she had collected in the forest. Noting my curiosity, she placed the basket on the ground and pulled at my backpack. I took it off, and she opened it. The eyes in her weathered face twinkled with prankish glee as she began shoveling the little orange balls into my backpack with both hands until it overflowed and the fruit bounced along the ground in all directions. I pulled out my wallet and offered her money, but she only strapped her load back on, gave me a last warm smile, and continued on her way. Try as I might, I failed to imagine that in not-too-distant times these laid-back, merry-tempered folks were still hacking off people's heads to use as fireplace decorations.

When I returned to the Fairy Cave, I found Hans Jr. in his usual Sunday afternoon state: dirty, blistered, and banged-up ("Dad, I fell 7 feet on the Rodeo route and smacked face-first into the wall! *It was fricking awesome!!*") The fruit was all gone, and the climbers were heading out for dinner at the Red Dragon, a popular coffee shop a few limestone crags away. Despite its misleading name, it is not a Chinese restaurant. The original owner had been Welsh, and his native flag had inspired the name. His origins were also in evidence in some of the fare he served, such as some of the best fish

---

88 *Apis dorsaa*

89 *Baccaurea macrocarpa*

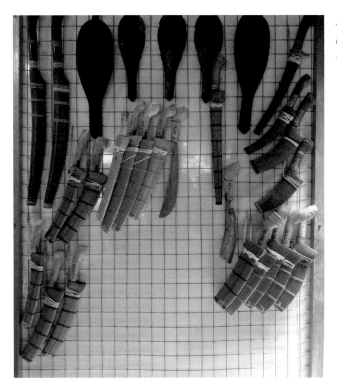

Parangs for sale at blademaster K.K. Fu's workshop, Bau

Sunset over Kuching

& chips in Borneo. His bacon burger, while supremely unhealthy, was so scrumptious that the climbers had named one of their routes after it.

As the light outside the Red Dragon ripened to mango, everyone performed the standard post-climbing ritual: pig out like heroes and then slump into python mode, as the effects of severe feasting are known in this region. After dinner we certainly bore more than fleeting semblance to the great serpent after ingesting a wild boar: distended bellies, slow digestion, and extreme torpor. Too stuffed to feel anything but pure contentment, it took us a while to regain our ability to rise from our seats. As we drove back to Kuching beneath a grand palette of equatorial colors riffling across the evening sky, we called life a win, and made plans for the next weekend.

* * * * * *

We had heard magical things about a forest behind a little jungle resort an hour from Kuching, and one sunny Saturday we set out on a father-and-son expedition to see for ourselves. After we had left the main highway, the roads became smaller, less traveled, often one-laned, and they all desperately needed maintenance. The scenery, in contrast, was spectacular. Cocoa and banana groves set off the kampung skylines of mighty durian and mango trees. Stout little churches squatted amidst short-stilted houses half-hidden behind outsized hibiscus and bougainvillea hedges. Like Odysseus' sirens tempting with color instead of song, their entrancing pastel blossom riots could be fatally distracting to passing travelers, who had to keep their eyes and vehicles on the road which by now had become a cruel joke. After some more gnashing of teeth and crushing of kidneys, the pothole jamboree mercifully ended in a wide-open space, the parking lot at Adis Buan Resort.

We had been forewarned that the management took a relaxed view of what constitutes a resort, and now we could testify to the veracity of that assessment.[90] By no stretch of the imagination was this Mar-a-Lago. The patrons, bless their hearts, couldn't have cared less, because all the essentials for a good time were in place here: a shallow, slow-flowing river to play in, half a dozen open barbecue huts under shady trees, and a few rough-hewn cabins to crash in after a hard day of carousing.

After paying a few ringgit at the entrance, we walked through the partying crowd toward the trailhead. The guests were mostly rural folk with open, inviting smiles. They intuited from our snake sticks and binoculars that we hadn't come for a cool swim and a hot dog, and took pity on us, offering drinks and barbecued things at every pit we passed. Politely but firmly, I kept declining one after another of these kindhearted gestures—no time for dilly-dallying, the jungle beckoned with quests and treasures! My son, naturally, regarded my Victorian melodrama as criminally wasteful at best. His despair over missing out on all those delicacies was tangible. I could see murder

90 That was in 2012. Since then, Adis Buan and its access roads have made much progress.

Trail at Adis Buan

in his eyes, and only my promise of a post-expedition, all-he-could-shove-down-the-piehole session at the Red Dragon prevented further escalation. (I also made a mental note not to let him bring his own parang in future.)

The path into the jungle had been built for hunting and foraging and was said to trace the river to its source at the top of Mount Serapi in Kubah National Park. Our progress into the jungle gradually replaced the noise from the resort with the songs of birds and cicadas, and soon we were alone with the forest. The trail was a bona fide obstacle course. Blackwater pools harboring catfish and gibbon-armed freshwater shrimp[91] had to be navigated via makeshift gangplanks made from loose tree trunks. Every ten minutes, it seemed, we arrived at the bank of yet another tributary to the main river. Cute little streamlets all, they were just a tad too deep and a skosh too wide to safely jump across, and they all offered the same two non-choices to reach the other side: tightrope it on a tottering bamboo pole, or clamber down to the creek for some good old-fashioned wading. Between water hurdles, we squelched through the trail's sandy mud. I found myself in awe of the people who traveled down this path for miles to find firewood and edible plants, extract hand-cut lumber, and track down and drag out wild hogs weighing more than themselves.

The obstacles kept coming, but our bellyaching didn't last. In Borneo as a rule, the scenery and the life it is filled with will outweigh any adversity the naturalist might face. John Muir found that "the clearest way to the universe is through a forest wilderness;" this heath forest, kerangas, was no exception. Compared to the biological opulence found in Borneo's rainforests, kerangas might appear like a desert; it's hot as hell, the ground is sandy, and there is none of that all-embracing shade the rainforest offers. There are trees and shrubs, but none of the lushness for which the island is better known. For all intents and purposes it is a desert, but it is a desert in Borneo, not Arabia's Empty Quarter. The dominant trees here were short, straight, and thin. They delighted with a coarse, reddish bark, and their sparse canopy leaked the sun onto the ground. Abundant light and poor soil had attracted an impressive proliferation of pitcher plants, almost all of them *Nepenthes ampullaria,* that curious vegan carnivore which prefers falling leaves over bugs for sustenance. The ones here were among the largest I had ever seen, and their colonies spread over the forest floor like an alien invasion. Their vines snaked up the trees and marked their passage with clusters of pitchers like little mottled cauldrons. Our path was often fenced in by dense stands of terrestrial bamboo orchids.[92] Many of them stood over 6 feet tall, and atop each whip-like stem swayed a large, long-snouted blossom in pink and white. Other, more humbly sized, orchids had attached themselves to tree trunks and offered their dainty flowers to pollinators. Fungi in all colors of the rainbow thrived on every surface;

---

91 *Macrobrachium* sp.

92 *Arundina graminifolia*

Bamboo orchids

ferns with leaves like moose antlers grew next to giant mosses resembling green toilet brushes. Estimations suggest that at least 40 percent of Borneo's orchids and as much as 30 percent of all Bornean plant species are endemic, and I wondered how any botanist could work here without going mad with pleasure.

The trail now ran alongside the main river, and we walked through a gallery of magnificent *Tristaniopsis* trees cooling the riverbank with their wide crowns. There were two kinds, one orange, one grayish-white, and their bark was as smooth as a surfboard; the trees peeled it off regularly to get rid of parasites and other unwelcome squatters, and beneath the silky, elegant trunks, the stripped-off bark lay on the ground in great untidy heaps. When Hans Jr. leaned against one of the carrot-hued trees, the trunk gave off a fine powder that clung to his skin and clothes. This finding boosted his mood considerably. He stripped to his Batman boxers, and then spent a good half-hour lovingly decorating himself in orange war paint, highlighted with accents from one of the gray-barked peeling trees, as he called them. Body art applied, he cut a nice spear from a sapling with his parang and then mugged for photos, fiercely grimacing and brandishing his weapons, and declaring himself Borneo's Last Cannibal. (Not the first nor the last person to confuse headhunting

Tristaniopsis trees

with cannibalism, but I did not correct his error. I was not sure if he had forgiven me for denying him all that food and drink earlier, and he still had his parang.)

During the makeup break, I had time to admire two of the world's largest butterflies. The exceptional size of some Southeast Asian species has earned them the name birdwings. They are swallowtails from the *Papilionidae* family, and while not necessarily rare, they rarely fail to impress the observer. A male Malay birdwing[93] the size of my hand stitched across the river. His forewings were midnight black, the golden-yellow hindwings framed in black embroidery. His flight path appeared erratic yet determined, and he reminded me of a Chinese sampan in full sail guided home by a tipsy skipper. Just a few yards away, another birdwing was drinking from a mud puddle. This was, hands down, Malaysia's most beautiful butterfly. The slender black wings of Rajah Brooke's birdwing[94] span almost 7 inches and are painted from tip to tip with a chain of electric-green shark teeth. The crimson head completes the majestic impression—this is truly the rajah, the king, of lepidopterans, and a whole group of these stunning insects at a watering hole, lazily flapping their iridescence around, is a thing of singular elegance. (The federal government in KL agrees. Despite the name's colonial implications, Rajah Brooke's birdwing is Malaysia's national butterfly.)

---

93 *Troides amphrysus*

94 *Trogonoptera brookiana*

*Wild ginger flower (*Etlingera coccinea*)*

Marching on, we watched a gang of least pygmy squirrels[95] zip up and down and back and forth between two trees like remote-controlled toys running amok. These mouse-sized balls of fur, a Bornean endemic, count among the world's smallest squirrels. Their tininess makes them almost too fast to watch, and the effect is sidesplitting. I have seen serious mammalogists crack up at the sight of these hyperkinetic critters and insist they hadn't seen anything this funny since that crazy rodent in *Hoodwinked*. Our badly suppressed guffawing soon destroyed the magic moment. The squirrels stopped their wild chase (I swear I could hear little brakes screech!); their noses whiffled in the air, and no sooner had they discovered us than they rocketed out of sight into the treetops.

We settled down for a picnic lunch by a bend in the river. Hans had made steak-and-egg sandwiches Emeril Lagassé-style (no greater parental joy than a child obsessed with celebrity chefs), and dessert was fresh *longan*, those smoky-flavored cousins of the lychee. While we ate, we enjoyed the Edenic setting and the soundtrack composed and performed by the birds, the insects, and the soothing murmur of the river slinking over its bed of rocks. Large red *Tristaniopsis* trees lined the opposite bank like sandstone pillars. Their color stood in perfect contrast to the dark green of their canopy. At their feet, sword-leafed bushes resembling frozen green fireworks

---

95 *Exilisciurus exilis*

[Left] Butterflies sucking on a sweaty backpack

[Below] Rufous-backed kingfisher

guarded the shore in a tight row. Close to the far bank, a rock the size and shape of a bowling ball stuck out from the flow. Two large purple butterflies sat on it, their wings wagging in the breeze. Two smaller butterflies, lemon-yellow, danced close above the purple pair like winged puppies with not a care in the world. The shallow river had worried the rocks into smoothness, and the sunrays flashed on their slick surfaces to the stridulations of the cicadas. It was all achingly beautiful; a true place for poets and romantics, and I felt blessed and favored for the privilege of being here.

Then I looked at the butterflies through my binoculars, and paradise turned into a Hieronymus Bosch painting. With that immediate intimacy a decent pair of binocs delivers, I was pushed face-first into reality: the butterflies weren't there for our spiritual delectation. With great gusto, the two larger ones were sucking the eyeballs off a dead crab, while the two smaller ones, playing yellow hyenas to the purple lions, were waiting for their turn at the gorefest. I stifled an impulse to gag. So, it was true what my lepidopterist friends had been telling me for years. Contrary to their illusory depictions in fairytales, Disney cartoons, and other reality twisters, most butterflies have revolting eating habits. To be sure, they do drink from flowers, but nectar alone does not provide them with enough salts and proteins. These nutrients are found in much less appetizing food items, including mud, rotten fruit, feces, and even blood, tears and decaying flesh. Any butterfly collector in Southeast Asia will tell you that nothing attracts the little beauties like fresh human urine, and *belacan*, that local fermented shrimp paste with the killer pong. Sweat is also an all-time favorite—I remembered a hike on a very hot day when a dozen of those little yellow guys landed on my shirt for a suck-and-run saltwater raid.

I put the binoculars down, and paradise reappeared. The afternoon heat was losing its bite now, and some birds had already returned from their siesta. A greater racket-tailed drongo in shimmering black sat on a nearby branch. Its tail consisted of two long wires with a small round feather at the end. It would dive off its perch to snatch insects in mid-flight, then return to its ambush spot to eat its prey, then preen until the next attack. From the trees on the other side came a long-drawn trill, slow at first, then quickly increasing in pitch and tremolo until it ended in a drill-like whirr. The caller was a black-and-yellow broadbill, one of Borneo's most striking birds. It was about the size of a house sparrow and looked as if a stoned Pixar artist had done a number on it with pastel crayons. The black head was accented by yellow eyes, a thick, white neck ring, and an almost comically broad turquoise beak. Long, fringed epaulets in canary yellow marked the bird's black shoulders, while chest and belly were kept in a tender peach tone. As we broke camp, an orange shuttlecock bulleted up the river, a rufous-backed kingfisher alarming the forest about the human danger with shrill staccato calls.

On the way back we discovered six little durians stacked up between two buttress roots. *Durian isu,* as it is locally known, is a wild species.[96] The fruit, smaller than regular

---

96 *Durio oxleyanus*

Wild durian species

durians, are round and greenish, with long thin spikes. They also lack the typical durian aroma; their flesh is less sweet, and is reminiscent of walnuts. Somebody had found these fruits somewhere in the forest and stored them here for later collection. While we were still speculating on the nature of the owners, three Bidayuh men appeared on the trail, soundless like jungle cats. They had the lithe muscles of track athletes and wore bandannas, parangs, and mismatched camouflage clothes. Their feet were shod in black shoes made from stiff, thick rubber. Nicknamed Adidas kampung, these are designed like soccer boots but with fat rubber cleats for walking on muddy terrain, and holes for good drainage during river crossings. In terms of durability and water resistance, no high-tech Western footwear compares. Adidas kampung are the ultimate jungle shoes— but, as detractors like to point out, only if you have wooden feet.

The men's rattan baskets held Ziploc bags with fresh plant cuttings. We had a brief friendly chat, and they told us they were in the employ of a local nursery for exotic plants. They had been inside the national park further up the trail, looking for new material to cultivate, and they proudly showed us their swag: gingers, orchids, begonias, and a rare red variety of *Nepenthes ampullaria*. One of the men had a hunting rifle over his shoulder. I didn't ask why he had brought it. There was no dangerous wildlife here that would warrant armed protection. Neither did I ask whether they had collection permits. They would just lie about it. But then they knew I wouldn't return to Kuching and sic[97] law enforcement on their nursery, because it would be pointless. And I knew they knew, so peace and harmony were maintained. As a farewell gift, they gave us two of their wild durians.

It's a platitude: on a cosmic scale, we're insignificant specks in space and time. Yet we are perfectly able to destroy most of our cohabitants before our own eventual

---

97 incite or command to attack

demise. Much has been written about nature's indomitability and our perceived frailty in the face of her powers. John McPhee felt "the raw, convincing irrelevance of the visitor" in Alaska, and to Alexander von Humboldt the Amazon rainforest was a world in which "man is nothing."

In the 21st century, few places are left where this still holds true. Maybe Antarctica, or the Himalayan upper ranges. But on the island of Borneo, former home to mighty jungles bigger than many European countries, legally protected nature is getting hammered by illegal human activity. The chainsaw is just one actor in the tragedy's large cast. I cannot remember the last time I was in a forest at night and heard no gunshots. Hunters with dog packs roam the national parks to the point that the park rangers will try to keep you from going on night walks. And thanks to the rise of budget airlines, Airbnb and CouchSurfing, there is a planet-wide boom of biopiracy involving foreigners who often cooperate with locals. These collectors—without any sort of collection permit—travel to remote corners of the globe to remove and bring home any exotic form of life that can be grown, kept, or mounted. My personal experience includes Russian orchid poachers, Japanese butterfly thieves, and Czech lizard larcenists, but those were just a tiny part of an endless worldwide cavalcade of self-styled nature lovers who know the price of everything and the value of nothing. Today, an old joke holds truer than ever:

> What happens when a new species is discovered?
> Two Germans buy a plane ticket.

＊   ＊   ＊   ＊   ＊   ＊

The Malaysia Nature Society is a community of citizens enthusiastic and concerned about the natural treasures of their homeland. Since its inception in 1940, the MNS has launched countless conservation campaigns, many with solid and far-reaching success. Hans Jr. and I had become card-carrying members of the MNS Kuching branch soon after our arrival in Sarawak. Most of the other members were mainly interested in birding but fascinated by our preference for snakes and similar varmints. Soon the society hatched an idea for a public nighttime jungle walk which I would lead. The walk was to be held in Permai, a beachfront-cum-rainforest resort bordering Santubong National Park north of Kuching. I was not familiar with the trail the MNS had selected for the event, so a few weeks before the actual walk we hiked the route with a few resort guides to learn the lay of the land and scout for interesting spots.

At first, things looked bleak. The monsoon season was upon us; it had rained the entire way to the resort. The rain had stopped when we arrived, but the forest was dripping with runoff. The trail was so narrow our shirts were soaked from rubbing shoulders with the wet greenery. Our expectations were measured; in these conditions, the chances of seeing any animals apart from hungry leeches were slim. This was doubly frustrating for my high school friend Marcus who had joined us. A nature photography nut, he was visiting us in Sarawak, and I had been hoping to show him as many rainforest splendors as possible.

Then the sun came out, both literally and figuratively. A beautiful creature straight out of *Jurassic Park*, if on a smaller scale, clung to a tree trunk at eye level. Down its back ran a flamboyant, comb-like crest of long, dense spines. This dollhouse dinosaur was something to behold, and the beast's eyes were something else altogether. They were very large, framed by orange rings, and held the world's bluest eyeballs. These looked like polished lapis lazuli, and evoked tales of Chinese dragons with gemstones for eyes. Our photography session ended when the reptile decided it'd had enough of the smelly primates and their annoying voyeurism. Or maybe it was its revenge upon our species for hobbling it with the graceless name of blue-eyed angle-headed lizard.[98]

The forest was coming to life now. Little crabs, as red and busy as fire engines, scurried in and out of the leaf litter, and we were watched by slender geckos equipped with long, sharp claws for a life spent hunting on tree trunks and mossy rocks. Rotten branches overgrown with orchids lay between the giant roots of a giant tree, and an equally giant liana coiled around the tree trunk from crown to root. From smaller trees hung smaller lianas graced with bouquets of blossoms and berries. Most of the creepers were grayish-brown, but there was also a bright green one. It was much shorter and thinner than the creeper it rested on, and it scanned us with a pair of tadpole-shaped pupils. Five feet long, thin as a whip and flat as a carpenter's pencil, the oriental vine snake[99] is perfectly outfitted for life in the trees. Its huge, forward-facing eyes sit in front of the pointy-nosed skull, where they provide a stereoscopic view ideal for hunting fast arboreal lizards. I picked up the snake to show my companions. It sat in my hand without moving, head and neck in the air. Like most snakes, it stuck out its tongue to scent the scene. Unlike most snakes, though, it didn't waggle that gray tongue around. The tongue just hung there in mid-air, straight as a ruler and motionless like the rest of the animal. Another clever adaptation to the arboreal lifestyle—if you want to imitate a twig, you'll want to look just as rigid.

I put the vine snake back on its vine, we took a few pictures, and then scrambled across an empty stream full of slime-covered boulders. My face connected with a small piece of wood hanging from above on a silken thread. I picked it off my wet forehead. It was just a bit of forest debris, a short, broken twig with a gnarled knob on one end. I was about to flick it away, when the knob extended eight legs and stared at me indignantly with a disquieting number of eyes. Without a hefty dose of luck, the odds of ever

---

98 *Gonocephalus liogaster*

99 *Ahaetulla prasina*

Blue-eyed angle-headed lizard

Oriental vine snake

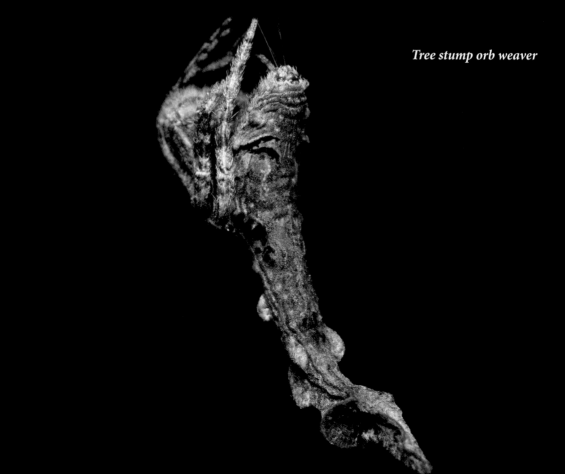

Tree stump orb weaver

meeting this spider in person are not in your favor. It is aptly named the tree stump orb weaver, [100] and like the mechanics of a Venus flytrap or the multifaceted eyes of a dragonfly, this pinnacle of mimicry might rattle your faith in the theory of evolution, if only just for one scary second. The little tree stump walked up to my elbow and looked around. Then it nonchalantly abseiled into the leaf litter and vanished forever. If it is still alive today, I'm sure it gets a kick out of telling its great-grand-spiderlings about the day it shocked five humans into briefly questioning their entire worldview. And when it tells that story, there will be a sparkle in its many eyes.

Presently, we came to a narrow brook, 10 feet wide and a foot deep. A line of smooth rocks formed a natural path to the other side. Hans Jr. was the first to cross. He had almost planted his foot on the third rock when he gave a blood-curdling yell and raced back like a child possessed, screaming distinctly unprintable things. I was baffled. My eyes raced to find the danger that had triggered his extreme reaction, but came up empty. Then I noticed that the rock he had flinched back from had two nostrils, and I zoomed in on the rest of the thing. The image hit me like a sledgehammer. Just below the surface, a 16-foot reticulated python lay stretched out along the middle of the creek, its tail end out of sight somewhere upstream. It was a very large example of the world's longest snake species, yet its marvelous camouflage pattern made it almost undetectable. The head partly stuck out from the water, and amid the visual jumble of the surrounding jungle textures it hadn't registered to me as anything else but a wet rock.

Hectic activity ensued. The guides retreated to a safe distance and debated whether to inform HQ about the monster in their forest. Marcus broke out his Nikon and took

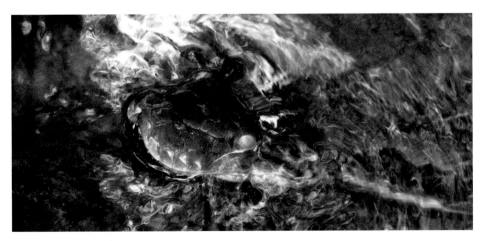

Reticulated python, Permai Rainforest Resort

---

100 *Poltys elevatus*

a few test shots. Hans' shock had subsided; now he was as thrilled as any 12-year-old face to face with a wild, man-eating snake. And so was I. But reality took over quickly. I had no idea how to proceed from here. After four years of playing with snakes in Taiwan, my snake handling and photography skills were comfortably past the greenhorn stage. Then again, few snakes in Taiwan are much longer than 6 feet. The snake before me was as long as my truck, weighed more than my wife, and had the strength of, well, *a really big python*. Above it all hovered the legends and myths surrounding *Malayopython reticulatus*: eater of deer; constrictor of men. A face filled with a hundred curved and serrated teeth arranged in six rows. Verily, this was the snake of snakes, and it filled me with love and terror in equal proportions.

The others looked at me in expectant silence.

This is what your big mouth gets you, I thought. Never missing an opportunity to pontificate on how beautiful and interesting and misunderstood snakes are. Now these people see you as just the guy they want by their side when they meet a gigantic python in the jungle. *I should have kept my trap shut.*

The others looked at me some more.

I took a deep breath, wished for a paper bag to breathe into, and attempted rational thinking. After all, this was just a snake. Sure, it was the biggest snake I had ever met, but a snake nonetheless, and it would behave like any other snake. Like those little green pit vipers, pythons are sit-and-wait hunters, so it would probably react to us like a pit viper: staying immobile while relying on its coloring for protection. I took out camera and snake hook and approached the lindworm like Siegfried the Timid Dragon Photographer. The python had not moved an inch since its discovery. It behaved as predicted, like a firehose-sized pit viper. I knelt next to its head and took a few photos. Now Marcus and the guides started photographing from a closer distance, and the python still did not stir. I had a strong feeling there was more to the snake's astonishing calmer-than-marble-ness than mere reliance on its battledress: supreme confidence in its power and skills. "Exquisite lack of industriousness" is how a journalist once described soccer phenomenon Cristiano Ronaldo's playing style. "It is not that he cannot run, or doesn't want to," the writer noted, "he is just in no hurry until he has to be." In its own realm, this python was the essence of Ronaldo.

Then trouble came to paradise, courtesy of Mister Hans the Snake Man. Hoping to pose at least part of the submerged python in a more interesting way for the cameras, I gingerly moved the snake hook beneath its head and tried to lift it out of the water. Woe, the hubris! The python's hulking muscles did not budge an inch. My efforts were akin to using a pipe cleaner to pry loose a floorboard. At this point, the snake began to take umbrage at my repeated privacy violations. Still in no particular rush, it gracefully U-turned its humongous body and slowly started to glide upstream. It probed a few hiding spots under the banks, but none were large enough to accommodate so much snake. Eventually it coiled up underneath a large fallen tree that straddled the brook.

The guides had called the resort's head office to report our find, and now a small army was panting up the hill to get a look at the goliath. This was the largest retic ever found in that forest, and everyone tripped over everyone else trying to get a photo of Ronaldo under the tree trunk; a few of them even sloshed into the brook for better shots (including, to my utter horror and chest-bursting pride, my own son). Lucky for the snake, the head guide soon shut the whole circus down. Everyone was ordered to leave, and the trail was closed off for two weeks to give the snake time to move deeper into the forest, where encounters and possibly conflicts between resort guests and giant snakes were less likely to happen.

∗　∗　∗　∗　∗　∗

Our other herpetological activities were also in full swing. I continued the snake education program I had started in Taiwan, giving talks at Kuching's schools, colleges, and various private and government institutions. Some of these events were covered by the media, and Kuching's small-town character soon taught me what it meant to be a weird fish in a small pond. After some news outlets had reported on my public snake presentation at the Sarawak Biodiversity Center, random strangers—supermarket cashiers, mail carriers—would inquire whether I was that snake-handling *orang putih* (white person) they had read about in the paper. My recognition factor was boosted by internet footage of that presentation. In addition to more educational segments, the video showed me desperately groping through my collar for a 2-foot snake deep inside my shirt while I gamely tried to keep the talk going. I had looped the snake around my neck as a prop, but the poor thing was intimidated by the roomful of humans and soon began looking for a hiding place. When my groping proved futile, I pulled up my shirt and caught the snake in mid-fall. I was quite proud of how I had handled the crisis in the best show-must-go-on spirit. With hindsight, though, watching a fat, half-dressed guy doing a spastic belly-dance with a terrified snake was probably not the sort of edutainment the audience had come for.

Educating humans about snakes is enriching; so is introducing people to the rainforest. But for sheer adrenaline, nothing beats cruising for snakes on lonely country roads. Statistics tell us that in areas with snakes and roads, the snakes will eventually cross the roads. It follows that driving on those roads will eventually lead to encounters with those snakes. In Borneo, the best time for this is at night, right after a hard rain. Not only are many snakes nocturnal, but they also like cooler temperatures and high humidity. The rain also brings out a lot of their prey, such as rodents (flooded from their holes) and frogs (duh).

Our cruising nights usually began with dinner at a cheap-and-cheerful 24-hour Indian restaurant on the outskirts of Kuching. Indians in the know had assured us that the curries there tasted just like home, and the Bengali head waiter dazzled with an incredible memory. He would take complicated multi-course orders for a party of eight without writing anything down, and confirm it all with a smile and a head waggle; in all the years I've eaten there he has never messed up a single item. This amazing feat would be made even more amazing by the fact that although he had been in Malaysia for most of his adult life he still spoke little else but Bengali, plus whatever Malay terms appeared on the menu. While we ate, the sun would crash below the horizon with equatorial abruptness, and by the time we had tipped the Memory King, the firmament outside had become what A.B. Guthrie called "more sky than a man could think." Light pollution is virtually unknown outside Sarawak's larger settlements, and on the way to our target road we frequently pulled over to soak up an outbreak of stars that defied the imagination—a ceiling drape of glittering gems woven so densely there seemed little room for the space between them.

Our go-to cruising road was a 10-mile stretch near the Indonesian border. Cutting through forests, agricultural land, and two tiny villages, it also runs along the bottom of Mount Penrissen, a small mountain range popular with biologists from Universiti Malaysia Sarawak (UNIMAS) in Kuching. Mount Penrissen is known for its natural riches and as a reliable place to find new species. The data we collected during our cruises in the foothills would complement the findings the scientists brought down from higher up.

The UNIMAS teams are often led by herpetology professor Dr. Indraneil Das, a transplant from Kolkata. Long before we moved to Borneo, I'd already owned all his field guides for the island, and after our arrival I sought him out and offered my assistance with slightly damp palms. For a citizen scientist like me, Prof Neil, as his students call him, is somewhat of a rock star. His desk is forever cluttered with innumerable jars containing pickled snakes, frogs, and lizards, all new to science and awaiting description, and he has probably forgotten more about the reptiles and amphibians of Southeast Asia than I will ever learn. After studying at Oxford and Harvard, he declined offers for post-doc work from both institutions; instead, he accepted a tenure at an insignificant little academy in Malaysian Borneo. The reason? "Because it's Borneo! What other reason would I need?" Indeed, even the UNIMAS campus is a naturalist's dream. Together with the golf course next door, it hosts some impressive wildlife that includes saltwater crocodiles and large raptors like ospreys, crested serpent eagles, and bat hawks. Several new dragonfly species have been discovered on campus, and the school's own swamp forest is so large that even a former director of the UNIMAS Institute of Biodiversity and Environmental Conservation, Professor John Beaman, once managed to get lost in it for an entire night.

In the field, Prof Neil morphs from dapper-suited, soft-spoken scholar of life sciences back into that highly excitable snake geek he has been since grade school, when he hid his first pet cobra in a shoebox under his bed to avoid catching hell from his mother. Science always reigns supreme for him, though, and he knew how to harness an obsessed amateur to the chariot of his research. In Taiwan I had begun to record data points about every snake I found. Date, time, location, the snake's length and life stage, and other information were all entered in a little notebook and later transferred to an Excel file. Apart from satisfying purely academic interest, the body of knowledge about the life forms in the area might someday inform decisions on infrastructural development, or thwart plans for another golf course. When I showed Neil the little spreadsheet I had prepared for the task, he gave me a "nice try" look and added another 16 data columns. Some of these new items made sense (GPS Coords, Behavior, Coloration Remarks), while others, like Distance to Nearest Forest in Meters, struck me as unnecessary. Neil's only reaction to my quizzical face was "Might as well do real science, eh?" (Over time, I figured it all out. Even why the moon phase is important.)

Not only was the information collection well organized; there were also protocols for our snake drives. We often invited interested parties—friends, visitors, scientists, fellow snake nerds—to join our cruises. The person riding shotgun occupied the jump seat. When the driver stopped for a snake, the jumper, armed with headlamp and snake hook, would leap out of the car and try to catch the reptile while the driver pulled over and turned on the hazard lights. If the jumper was successful, and traffic allowed it, the driver then greenlighted the remaining passengers to pile out and do their assigned duties. We had a big blue science duffel bag filled with hanging scales, thermometers, barometers, GPS devices, measuring tapes, field guides, cameras, high-visibility vests, and a 2-gallon container of formalin to marinate roadkill (careless drivers keep bringing new species to light). The script for a scientific encounter with a road-crossing snake ideally reads as follows:

> The driver suddenly stomps on the brakes.

Driver: Snaaaaake!

Jumper: What the *hell*, man? I almost smacked my head into the windshield!

Driver: Quit whining! See that sunbeam snake over there? Get out 'n' get it—go, go, go!

> Jumper mutters a vicious curse under his breath and hurries out to catch the snake. The snake shoots off, and the backseat turns into a soccer stadium as the backseat passengers cheer and jeer.

Passengers: Let's go, buddy, get that snake! Come on, man, you can do it! Oh, for Christ's … *you're letting it get away*! Would you *look* at that *fool*?

The jumper catches the snake and triumphantly thrusts it aloft.

Jumper: Got him!

The driver pulls over and turns to the people in the backseat.

Driver: Let's do science, everybody!

Everyone leaves the vehicle, the science duffel is fetched, instruments are handed out, and the snake and its surroundings are measured, recorded, and photographed. The snake is then released, everyone climbs back into the truck, and the cruise continues.

This scenario, of course, is known as "best case", that evil euphemism for "highly unrealistic." Most of the time, Murphy's was the law of the land. Snakes would slink off the road before we had even stopped, or they didn't cooperate, or gave us the slip during the shoot. Even species that were easy to catch and known as cooperative sometimes disappointed—sunbeam snakes, for one. An adult *Xenopeltis unicolor* is some 3 feet long and leads a fossorial lifestyle, meaning it spends much of its days underground. At dusk it emerges to hunt frogs, small mammals, and the occasional fellow snake. At first, a sunbeam's color appears brownish-nondescript. Once you shine your flashlight over its body, its scales burst into a trippy kaleidoscope of iridescent colors. The nonvenomous sunbeams are among the slowest and most docile species in Borneo, and do not seem to mind being picked up. Their cute wedge heads and stuffed-toy eyes often create instant trust even with folks not accustomed to the company of legless reptiles. That makes sunbeams the perfect snakes to show off to civilians (those strange people whose lives do not revolve around snakes). During our early cruises, my greatest joy was to put a sunbeam in the hands of people who had never touched a snake before, and see their eyes light up at the animal's beauty and good nature. I hastily abandoned that practice when I found out that sunbeams are not that different from other animals—when enough is enough, they will fight back. I learned this the hard way on two consecutive cruises, when I had to use my first-aid kit on two of our guests. They had been viciously bitten by sunbeams whose cuteness had baited them into petting the snakes with a little too much enthusiasm.

With dog-toothed cat snakes, in contrast, you would get exactly what it says on the label—the name leaves little to the imagination. *Boiga cynodon* is a snake hater's classic foe: 8 feet long, bulging eyes with vertical, cat-style pupils set in a large, angular head, two pairs (yes, *two*) of enlarged front fangs, and an additional set of venom[101]-dripping teeth in the rear of the mouth, this snake is the stuff of most excellent nightmares. Its

101 Not lethal for humans.

behavior complements its anatomy: if it's not satisfied with your level of scaredness, it will inflate its neck and the first few feet of its body for additional effect.

Spotting and catching an adult *B. cynodon* was always good for some fine excitement. There would be no real hurry to get out of the car; 8 feet of snake takes a while to get off the road. But convincing this species to donate a few minutes of its time to a worthy scientific cause would require grit and reflexes. Ideally, this was done wearing welding gloves, what with all those crazy fangs. When at length we held the snake in our loving arms, the real problems began. Where to photograph such a long thing? There were no clearings or picnic spots in the jungle along our cruising road, and a photo shoot on the road, not a problem with smaller snakes, presented a traffic hazard. In such cases we often transferred our find to a special snake bag, made from heavy-duty cotton and fitted with drawstrings and double-stitched seams, and brought it back to Kuching. There, we would photograph it on a park lawn the next morning, and later return to where we had met it, and release it.

Taking pictures of large snakes in a public park is a three-person job. The photographer needs an assistant to pose the reptile and keep it from escaping. (The hat-on-the-snake trick obviously doesn't fly with big specimens; although I've met a few Australians who approach the issue by carrying large trashcan lids.) The third person deals with public relations. Photographing snakes of any size in public can produce gaggles of civilians who increase the irritation levels of the animal and the photographer. They tend to ask an infinity of questions and are full of well-meant suggestions. Sometimes I felt chatty and charitable and would do a little show-and-tell with the snake, answering their queries and addressing their comments. At other times I just told the crowd we were working on an important piece for *National Geographic* and—so sorry!—really couldn't have any disturbance right now. (I'm still surprised that actually worked sometimes.)

Frontline combat, work on a movie set, and road cruising for snakes have one thing in common: they all involve long periods of tedium peppered by sudden outbursts of frantic action. To stave off the perils of road weariness during long drives, we sometimes placed snake-like twigs on the road. Without fail, these adrenaline sticks would re-energize us when we spotted them on the next pass. No matter how bushed I am after five hours of night driving, nothing wakes me up like a snake on the road. In a parallel to gambling, the madness of the unexpected is the main reason why a certain breed of people will gladly waste sinful amounts of time and fuel driving endless loops in the dark: what might lie around the next bend? Nothing, again? Never mind, there's always the bend after that, and possibly the next addition to your life list.

Or even more than one lifer. On one of the best nights in our road-hunting annals, we connected with two of our most-wanted target species. After a heavy rainstorm, the cruising road was now slick with water and thick with frogs. We always drove with open windows to enjoy the sounds and songs of the night things, and tonight we were treated to an amphibian blues jam at ear-numbing decibels. As we snailed our way through the frogs, mindful not to croak any, we saw a huge green individual stand out from the others like a Granny Smith-colored Saint Bernard in a pack of brown Yorkies. We could not believe it. Here in the middle of an asphalt road, far away from its home in the treetops, sat a legend of natural history. It had rough skin and grossly oversized feet. They were large enough for a small duck, and their digits were connected by yellow webbing so flappy it threw folds. In the 19th century, this frog, then unknown to science, had fascinated Alfred Russel Wallace so much that he presented it in *The Malay Archipelago* as an example for evolution's step-by-step progress:

> One of the most curious and interesting reptiles which I met with in Borneo was a large tree-frog, which was brought me by one of the Chinese workmen. He assured me that he had seen it come down in a slanting direction from a high tree, as if it flew. On examining it, I found the toes very long and fully webbed to their very extremity, so that when expanded they offered a surface much larger than the body ... This is, I believe, the first instance known of a "flying frog," and it is very interesting to Darwinians as showing that the variability of the toes which have been already modified for purposes of swimming and adhesive climbing, have been taken advantage of to enable an allied species to pass through the air like the flying lizard.

Wallace's flying frog,[102] named after the great naturalist, is probably the most famous of the region's many gliding animals. When spread, the webbing between toes and fingers turns the feet into parachutes that allow the frog to glide distances up to 50 feet. This species is normally found high in the canopy and only descends to ground level when searching for a mate, or to lay eggs. Judging from its size, this one was a possibly gravid female. But what business did she have on a road? Had the rain tempted her into venturing out onto the warm blacktop? Whatever the reason, finding this arboreal frog in the middle of the road was an almost impossible stroke of luck. We took an album's worth of photos, then Hans Jr. nudged the frog into the safety of the forest. (When you're done, always help your findings off the road—you'd be surprised how many people love to roadkill for sport.)

Four hours later, long past midnight, the flying frog was still the only thing of note we had discovered all night. All we kept seeing were boring, flightless frogs whose asphalt fetish forced us into endless swerving maneuvers, and two giant earthworms upon whom we wished a pox for their audacity to look like snakes. I was exhausted from the long drive, and my eyes burned from constantly scanning the tarmac for creatures. We had

---

102 *Racophorus nigropalmatus*

Wallace's flying frog

reached a section of the road that was all tight bends and steep embankments, shrouded by trees and wild with vegetation. String curtains of thin yellow air roots hung from low branches. When a car passed through these curtains, they caressed it with a soothing whisper. Sometimes, when overfatigue had brought me to the edge of my senses, I could hear actual words. Right now, my wiped-out brain convinced me that the roots were whispering to me again; this time they were quoting Orson Welles:

> Almost we are persuaded that there is something, after all, something essential waiting for all of us in the dark alleys of the world, aboriginally loathsome, immeasurable and certainly nameless.[103]

In some cases, a hard swig of extra-black coffee from my extra-bottomless thermos would chase the fatigue monster back under the truck. But I was too far gone tonight. Home was still 30 miles out, and my current narcoleptic state was a danger to everyone on the road. The only remedy was a power nap. I parked the truck under one of the root curtains, reclined my seat, and told Hans Jr. to wake me in half an hour.

Two minutes later, he shook me awake with a strange announcement: "Dad, look— someone left a neck pillow on the road."

There is no worse time to wake up than when you've just drifted into sleep, and I jerked upright in the foulest of moods. "You wake me to tell me there's trash on the road? Are you out of your …?" The sight of the pillow silenced me. A few yards away, it lay puffed and shiny with wetness, and it did appear to be one of those fluffy sausages you sling around your neck during airplane rides. On second thought, though, it looked a little too long and a little too thin for a travel pillow. I couldn't make out the color, but it seemed to be some kind of animal print. Most notably, the end pointing in our direction was strangely tapered. Like a snout.

It woke me up like a bucket of ice water. "Son," I said almost inaudibly, "I don't think that's a neck pillow."

"That's why I woke you." Hans squinted a little harder at the puffy roll. "Short-tailed python?"

"Think so."

We slowly opened the doors and slunk onto the road like frogmen into enemy waters. The closer we got to the pillow, the clearer its details became. Two little yellow coals looked at us from the tapered end. That end also had a long mouth, and a row of what looked like holes in the lips: heat-receptive scales for locating prey. The animal print was snakeskin-boot realistic. Hans had nailed it; it was a Borneo short-tailed python. In many regards *Python breitensteini* is the opposite of its giant reticulated cousin. Not just the tail is short, but at an average of 4 feet, the snake's entire length is not exactly world

---

103 Unfilmed script for *Heart of Darkness*

record material. Its rubenesque bulk, however, fully compensates for the shortness. A small head and a tiny tail bookend a heavy, pumped-up body that looks like a blimp made from snake leather.[104] Short-tailed pythons carry a reputation for having a temper even shorter than their tails, and keepers of captive specimens had told me troubling tales about the snake's feeding habits. Instead of peacefully strangling its food like most pythons, a shorty will sometimes insist on killing the poor mouse, rat, or rabbit (depending on the snake's size) by repeatedly slamming it against the cage wall with the fury of a hundred demons.

The snake lounged on the asphalt unperturbed, and monitored our approach with slow undulations of its pink tongue. Relaxed and peaceful though the serpent appeared, gorgeous even in its marbled coat of chocolate and cream, that little jukebox in my mind insisted on playing Darth Vader's Theme. I had a bad feeling about this. Mindful of the warnings about the snake's attitude, I had prepared a snake bag. I was not going to let a python with short-snake syndrome and anger management issues give us all sorts of grief during measuring and photography, or hand us the utmost loss of face by escaping into the dark, undocumented. This was our first *breitensteini,* and I would make sure everything went smoothly. We would put that pretty snake in a soft, white cotton bag, store it overnight in a cool, dark room in our house, and tomorrow, when Shorty had enjoyed a good night's sleep and was in a fabulous mood, we would take pretty photos of it in our backyard.

The next thing I remember was four profusely bleeding lacerations that suddenly appeared on the back of my right hand. I also remember thinking *Of course, they have four rows of teeth in their upper jaw. Silly me,* and cursing myself for forgetting the welding gloves. The plan had been simple. Hans would open the snake bag while I lifted the coiled python—right hand around the neck, left hand guiding the middle— placed it in the bag and tied up the drawstrings. But plans have minds of their own. When I picked up the plump cutie by its midriff, it twitched its little tail once, like a dreaming kitten, and then released the fury. The head shot out from the coil, whipped around, and chomped down on my right hand, raking four deep rows into my flesh as it pulled back. Fearing it would get away if I dropped it, I kept holding the python by the middle with my bleeding hand while I tried to secure it behind the head with the good hand, with heroic contempt for further gory consequences. The front part of the snake thrashed in the air like Medusa's curls on a bad hair day, snapping at everything with great ferocity while the rear supported the frontline efforts with chemical warfare. Twisting and writhing to escape my grip, the python engaged its waste disposal system and sprayed me from head to toe with musk and fecal matter. The fetid bouquet had to be smelled to be believed. Within seconds, I looked and reeked like a latrine cleaner after a bad workplace accident. But against all good sense, I was dead set on not letting this

104 All three Southeast Asian short pythons—*P. breitensteini, P. curtus,* and *P. brongersmai*—are extensively harvested for leather; an estimated 100,000 individuals are taken for this purpose each year.

charming animal slip through my fingers, slimy with blood and feces though they were. My son had retreated into the shadows, pale with horror. He was still holding the snake bag open, but more from shock than sense of duty.

I snarled at him, "Get closer, dammit!" and finally we bagged the beast. When I tied the bag, my triumphant expression turned into a pained grimace when the python, for good measure, slashed my other hand through the bag cloth. On the way home, we kept the windows open again. Only now for a different reason. (P.S. During the long photo shoot on my lawn the next day, the snake was as placid as an overfed housecat. Go figure.)

* * * * * *

There is more to road cruising in Borneo than mad snakes and aviating amphibians. Plenty of other wildlife is around to enchant non-herpetologists. Bugs, for example. After photographing a small snake on the road one night, I returned to the car to make my first acquaintance with a night wasp.[105] More precisely, my behind did. Night wasps are unusual in their family in that they are active between dusk and dawn. Like many nocturnal insects they are attracted to light. When I stepped out of the car to deal with the snake, I left the cabin light on and the door open, providing the wasp with motive and opportunity. It was exploring the driver's seat when I climbed back into the truck, and it escaped my notice. It did not escape my big butt, though. Before I mashed the poor insect into the upholstery, it had time for one last-hurrah bayonet strike. I learned a lot that night. I learned that night wasps administer a serious sting that hurts like a mother, and seemingly forever. I also learned that before you let a night wasp hit you in the rump you should see that your truck's suspension system is up to snuff, or the two hours home will feel like two eternities. And from now on I would keep the passenger cabin in complete darkness at all times.

Borneo's insect fauna has been estimated at around 50,000 species, with thousands more waiting to be discovered. There are records of over 700 ant species, 12,000 kinds of butterflies and moths—and, with over 370 species, over 12 percent of the world's stick insects, including Chan's megastick,[106] with a body length of over 14 inches. The sheer variety of Borneo's bugs is enough to make a grown entomologist cry. (One might assume that frequent contact with fantastic wildlife will gradually diminish a naturalist's capability for pure, childlike amazement. There must exist, one argues, a natural defense mechanism that numbs the brain to continuous sensory overload. But I have yet to meet a biologist working in Borneo who isn't living proof to the contrary.)

By "bugs," I do not mean insects alone; the island is a kingdom for invertebrates of every conceivable sort. Like big hairy spiders. I *love* big hairy spiders. (There, I said it.

---

105 *Provespa nocturna*

106 *Phobaeticus chani*

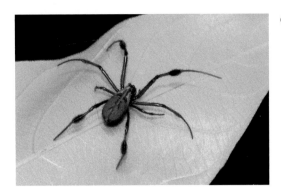

Opadometa sarawakensis

Do with it what you will, Freudians.) Borneo is a hotbed of tarantula diversity. New species are regularly found, such as the blue-legged knockout feted as the World's Most Beautiful Spider.[107] But after a year of countless forest walks, I still had not found one hair of these wonderfully weird plush creations. Many tarantulas spend their entire lives with their butts in a burrow, looking out in the hope a meal will stroll by close enough to catch. They are shy and sensitive to their surroundings, they love dark nooks and crannies, and I found them impossible to find. When I finally met my first wild tarantula, I reacted to it like a ten-year old girl to her first pony. Not only did the spider itself excite me, but also the way it revealed itself to us: eight-legging it across our cruising road. Half my mind exploded in celebration, while the other half tried to explain away what I was seeing. Up to that moment it had been my considered opinion that tarantulas never leave the dark, damp safety of the forest, and most certainly do not jaywalk across moonlit country roads. But there it was: a very big, very hairy spider on the road right before us, and it was staring into our headlights.

Our expedition gear included a Faunarium™, a small plastic terrarium with a pop-on lid that we used to transport small animals to more photogenic settings. Now I needed it to secure the tarantula. While Hans dug for it on the truck bed, I tiptoed toward the spider. It still sat with its six frontal eyes trained on the car, while the two lateral ones checked the roadsides. Its cephalothorax (often erroneously thought to be the head, but actually a fused head and thorax) was huge and its abdomen slender, and it had the comely long legs of an octopedal thoroughbred. It was dressed in black velvet; only the abdomen was mouse gray. Keeping my camera aimed at the animal, I slowly duckwalked toward it, looking like Chuck Berry in cargo shorts after gaining 100 pounds and ditching the Gibson for a Pentax. I kept shooting in rapid-fire mode, fearing the tarantula would scoot off the road at any given moment. It was still in position, but I was getting antsy; I wanted to cover it with the upended Faunarium to keep it in place to craft better shots. I was unfamiliar with the flight-or-fight psychology of big hairy spiders, but if it chose the

107 *Birupes simoroxigorum*

165

flight option I certainly was not going to grab this one with my bare hands. Apart from allergic reactions, most tarantula venom is not considered dangerous to most humans, but I didn't want to take any chances with Black Velvet here. Discovering a new big hairy spider species with unprecedented toxicity only to get killed by it on the spot was not my idea of scientific glory, even if they named the darn thing after me.

Hans walked up behind me with the Faunarium. The tarantula shifted a little. Evidently, it regarded my son as one human too many for comfort. But it stood its ground like a boss. The six hind legs were firmly planted, and the two front legs and pedipalps raised straight up in the air, pointed at us and ready to rumble. I remembered an illustration in a high school history book that showed a group of Hannibal's war elephants clashing with Roman infantry. Some elephants were trampling their terrified opponents into the muck, splintering spears and shields; others had grabbed soldiers with their trunks and were flinging them away like rag dolls. The biggest elephant in the unit was rearing up into a panic-inspiring pose, trunk in the air like a whip, and about to come down on two screaming legionaries. Right now, the tarantula looked like a spitting image of that war elephant and gave off the same irate vibe. And it was armed. Beneath the frontal eye cluster glistened two large, black fangs the shape of

Malay reddish-brown tarantula (**Coremiocnemis valida**)

tiger canines. They would administer the venom, and they were thick enough to leave a pair of bleeding holes in my flesh. Even if I avoided full contact with the spider, it could still fire off a cloud of urticating hairs. (*Urtica* is Latin for nettle, and tarantulas are notorious for their skills with this sneaky weapon. The hairs can embed themselves in skin and eyes and cause great physical irritation and discomfort.)

I reckoned that right now would be a good time to quarantine the spider. Hans placed the little plastic terrarium over it, and I let out a sigh of relief. Now for some proper camerawork. I took out wireless flash and diffuser and prepared the shoot. Once I had set up a shot, Hans lifted the terrarium, I took a few photos, and the box was replaced until I was ready for the next angle. After a few of these maneuvers, the tarantula performed a cool trick. It slowly pulled its legs under its body like an eight-fingered hand curling into a fist, ceased all movement, and now appeared to be lifeless. Many animals, vertebrates and invertebrates alike, practice thanatosis, also called tonic immobility, the art of playing dead. The idea is to render the pursuer unresponsive to its victim, as most predators only catch live prey. I had seen this behavior in snakes and beetles before. Most animals playing possum take a while before reviving themselves, so we put a few leaves in the terrarium, added a wet, balled-up tissue as a water source, and moved the tarantula into its temporary home. This we hid under some vegetation and continued our drive in the hope the spider would have resumed normal operations when we returned.

When we retrieved the Faunarium™ three hours later, the tarantula still looked as dead as a doornail, legs contracted in that death curl typical for expired spiders. I put on a welding glove, opened the lid, and touched the arachnid ever-so-lightly. No reaction. I pushed it a little. Nothing. I slid a leaf underneath its body, lifted it up, then lowered it again. Still looked pretty dead. An uneasy feeling crept up on me. What if this was not an act, after all? I felt as guilty as Cain. What had we done? Had we stressed the spider to death with our endless camera flashes, or with our sheer presence? With great apprehension, I called a friend in Kuching who kept dozens of tarantulas in his basement, all neatly lined up in individual acrylic cubes. It was well after midnight, but I knew he kept vampire hours, and he picked up on the second ring.

Before I had even finished my story, I could hear him break into a big grin: "You picked the best month, but your timing was awful. That was a male. They come out this time of year to search females to mate with. That's why he was out in the open and crossing the road. But once they've found a suitable lady and have done their procreational duty, they will die not long after."

With a heavy heart but a clearer conscience, we took a few more shots of the deceased, and then gave him a sky burial by the road. His life was over, but his remains still had a purpose: for many of the creatures in this forest, a big, hairy, freshly dead spider is a much-appreciated feast.

Farewell, Black Velvet. We never knew what species you were.

* * * * * *

At the far end of the cruising road stood a low concrete building with three parallel storefronts. The one in the middle was bricked up, but the mom-and-pop joints flanking it were still doing brisk business when we pulled in for some R&R at 1 a.m. on a Sunday. The two shops looked similar. A big beverage refrigerator with a glass door, shelves for homemade yam chips and industrial junk snacks, and a small gas stove on a side table to cook instant noodles, the single item on the menu. If you asked nicely, they would also sell you arak, the region's indigenous white lightning. Arak is crudely, but effectively, distilled from rice wine (*tuak*), and no connoisseur of fine spirits would use it for anything but dressing wounds and degreasing engines. But at two US bucks a quart, this 120-proof rotgut is the ultimate party fuel. We sat under the shop arcades and ordered iced Coke with fresh lime. While we waited for our drinks, we messed with the pale, finger-sized Asian house geckos[108] that swarmed the wall between the neon signs, hunting everything that moved. During our tours I carried a laser pointer to show the location of arboreal animals. When you ran the green dot along the gecko wall, two or three of the lizards would always skitter after it like excited reptilian kittens.

That kept us amused for a while, and when our drinks arrived an impromptu sports event began on the road: a drag race, Mad Max style. Two shirtless sixth graders in swimming trunks and flip-flops lined up their mopeds, one to each lane. On the count of five they howled off toward a finish line drawn in yellow chalk 100 yards away. Both were going in the same direction, so one of them faced possible suicide by oncoming traffic. Even more exciting, the rules seemed to require keeping the front wheel in the air for the entire distance. I was very much impressed by their skills. I have never been able to hold a wheelie for more than 10 yards, and I always wiped out the bike. Peter Matthiessen would have called the two kids "innocent of fear and common sense," but I looked at the spectacle from a kinder angle—they were just bored in the boonies. Internet reception wasn't too good out here to begin with, and maybe the kids' data plan had run out, followed by their top-up funds. Anything at all, then, to spice up Saturday night.

The cars in the parking lot reflected an automotive culture seen in many rural corners of the world. There were three dominant models: the aged but well-maintained workhorse pickup, the ancient rattletrap held together by a string and a prayer, and the tweaked-out Japanese compact car with garish manga decals, over-tinted windows, and an exhaust pipe in which a cat could overnight. The patrons at both shops were all male, either old or teenaged. The sole exception was a mop-haired guy in his forties with gin-blossomed cheeks and verbal diarrhea, both most likely induced by the large missing quantity of arak in the bottle on his table. He was well away with the fairies and

---

108 *Hemidactylus frenatus*

talked at operatic volume to everyone who caught his eye. In turn, everyone ignored him. The old men quietly nursed cans of smuggled Cambodian lager. Their faces spoke of long days and short lives, and they stared without seeing at the TV set on top of the beer fridge where a badly pirated copy of *Rambo IV* was blaring away, the action on the small screen largely obscured by Malay and Chinese subtitles. Unlike the old-timers, the teenage boys were really into the movie. They greeted every bad guy's gruesome end with lusty swearing, and the disembowelment scene in the final minutes was celebrated like a soccer goal.

I couldn't think of a better place for a midnight Coke-and-lime.

In Sarawak, medieval culture often exists in harmony alongside the Third Millennium. An example: like many Bidayuh settlements, Annah Rais, a longhouse cluster a few miles from where we were sitting, has a small *baruk,* a round thatched building on stilts. Its pointy roof caps a single room that serves as a display hall for headhunting trophies. The skulls often dangle in the center of the room and greet the visitor at eye height. The cramped conditions in the headhouse at Annah Rais force you to look eye to eye with an iron cage holding a dozen brutalized human skulls. The ghoulish atmosphere is enhanced by a blue glow that intensifies the creepiness of the severed heads. But this eerie blue light is not a haunted-house effect put on for the tourists—it comes from the wall-mounted, Plexiglas-encased wi-fi router that provides internet access to the longhouses.

Familiarity with both ancient and modern concepts was also manifest in the thoughts of the shop proprietor who had now come over to sit and chat with us. Albert knew us from many late-night visits, and, as was his custom, he started the

Baruk (skull house) in Annah Rais

conversation with "Mr. Hans and Mr. Hans! What snakes did you find tonight?" After reporting our tally to him, we chinwagged a bit about this season's sensational durian harvest, and the recent landslide 10 miles from here that had pushed a 50-yard stretch of the main road into the valley, missing a farmhouse by a hair.

He leaned closer, and his face tightened into importance. "What do you think about doing a little business together?"

Business? Would he like us to sell his surplus durians in town? Or hand out promo fliers for his shop at the Lodge School and the Waterfront bars?

"No, no. I'm talking about snakes. I like to eat snake meat. In fact, most everyone here likes snake meat. We've been eating it since the dawn of time. Not the small ones, of course, but anything bigger than, say, 3 feet, if it's not too skinny. No whip snakes, obviously. Pythons are best. But big ratsnakes will also do. So, I was wondering … when you find one of those, after you're done with your photos, would you sell it to me?"

His proposal didn't entirely take me by surprise. Once or twice before, when photographing a python, a passing motorist had stopped and inquired if we would donate the snake to him after the shoot. An understandable request: even a young *Malayopython reticulatus* makes for a lot of curry, and apart from the constant choking hazard from its hundreds of fishbone-like ribs, it is supposed to be a pretty decent meal when cooked the right way. But why bother with a ratsnake, which is more scales and bones than anything else? And what was wrong with pork chops and drumsticks, anyway?

"Pigs and chickens, ha!" Albert scoffed. "They're all injected with hormones and antibiotics and God knows what other devilry! My wife always says: 'When you need medicine, you eat pork. Got all the medicines you need.' But snake meat is fresh and natural!"

His argumentation was compelling, but I wouldn't poach wild animals for him or anyone else. I tried to reason him away: "You realize that wild snakes are full of internal and external parasites, yes? Ticks and tapeworms and stuff?"

"Sure, sure, but no worries, we always deep-fry them and add lots of chilis, make sure everything is sterile. Haha!" He clapped his hands at his own cleverness.

I couldn't argue with that. But I still wasn't going to commodify the local wildlife. I needed to be diplomatic about it, though; I didn't want us to become *personae non gratae* here. So, I chose the Way of the Wimp. "Tell you what, next time we find a suitable snake, we'll bring it to you, and you can decide if you want it. We'll talk money then."

Albert was happy. We shook hands, he bought us another round of limed-up Coke, and we parted in good spirits.

Luck is a fickle mistress, though. From that night on, all we ever found on that road were snakes smaller than 3 feet. I suspect Albert knows why. Lately, there's been a certain lack of freshness in the limes he serves us. And the glasses aren't quite as full as they used to be.

* * * * * *

"There are no vegetarians south of the border." Many Sarawakians hold this opinion about Kalimantan, the Indonesian part of the island, and the least economically fortunate of the three countries on Borneo. Hunting for sustenance has become largely unnecessary in Sarawak. But old traditions hold sway in the countryside, and for the last 40,000 years, the most popular game has been wild boar. Not just because it's drug-free, but public sentiment strongly sides with Ted Nugent: no better pork chops than the ones you've killed and grilled yourself.

In these forests there are two kinds of pigs. Feral pigs are escapees from hog farms and can reach proportions to rival their monstrous cousins in the southern United States. *Sus barbatus*, the Borneo bearded pig, looks very different. It is small and slender, probably an adaptation to life in dense forest undergrowth. Its claim to fame is a comically bushy Amish beard that runs from the ears to the lips and is often complemented by a thick tuft of long white bristles sprouting from the top of the snout like an enormous shaving brush. In Bako National Park with its strictly enforced hunting ban, bearded pigs move fearlessly among the visitors. They often join forces with local organized crime, the long-tailed macaques, in raiding unattended backpacks containing food. The monkeys nimbly open the zippers and remove everything that looks and smells edible, while the pigs prefer a more muscular method—they grab the packs and drag them into the jungle, their little piggy tails whipping in the wind with glee.

Borneo bearded pig (photo, Christoph Lepschy)

Boar hunting can be perilous. Charles Hose argued in 1929 that the bearded pig was not to be trifled with: "He has a better claim than any other beast to the title 'King of the Jungle', for he fears neither beast nor man." My personal experience supports this opinion. I once witnessed an ugly scene that started in the parking lot at Permai Rainforest Resort where three stray dogs attacked a bearded boar that had ventured out from the jungle. The pig immediately retreated and led the mutts into the forest. Once out of sight, the animals started to battle by a small creek just inside the tree line. There was wild splashing, barking and yelping, and the occasional grunt and squeak from the boar. The barking weakened. Then I heard only two dogs. Then one. Then silence. I waited 15 minutes before going in to check the war zone. The pig was gone; so was one of the dogs. Its two comrades lay mangled by the creek. One was still breathing, but only just, through what looked like a sucking chest wound.

Hunters in Borneo use packs of trained dogs to find bearded pigs. The hogs often travel in groups and, when cornered, will try to dispatch the dogs first. Neutralization tactics against the hunter involve rushing him, ramming the tusks into his scrotum, and then swinging the head upward to eviscerate the man. The animal's savage courage is its main survival tool, but the pig's chances are often improved by the huntsman's inadequate weaponry.

Firearms are strictly regulated in Sarawak, yet in the bush you wouldn't think such legislation existed. Many hunting rifles and shotguns are handmade in Kalimantan and snuck in over the mouse trails. Their craftsmanship can be questionable, and their use requires caution. Many cartridges are hand-filled with homemade propellant, and sometimes the guns backfire. An elderly hunter from Annah Rais told me he had given up on the pastime because "these DIY guns are just no good. Just last Saturday night, I stood ten paces away from a big sow. The dogs had her in a corner. I aimed and shot, but the bullet flew past the pig on a bent trajectory! I used to hunt with my father's Lee-Enfield—now that was a fine rifle—but the government took it away from me long ago. To hell with it all! I'll get my pork from the market from now on."

Hardcore "live to hunt, hunt to live" Nimrods are not deterred by such minor technical details. Every time we went on a snake cruise we saw people with various kinds of firearms, either entering or leaving the forest on foot, or motoring to other hunting grounds. On occasion, we would encounter fellow road cruisers. One group patrolled our stretch of the road in an old white van. The driver kept the vehicle at a steady 10 miles per hour while the passengers looked for prey. The man behind the driver swung his flashlight through the roadside trees, and his friend on the passenger seat kept his beam on the asphalt. The first time we saw them pull over for a pit stop, I parked behind them, walked up to the driver's window, and introduced ourselves and our purpose here on the road. The man in the passenger seat was clearly the leader of the trio. His craggy face and arak breath made me think of Keith Richards on an unproductive day, and he looked older than he probably was. The single-barreled shotgun between the front seats completed the picture. He didn't seem terribly interested in befriending us, but he did ask a lot of gruff questions about our night. In my naïveté, I told him about the animals we had seen earlier. His stony face became almost animated when I mentioned the young leopard cat that had exploded away from a roadkilled rat when our car came into sight. The man's approving facial twitch slapped me back into reality; I remembered that barbecued leopard cat is considered fine dining around those parts. He demanded detailed location info for the cat sighting; I lied about it. Then I asked him what sort of animals they were looking for. I was expecting the usual: wild boar, pythons, maybe flying squirrels. A rictus of a smile stitched across those crags when he rumbled, "Anything that crosses the road."

I was too shocked to inquire further. *Anything?*

Later I told a local biologist about the incident, and he nodded. "Yep. Anything. He meant that. They shoot first, then figure out what to do with it. If they care to bother at all. Sometimes, people traveling by boat along the rivers shoot everything they see out of the trees and don't even pick it up. Monkeys, hornbills, bats, squirrels … anything indeed. For no other reasons than boredom and ignorance."

I eventually found some comfort in a conversation with Oswald Braken Tisen, a take-no-prisoners conservationist and at that time deputy general manager at Sarawak Forestry. Growing up in rural Sarawak, he used to go hunting "all the time. But today, when I show my children a monkey or a python, they don't think it's food. It all comes down to education." There is still hope for Sarawak's wildlife, but for that hope to blossom, education needs to hurry up fast.

⁎ ⁎ ⁎ ⁎ ⁎ ⁎

During our snake cruises we never saw any pigs (too smart, too wary, too cunning), but there were other mammals. Bats were the most obvious family. With close to 100 species, they are Borneo's most common mammals. They range from tiny microbats that hunt airborne insects by echolocation, to puppy-sized fruit specialists with a 3-foot wingspan. Our truck's roof lights attracted insects, the insects attracted bats, and these often performed their dogfights inches away from our windshield. Insect-catching bats are famed for their expert use of echolocation in high-speed chases and hair-raising maneuvers, but they are not infallible. It didn't happen often, but once it happened twice in the same night: a bat ricocheted off the glass, its kite-strutted wings splayed out as it somersaulted through the air, and just before it hit the ground it righted itself and regained control over its flight path. On even rarer occasions, a bat would smack straight into the roof lights and slide down the length of the windshield, ending up stunned on the hood. One of the many fascinating facts about bats is that they have been shown to carry more than 60 viruses classified as zoonotic, i.e., transmissible to humans. Among them are HIV, SARS, Covid-19, and Ebola, which is why we always put on our welding gloves before carefully removing the little daredevils from the hood and placing them on low branches to facilitate their takeoff after regaining consciousness.

The road wound through plenty of forest, but the area was too populated for Borneo's charismatic megafauna—the sambar deer, orangutans, sun bears, and clouded leopards—which mostly live in remote places with less hunting pressure. The mammals we did find on this road were less illustrious and generally smaller, but they intrigued us in their own ways. *Trychis fasciculata* was a regular. The first one we encountered came trotting out of the bush to cross the road, and we had no idea what it was. In mid-crossing, our headlights confused it. It changed its mind and ambled along the median strip instead. We followed at a close distance. When you drive at 5 miles an hour behind an animal fully illuminated by your high beams and roof lights, you get a very good look at it, but we couldn't make heads or tails of this one. It looked like a big, ugly rat, but something felt wrong about the rat theory—it just didn't look rat enough. Only one thing was sure: this critter was no kind of aesthetic triumph.

I called Chien Lee and described the creature before us leading the way like a hairy little Follow-me car. "It's large, gray, and disheveled, with long, thick, unkempt hair, and a bottle brush at the end of its ratty tail."

There was a chuckle at the other end of the line. "That's not a rat, it's a porcupine. A long-tailed porcupine, to be precise."

The porcupine chose this moment to scurry back into the forest. I felt cheated. I knew there were *real* porcupines on the island, with big beaver bodies and orange teeth and bristly skirts made from those arrow-sized, barbed quills; all the stuff you would expect from a proper porcupine. Instead, we got … this? *Their Skid Row cousin?*

My disappointment with this very unspectacular, and therefore in my eyes un-Bornean, mammal lifted with our first moonrat. We were driving through a kampung later that night when a small white dog ran onto the road, chased by a bigger, brown dog. Noticing our approach, the white dog came straight at us to hide beneath the truck. The brown dog, clearly a smarter breed, balked at the insanity of running under a moving vehicle and broke off the chase. When the white dog disappeared under the car, right beneath my open window, the air was briefly hideous with ammonia and rotten garlic, and at the last glimpse I discovered that it wasn't a dog at all. It looked like a giant shrew—long, tapered muzzle, long whiskers, tiny eyes. Its pelt was the color of freshly fallen snow.

My confusion knew no bounds. Was this actually some kind of shrew? And what was up with that crazy smell? I did feel lucky, though, because that animal was definitely an albino, and albinos are rare in tropical forests. As a rule, they don't last long—their bright white color advertises them to predators. For that reason alone, it was a very nice find, whatever it was.

Over the next few weeks the albino theory evaporated fast with every additional pristine-white moonrat we found. *Echinosorex gymnura* is a mostly carnivorous member of the order formerly known as Insectivora, which also included shrews, hedgehogs, and bats. The subspecies *E.g. alba* (Latin for white) only exists in Borneo, and it only comes in one color: white. The color doesn't make sense for a forest animal until you realize it's an aposematic warning. Aposematism, from ancient Greek, meaning something like "approach at your own peril," refers to an animal's appearance, which signals to predators that it's toxic, dangerous, or distasteful. Moonrats might be bluffing about the first two, but their awful stink does suggest a disagreeable gastronomic experience. It also suggests that the brown dog must have suffered from a serious olfactory dysfunction.

Borneo's small-mammal fauna is rich in extremes. It includes the binturong,[109] a.k.a. bearcat, a carnivore that looks like a big shaggy dog and lives in trees, and the banded linsang,[110] a classic-Disney beauty with a zebra coat so spectacular that Cruella DeVil would have deforested all of Borneo just to get her hands on every last one. For me, though, the crowning glory of the island's mammalian weirdness is a creature that is almost devoid of the common denominator of most mammals, namely fur. Instead, it is covered from the tip of its nose to the end of its tail in something Nature usually reserves for reptiles: keratin scales. To visualize this animal, start with a pinecone about as big as a Scottish terrier. Add four short, stubby legs, then put three heavy-duty claws on each forepaw. Attach an ice-cream cone, pointy end out, to one end of the pinecone. Once you have glued two almost human-like ears, a dog's nostrils, and a pair of beady eyes to the ice-cream cone, you're done with the head. On the other end, add a long, flat tail. Finish the animal by covering all of it except eyes, ears, nostrils, and underside in thick, mud-colored scales. Voila! you just created a pangolin, or scaly anteater.

The pangolin's bizarreness doesn't end with its appearance. It has no teeth and lives on a diet of ants and termites, whose nests it excavates with its powerful claws and raids with a sticky tongue that is longer than its entire body and needs to be stored in an abdominal cavity close to the pelvis. The pangolin can shut its ears and nostrils to keep insects out while feeding. It is believed that one pangolin consumes over 70 million ants and termites in a single year. When threatened, pangolins roll up into an armored ball held shut with powerful muscles. A baby pangolin travels around with its mother by riding on the base of her tail.

And the bizarrest fact of all: the pangolin, a creature most people have never even heard of, is the world's most trafficked nonhuman mammal.

But more on that shortly.

---

109 *Arctictis binturong*

110 *Prionodon linsang*

* * * * * *

There is only one woman in the world to have named a planet. There is only one person in the world that has been struck by re-entering space debris. And on Monday, June 25, 2012, I believe I also became a member of the exclusive club of World's Onlys: I am the only person in the world whose pet snake was liberated by a pangolin.

Most of Sarawak had been without rain for two weeks, a small catastrophe this close to the equator—huge ditches dried out within the first days, and people in the backcountry ran out of rivers to commute on. It is not a situation conducive to finding reptiles, but I had learned to approach the cruising area with serenity. I probably wasn't going to see anything but bats today, but it's always therapeutic just to be in the forest. As anticipated, after two hours of driving I still hadn't seen anything but bats. Then came a twist of fate. Like with a Jesus encounter (seeing His face burnt onto a piece of toast, you know, or Him standing in front of you in the checkout line, counting His change), suddenly all my troubles were faint memories, and angels poked their rosy-cheeked faces through the night sky and let rip a glorious hymn in praise of whoever up there had commanded the pangolin to cross the road right in front of my car.

A pangolin's silhouette is unmistakable. This one had come moseying out of the grass as if leaving a pub with the intention of grabbing a final nightcap at the Swan and Bulldog across the street. An American mammal researcher working with camera traps all over Borneo once told me that statistically, the chance of meeting a wild *Manis javanica* is slimmer than encountering a sun bear (almost nobody I know has ever seen a wild sun bear). The reason is that in Malaysia pangolin meat currently sells for US$80 per kilo, and the scales for much more, thanks to seemingly irrepressible medical superstitions prevailing in China and Vietnam. The animal's parts are believed to possess all sorts of medicinal powers, and its meat is considered a delicacy. Their highly specialized diet and behavior makes them difficult to breed in captivity, so Asia's voracious appetite for pangolins needs to be quenched through poaching. The Sunda pangolin is the only species in Borneo. Hunting and keeping these animals is illegal in Malaysia, but enforcing wildlife protection laws can be a challenge in Sarawak, a huge state with a population density of just 60 people per square mile.

There are eight pangolin species in the world, four each in Asia and Africa. Scientists have designated all species of pangolins as being at risk of extinction. All of them were uplisted to CITES[111] Appendix I in 2016. By most conservative estimates, 10,000 pangolins are trafficked each year. Pangolins only bear one young per year at best, and the excessive hunting at this scale will most likely lead to their disappearance within the next decade if nothing drastic happens to prevent it. In Vietnam, pangolins

---

111 Convention on International Trade in Endangered Species of Wild Fauna and Flora

are now practically extinct, and every year Asian law enforcement nabs entire shipping containers of pangolins earmarked for the pharmacies and restaurants of China and a few surrounding countries. On April 3, 2019, in the world's biggest single haul in recent years, Singapore authorities seized almost 13 tons of pangolin scales taken from an estimated 17,000 pangolins. Total value: almost US$38 million.

What's so irresistible about pangolin products? For starters, they're supposed to be good eatin'. CNN journalist John D. Sutter, reporting undercover about pangolin poaching in Vietnam, wrote in a piece called The Most Trafficked Mammal You've Never Heard Of:

> "We keep them alive in cages until the customer makes an order," explains a chef from the Chinese province of Guangdong to *The Guardian*. "Then we hammer them unconscious, cut their throats and drain the blood. It is a slow death. We then boil them to remove the scales. We cut the meat into small pieces and use it to make a number of dishes, including braised meat and soup. Usually, the customers take the blood home with them afterward."
>
> Preparation options [in a Vietnamese restaurant] included: "blood wine," "stir-fried pangolin skin with onion and mushroom," pangolin "steamed with ginger and citronella," pangolin "steamed with Chinese traditional medicine"; and, for the unadventurous, the people who would rather eat pangolin at Chili's, there's "grilled" pangolin, too.
>
> As the waitress explained (…) the staff would bring the pangolin out to the table live—and slit its throat. Right in front of us. You had to order it whole, at a minimum of 5 kilos (11 pounds). Price: $350 per kilo. Or $1,750 for the whole beast.

The exorbitant price is another reason to dine on pangolin: you don't really eat it because it's delicious (opinions on the taste vary wildly), but because it's fabulously expensive and by ordering it you show off your social status.

Then there are the alleged magical health benefits. For such a small animal, the pangolin is supposed to have a vast number of medicinal uses: the fetus is consumed as an aphrodisiac, as is its blood. Pangolin scales are ground up and eaten as a treatment for problems with lactation, blood circulation, and cancer. Dipped in alcohol and rubbed on mosquito bites, they supposedly stop the itching. (Reality check: like the horn of the rhinoceros, another animal brought to the brink of doom by Asian superstitions, pangolin scales are pure keratin, the same stuff your hair and fingernails are made of. If all the hype about rhino horn and pangolin scales were true, people would be able to cure their malign tumors just by biting their nails.)

And just when you thought it couldn't get any weirder: some people carry the dried tongue in their pockets as a good-luck charm.

Before Covid-19, a virus supposedly carried by pangolins, the Chinese government used to encourage all this. In June 2019, Rachael Bale of *National Geographic* magazine stated in a Wildlife Watch article:

> In China, where such treatments continue to be sanctioned by the government, more than 200 pharmaceutical companies produce some 60 types of traditional medicines that contain pangolin scales, according to a 2016 report by the China Biodiversity Conservation and Green Development Foundation. Every year Chinese provinces collectively issue approvals for companies to use an average 29 tons of the scales, which roughly represents 73,000 individual pangolins.

Whether these treatments work matters little; what matters is that people believe they do. The pangolin's market value suggests that their belief is strong.

All eight pangolin species are on the critically endangered list for no other reasons than selfishness, ignorance, and the market dynamics these factors create. The odds of discovering a pangolin in the wild were towering against me. And yet, the one loping across the road right here was already the second specimen I had seen on this road in six weeks. The first one got away because my son had been reluctant to grab it: "I was afraid he'd bite me!" During our last session with a scaly anteater back in Taiwan, I had apparently neglected to tell him that these animals have no teeth. Their mouth is an empty structure through which the tongue travels out into the night forest to lap up bugs and water.

I would not permit another humiliation at the hands of a little ant-eating artichoke. Not that it's difficult to catch them—being mostly arboreal, pangolins knuckle-walk the Earth on their claws in an ungainly, plodding gait. Of course, the drama queen in me couldn't just get out and pick the thing up. That would have lacked flair. So I let the beast slide into a roadside ditch and had to clamber after it, banging my shin something awful in the process, and just before Scaly Pants could disappear into the ferns, I managed to grab it by the tail in a dramatic lunge that almost threw my back out.

Now I had my first Malaysian scaly anteater. Where to photograph it? The high frequency of passing mopeds ruled out a photo session on the spot. Every time a bike buzzed by, I had to swivel my headlamp away from the pangolin—now on the truck bed in full conglobation—to keep entrepreneurial locals from sensing a business opportunity. The little stinker (their anal glands secrete a pungent fluid used for defense and to mark territory) was a juvenile, about the size of a large cat, and fitted nicely into a medium snake bag. Fearing it would tear the cotton apart with its backhoe claws, I put the bag on the floor on the passenger side and kept a keen eye on it for the rest of the drive.

The Chinese pangolin we had found in Taiwan a few years before had readily given a nice floor show even in daylight. I planned to take some pictures of its relative in my garden and release it later in Kubah National Park. To that end, I asked a friend and pet shop owner in Kuching to lend me a dog cage for a few nights. I moved the pangolin inside, placed the cage in the little storage room under the stairs in our house, and went to bed happy as a clam.

The next day was a Sunday, climbing day for Hans Jr. We brought the pangolin to the Fairy Cave wall, and after showing it to the climbers (to a chorus of "How cuuuute—make sure the villagers don't see it!"), I took it to an abandoned orchard full of pretty rocks to photograph it. The pangolin was still balled up, so I placed it on one of the mini-crags and hid behind a tree. After half an hour of waiting for the keratin sphere to do something exciting—actually, to do *any*thing!—I switched tactics and hung it on a low tree branch by the tip of its prehensile tail, hoping it would give up the ball. But no. Pangolins are so muscular they can probably hang from a tree until the next ice age. When the sun started to bake us near noon, the ant freak was still tightly wrapped up, and I decided to take it back home again and photograph it at night in my backyard. They are nocturnal, I reasoned, so they should be more active by night.

That also didn't pan out as envisioned. After picking up Hans at the climbing wall, we topped off the day with some fruitless road cruising, and when we came home we were too tired to photograph anything. I caged the pangolin again, hoped for tomorrow, and turned off the lights.

The following morning, I opened the storage room door to an empty cage and a rolled-up pangolin sleeping in a dark corner of the room. There were no visible clues as to how the beast had escaped from its prison—no twisted wires, no busted door, no ripped-up bottom. Against my better judgment, I put the animal back in the cage, took my son to school, and started my workday. Later that night a few friends came over to watch the photo shoot. At 8 p.m. we took the pangolin ball into the garden, placed it on the lawn, stepped back and waited. An hour later, even the most rabid optimist among us admitted that the animal had no intention of gracing us with its unfolded presence. Were these Sunda pangolins more introverted than their Chinese kin? We had no way of knowing. But I did know there was no point in waiting any longer for the creature to do its song and dance for us, because it was not going to happen. I would release it in the wild again first thing tomorrow. Feeling terribly guilty about keeping Scaly Pants in such an unnatural environment for two days, I didn't put it back in the cage (from which it would have Houdinied anyway) but instead gave it the run of the storage room and bade it good night.

At the stroke of midnight, I woke up from a tremendous crash downstairs. I tiptoed down the stairs with great trepidation, expecting a gang of parang-wielding meth

Sunda pangolin in battle mode

heads tearing up the living room in search for valuables. But the den was quiet. Some faint noise came from the storage room, though. I opened the door and stepped into Armageddon. Three tiers of wooden boards along the wall of the storage room served as hold-alls for rarely used stuff. The top tier had held a big transparent plastic crate-on-wheels which we used to stash large snakes overnight. The crate's current occupant was an adult dog-toothed cat snake. Right now, neither crate nor snake were on the shelf. The pangolin, a powerful climber, had pulled itself up to the top tier, from there onto the snake crate, and then overbalanced and fell, pulling the crate down with it. Now the crate was on the floor, upside down, with the snake zooming around inside, hissing and inflating its neck in great agitation. The pangolin sat next to it, shaking like a leaf from the fall. After putting things back in order, I discovered a gift the pangolin had left me: a turd that would have made a Great Dane proud. It boggles the mind how such a small animal can produce such a massive mound of crap on an exclusive diet of tiny insects. I cleaned up that mess too, removed an old TV set I suspected of facilitating the pangolin's ascent, and went to bed again. At 6 a.m. the next day, I went straight to the storage room to see if everything was hunky-dory.

It was not.

The same End-of-Days scene I had witnessed during the night had rematerialized, as if I had never picked up the midnight mess (there's a movie idea: *Pangolin Day*, starring Bill Murray). The snake crate was on the floor again, again upside down, but this time the lid had popped off and the snake had escaped. In addition, all other items formerly crowding the shelves were now also on the floor, bent, shattered, or otherwise violated. The culprit itself was snoring sweetly at the far end of the upper tier, curled up into a most adorable scaly ball. The snake, on the other hand, was gone. Over the course of the night, besides cleaning out the shelves, the toothless demon-incarnate had clawed an inch-wide hole through the bottom of the door. Cat snakes can be very long, but most of them are also very slender, and my house guest had slithered through the hole into my office, and thence under the garden door to freedom.

Despite my ongoing desire to produce usable images of the pangolin, I could not wait to get rid of it now. I will admit an infatuation with all anteaters and a deep compassion for their plight, but their wicked pairing of physical power and inquisitive mind was more than I could handle. Into a snake bag the little wrecking ball went, and off it was to Kubah National Park. Most illegal hunting takes place close to the inner park perimeter, so I walked deep into the forest to release the pangolin. On the way I crossed a little rivulet. It was very shallow, thanks to the drought, and it gave me a wonderful idea. Although the pangolin had always been in reach of a full water bowl, it hadn't drunk much during its stay at our house. And pangolins need and love to drink a lot. Why not put it in the water and see what would happen? The stream was less than 2 inches deep, so I lowered the beast into it, on its back, making sure the head stayed above the surface. Then I stepped back and waited. Again.

Sunda pangolin

This time I struck pay dirt. After a few seconds, a long, pink, ropy tongue emerged from the pinecone and began lapping up the cool stream water. Slowly, the animal began to uncurl. It walked around, moved in and out of the water (pangolins are surprisingly good swimmers) and explored its surroundings at a leisurely pace. Incredibly, it fully ignored my presence, and I took hundreds of photos of this fantastic thing in a lovely natural setting.

Time is running out for pangolins. The earliest pangolin fossils date back to the epoch shortly after the dinosaurs went extinct. It is believed that pangolins are some of the earliest mammals, having evolved about 60 million years ago, and not changed a bit since. Living fossils like pangolins allow us a glimpse into a world unimaginably far back in the past. But within less than 20 years, growing prosperity in formerly underdeveloped countries has brought these genetic witnesses of a long-lost world dangerously close to the end of their run. As many as one million have been illegally traded within Asia in the past 10 to 15 years, and in the last two decades, the number of pangolins worldwide has dropped by about 90 percent. As with all poaching and overhunting, education is the answer. In the case of the pangolins, it will be an uphill battle against millennia of deeply ingrained superstition.

*   *   *   *   *   *

Malaysia's laws governing the foreigners within its borders often seem conflicting. With a three-month tourist visa you are allowed to purchase and register a car; you can even own a house on Malaysian soil. At the same time, it can take decades to receive a Malaysian Permanent Resident Card, even if you've been married to a Malaysian national the entire time. Malaysia, My Second Home (MM2H) is a government program that allows foreigners above a certain age to stay in Malaysia for a period of ten years, with the option to renew. A successful applicant may bring a spouse, an unmarried child under the age of 21, and parents who are over 60 years old. The tax-free import of one automobile is also permitted. In return, the government demands a permanent deposit of 150,000 ringgit (around US$38,000 in 2021) in a local bank, plus a monthly income of at least 10,000 ringgit. Hans Jr. had a student visa, and Lisa would receive a resident permit called a social pass, on the grounds that her children attended a Malaysian school. For myself, MM2H would have been the logical choice, since we had planned on staying in Sarawak for at least a decade, but my finances didn't quite allow it. A social pass was no option either. In the outdated thinking of Malaysia's immigration laws the male head of the household was the breadwinner of the family, and therefore only eligible for an employment visa, and said employment had to be with a company registered in Malaysia. As the owner of an online-based business I neither had nor desired such a location-based job. But my German passport allowed me to leave and reenter Malaysia every three months, so I arranged all my travels around my visa expiry dates. If no business or leisure trip was scheduled close to the date I could either fly to Singapore and spend a weekend with friends, or opt for the cheaper alternative and drive across the Indonesian border into Kalimantan for a cup of horseshoe coffee, a new stamp in my passport, and, on some occasions, a bit of adventure.

For our next visa run I chose the Kalimantan trip. We had never been to Indonesia before, and entering through one of its true backwaters sounded wild and poetic. Our Malaysian friends were full of dire warnings: "Make sure to cross the border with a full tank—Indonesian diesel is diluted with water and will ruin your engine! Avoid military roadblocks like the plague—they're just shakedowns for money and a fast track to jail! Keep your car in sight at all times—they'll jack it in broad daylight!" I would be lying if I told you that these suggestions did not unnerve me.

The 60-mile route to Tebedu, the border town on the Malaysian side, first took us to the start of our snake-cruising road then hung a hard right into a landscape dominated by limestone cliffs. Here, the narrow country lane took us up the steepest possible ascents, then dropped us screaming into the valleys beyond. On the far side of the hills, back in the safety of the flatlands, the road connected with a well-built four-lane highway. At its terminus was an open gate where a large sign informed the traveler that the gate, and with it the whole border crossing, opened at 6 a.m. and closed 12 hours later. There was also a gas station. Remembering the warnings about the stepped-on

Indonesian fuel, I filled the tank while Hans bought snacks, sodas, and a pair of plastic wraparound shades with multicolored lenses that made him look like a giant horsefly. Now we felt ready for Indonesia.

After receiving our Malaysian exit stamps at a concrete hut behind the gate, we drove across 50 yards of meticulously swept border to the Indonesian immigration building. The Kompleks Imigresen was impressive in its own right, not just for a tiny backwater village in one of Indonesia's most backwater provinces; three stories tall, with a steep roof, and decorated in elegant indigenous motifs, it put most border posts in Europe to shame. A grim-looking fellow in an intimidating uniform (Police? Armed forces? Tactical paintball?) assigned us a parking space, and we walked into the visa office. The ambience was dim and muggy, and it was eerily quiet. While we waited for our application to be considered, a short, potbellied cop at a corner desk watched us with an expression even grimmer than that of his comrade outside. He was a caricature of a tropical tin-pot dictator, attired in a black uniform starched to cardboard, pants tucked into combat boots fiercely polished into shaving mirrors, and the kind of sharply peaked cop cap generally associated with SS officers and Latin American tyrants. His face was obscured by a Pancho Villa mustache and a pair of reflective aviator sunglasses. I looked for a gold-plated .44 Magnum Desert Eagle on his hip, but the holster was empty.

The officer pointed at Hans Jr. and beckoned him over. As my son approached his desk, the man removed his glasses, revealing elephant-grade eye wrinkles, and pointed at my son's multihued horsefly shades. Hans looked back at me, visibly worried, then handed them over. The cop, still less expressive than a slab of granite, put them on and checked his reflection in a half-blind wall mirror. What he saw transformed him fundamentally. He broke into a huge grin that deepened his wrinkles to worrisome levels and began to pose for the mirror in a variety of ridiculous stances which he accentuated with an even greater variety of ridiculous faces. He turned to us and, lacking much English, asked in pantomime how much the horsefly glasses would cost. I sensed a chance to sneak into his good graces. I cast a glance at Hans Jr. to check, then with both hands outstretched, palms up, I mimed back, "Nothing. They're yours." His joy was beyond belief. He shook our hands as if he wanted to tear our arms off, and insisted we take a flurry of photos with him. In his ecstasy, he even made the other visa applicants in the room, two middle-aged Vietnamese ladies of the night, join us in the photo op. After that, everything happened fast: Captain Horsefly shouted into the backroom, keyboards clickety-clacked, and after we had donated a few fingerprints to the Kepolisian Negara Republik Indonesia, plus 50 US bucks in administrative fees, our visas were ready.

A group of money changers followed us back to the parking lot. We changed about 100 ringgit (roughly US$24), and Hans was agog at the brick-sized stack of notes we received in return—*three hundred thousand four hundred and seventy-one* Indonesian rupiahs. His astonishment later only grew at the prices for everyday goods: 8,000 rupiahs for a soda or a cup of coffee, 25,000 for a bowl of noodles. Yet all these things were still much cheaper than in Sarawak, and I used the opportunity to introduce my son to the concept of inflation.[112]

Kalimantan differed from Sarawak in other ways as well. Steeply gabled official buildings resembling wooden spaceports competed for attention with futuristic churches and golden-domed mosques. Even the simplest of residences were painted in all colors of the rainbow, and flags and banners flapped in the wind everywhere. Less attention had been paid to the state of the roads. Some of the potholes were the size of small strip mines, and the roadside grass, so painstakingly manicured to English lawn specs in Malaysia, flourished at jungle strength here, and encroached onto the asphalt wherever its path wasn't blocked by piles of garbage.

We stopped in a small town for lunch. English is often a dead language south of the border, but in the little buffet-style restaurant we had picked communication was easy. We just pointed at whatever tickled our fancy, and a round and friendly lady would pile it onto our plates. There were delicious tofu and tempeh dishes, fresh greens, and some of the best fried chicken I will ever have. In a welcome change from most Sarawakian cooking, much of it was liberally spiced with chili peppers. For those who favor the higher ranges of the Scoville scale, a condiment table offered various bottled hot sauces, saucers heaped with chopped bird's eye chilis, and a little jar of evil green goop labeled Saus Cabai Hijau, which I think means bowl of pain.

I capped off the delectable repast with a mug of horseshoe coffee. It is unlikely that Western novelist Louis L'Amour ever enjoyed a cup of joe in Indonesia, but, knowingly or not, in *The Daybreakers* he described it to a T: "Up in the hills we like our coffee strong, but this here would make bobwire grow on a man's chest in the place of hair."

The Indonesians would probably just shrug; for them it's their everyday java. Here's the recipe:

> Pour a generous measure of freshly ground coffee into a cup.
> Fill cup with hot water.
> Wait until the grounds have settled.
>
> Place a horseshoe on the surface. If it sinks, the brew is too weak. If it floats, carefully blow the horseshoe to the other side of the cup and enjoy in small sips.

A horseshoe shortage in Kalimantan forced me to forgo the test, but it didn't really matter. After all these years, I have yet to find a cup of Indonesian roadhouse coffee that fails to raise the dead.

---

112 In 2018 I went on a ten-day birding tour in Indonesian Papua, which cost US$880 per person, flight not included. We had been advised to pay the host in cash, and I have a photograph of me counting out the money on his dining table: 13,000,000 rupees in 65 stacks of 200,000. The bills almost covered the entire table.

I needed to use the restroom and was directed toward the back of the house. After a slippery walk through a lightless corridor I arrived at a tiny room, featureless but for a pail of brown water, a small window, and a hole in the wooden floor. The hole's circumference roughly equaled that of a human butt, and the view through it was unobstructed by any plumbing fixtures. I like an unobstructed view as much as the next person, but this one made my lunch crawl right back up my throat; 25 feet below me, an open septic tank that at one time had been a river paraded trash, sewage, and other godawful things through the town. The back of the restaurant projected out over the water and was propped up against the riverbank by stilts. The neighboring buildings were designed in the same fashion. In a fine display of architecture simultaneously facilitating and emulating a basic human need, the butts of all the houses teetered above the abyss, ready to eject any and all refuse into the cesspit below whenever the need arose.

Border village in Kalimantan, Indonesian Borneo

Two minutes after leaving the restaurant, we ran into our first roadblock. I was scared. For quite a while now, we had been living on the doorstep of this galaxy of almost 18,000 islands, populated with 264 million people from over 600 ethnicities speaking 700 languages. But apart from its fauna and flora I understood next to nothing about Indonesia. My slender grasp of its society and history was tainted by wild backpacker stories, bad movies, and the decidedly negative opinions of many Malaysians. Through the dark glass of all these warped prejudices, I perceived Indonesia as a country with a seriously underdeveloped sense of democracy, a long line of totalitarian regimes, and zero regard for the ecological value of its natural treasures. There appeared to be no rule of law, and anyone in a uniform needed to be regarded as corrupt to the bone and happy to abuse their power and throw you in a rat-infested dungeon for the rest of your natural life. I was very scared indeed.

The roadblock was simple, but effective. An armored truck was parked across each lane, leaving just enough space for a car to squeeze through between the two trucks. A dozen helmeted guys with POLISI stenciled on their ballistic vests slouched in various poses in, on, and around the vehicles. Fresh sweat darkened my shirt. They were toting assault rifles, and I had visions of my son and me prone on the asphalt, hands zip-tied behind our backs, boots on our necks, while the cops took our truck apart, looking for loot. I rolled down my window, took off my sunglasses, and tried to force a winning smile. (Hans Jr. told me later that it wasn't much of a smile. According to him, I looked as if I was passing a durian through my urethra.) One of the officers leaned into the car, took a quick look around, and, to my surprise, showed me how a genuine smile should look like. "Sorry, no English," he said, almost bashfully, followed by something in Indonesian. The only word I understood was *kemana* (where to)? My brain, still panic-frozen, produced a random answer: "Pontianak!"—Kalimantan's capital, a few hours south. The man stepped away from the car and waved us through, still smiling genuinely. I was trembling with relief. It took a few miles before my desperation fully disappeared and my heart rate returned to a safe range. And just when life was back to fine and dandy, and Kalimantan's lovely countryside was sailing past us at a smooth 30 miles per hour, a very large cop on a very large motorcycle pulled alongside and motioned me to pull over. His immense proportions told of years of hardcore bodybuilding. All my fears of decomposing in a third-world jail came rushing back to my mind where they mixed with flickering scenes from *Midnight Express*. The officer walked over to my open window, took his mirrored sunglasses off (are there really no other kinds in Indonesia?), and asked, in a kindly tone and in surprisingly good English, "May I see your international driver's license, please?" I had been convinced he would smash my brake light with his sidearm and write me a huge ticket (to be paid in cash on the spot, of course), or skip the small stuff altogether and rob us at gunpoint, throw his bike on the truck bed, and drive off with my pickup. But no, he just wanted to see my driver's license, the international one. *Please.* When he passed it back to me, he explained, "Many foreigners are not aware that their licenses from back home are often invalid abroad. In such cases, there is no accident insurance. I just wanted to make sure you had everything covered. Have a pleasant stay in Indonesia, gentlemen!" He tipped his helmet, winked at my son, and walked back to his ride, a leather-clad giant as gentle as the Buddha himself. I sat in shock for a while. Where were all the rogue, bad-hombre coppers everyone had told us about?

The village life around us soon distracted me from my bewilderment. Next to us was a mom-and-pop store with wooden shelves outside. They were tightly packed with identical unlabeled glass bottles that all contained the same golden liquid. I wondered why this tiny shop stocked so much cooking oil. Who would they sell it to? This was the butt-end of Indonesia's nowhere, the frontier, sparsely populated and hardly developed.

A boy on a moped answered my question. He stopped in front of the shelves, hollered into the shop, and took off the lid of his gas tank. The shop owner emerged, unscrewed one of the bottles, and, to my consternation, poured the cooking oil into the tank. Suddenly the warnings about the diluted fuel made sense. Gas stations were rare here, and often beyond the reach of small motorcycles. The shop owners would buy fuel in large quantities at the stations and transfer the stuff into bottles back home, sometimes adding a little H_2O for a little extra profit. It also explained the frequent news about fuel shortages at Kalimantan's filling stations. Whenever a tanker truck restocked a station, the shop owners from the area would swarm in and buy up the entire supply within hours.

About a dozen kids in navy-blue school uniforms were horsing around at a bus stop. A small white school bus arrived, and they all came to order and climbed onto the bus, one by one, in a disciplined fashion. The interior was already fully occupied with students, so the newcomers scrambled up onto the roof via a ladder fixed to the back door. A girl slapped the windshield twice from above, and the bus drove off with the new passengers sitting cross-legged on the roof and continuing their horseplay. As the bus swayed across the bridge before us, Hans and I looked at each other, speechless. How on Earth could anyone allow this …? Before we could start a discussion about fatalism and determinism as major influences on traffic safety doctrines in developing countries, we were distracted by more weirdness: mooing, clucking, and barking. The noise was distant at first, then swelling. The racket had reached an unpleasant level when another small bus swung around the corner. A number and a destination sign marked it as public transport. The farmyard riot came from two loudspeakers on the roof of the vehicle, which pulled into the bus stop whence the schoolkids had just departed. A few people hustled toward the bus from various directions. The driver patiently waited until they were all aboard, then swung back onto the road and took his bizarre musical number with him.

It was now mid-afternoon and time to return to Malaysia. We passed the roadblock again, where the friendly officer recognized us and motioned us through. In Entikong, the border town on the Indonesian side, Hans Jr. requested a second lunch, and we stopped at a little noodle house. The shop sign promised three kinds of noodles—wheat noodles, rice noodles, and glass noodles. The sign failed to mention that all three kinds were served together in one bowl. The concept took a little getting used to, but the broth was rich and spicy, and smoothed over our initial misgivings. As we slurped our three-noodle dish, a young man came in and asked politely, in English, if he could sit with us. My scalp prickled faintly—the other tables were all unoccupied—but my curiosity wrestled my paranoia to the mat. The man wore cargo pants with a black-and-white camouflage design, and a black tank top with the logo of an Indonesian death metal band. A pair of mirrored sunglasses (*hand to God, I am not making this up!*) hung from his necklace.

He thanked us for letting him join us and introduced himself. I have since forgotten his name, but what he said next will forever be tattooed on my memory: "I can get you anything you need. *I am the Number One Gangster in town!*"

I thanked him for his generous offer, told him we were about to leave Kalimantan and not in need of anything, and asked him to tell us about himself. This proved to be a smart move, and the next half-hour was pure entertainment. He told us engagingly fake-sounding stories about his cross-border smuggling jaunts, sprinkled with real facts about Kalimantan and its history. When he found out that Hans Jr. and I spoke Mandarin, he whistled at the entrance, and a man sitting on the steps outside came in. Number One Gangster introduced him as his friend, Mr. Lu. "He is Chinese, and he even speaks it!" Mr. Lu, too, rocked a death metal tank top, but from a different band. He also shared his friend's love for Kalimantan and its history and took over the talk with an in-depth look into present and past of the local Chinese community.

At one point I asked "So, are you guys full-time smugglers, or do you also keep regular jobs?" Their faces fell, and they exchanged furtive looks, as if unsure who should break the news to me.

"We have no jobs at all," Number One Gangster admitted with sudden frankness. "Smuggling opportunities come only once in a long while. Mostly we hang around the border crossing and help people fill out their visa and customs forms, for tips. Some are illiterate, you know." The bandit mystique, held up so bravely until now, crumbled into dust. I felt bad for him, and my expression probably gave it away, for Mr. Lu's took it as his cue to ask me for 20 ringgit "for arak." No excuse, apology, or explanation given. I gave him 10 ringgit—they had provided interesting knowledge about their home, after all. Mr. Lu handed the money to Number One Gangster and told him to get a bottle. When Hans and I left the restaurant, both men were sitting on the steps again, and toasted to our health and generosity.

In *The Last Train to Zona Verde*[113] travel writer Paul Theroux notes that "all national boundaries attract … rejects and immigrants and fixers. At this limit of the country, far from the capital … [p]eople did whatever they could get away with."

A Malaysian friend with rich experience in Kalimantan would later agree with this assessment. "You weren't conned," she said. "It's just the way they are—poor and desperate."

Crossing the border back into Malaysia, we couldn't find anyone on the Indonesian side to issue us exit stamps. We drove over to the Malaysian side, but the Malaysians refused us entry without proof of exit from the other side. We parked the car in Malaysia and walked back into Indonesia to carry out a more thorough search. And right on that empty, meticulously swept stretch between the two countries, we found, of all things, a snake. It was a reed snake,[114] just a few inches long, but with a beautiful metallic-black body and a handsome orange collar. Its pose suggested defense readiness: head and frontal body reared up, mouth open. In this *come-git-some* position it sat on the hot concrete, deader than dead. The sun must have flash-fried it on the concrete expanse and ended its life in this strikingly alive-looking pose.

Hans picked up the baked snake, carefully put it in his backpack, and said, "Isn't this the weirdest end to a totally weird trip?"

---

113 ISBN 9780544227934

114 *Pseudorabdion albonuchalis*

6 FAMILY TIME IN SARAWAK ...

The book of nature has no beginning, as it has no end. Open
this book where you will, and at any period of your life, and
if you have the desire to acquire knowledge you will find it
of intense interest, and no matter how long or how intently
you study the pages, your interest will not flag, for in nature
there is no finality.

Jim Corbett

On a hot and muggy afternoon in June 2013, Lisa and Karl walked out of Kuching
International Airport and back into our lives. Our younger son had finished elementary
school in Taiwan and would now join his brother at the Lodge School.

Karl's generous nature and love for all creatures big and small increased his new
social circle rapidly, if not always to the approval of his superiors. A week after his
arrival at Lodge, the principal took me aside: "Mr. Hans, could you please tell your
son that next time he brings a scorpion to school, he should please deposit it at the
office during class hours?" The previous evening, a neighbor had found an Asian forest
scorpion[115] under his living room couch. Aware of our family's nature obsession, he
stuffed the 5-inch arachnid in a Tupperware container and presented it to my delighted
sons. Karl was eager to share the joy with his friends, and maybe make a few new ones
in the process, and the next morning he took the black beast to school. Karl's curious
classmates immediately commandeered the little horror-in-a-box and paraded it
through a dozen classrooms over the course of the day. Shortly before 4 p.m., the
container ended up in Karl's hands again. By some miracle, the lid was still in place,
but the box had taken damage, and the scorpion's stinger stuck out from a crack in the
corner, ready to envenomate any comers.

Karl's fondness for wildlife could also cause conflict with his peers. One day he spotted
a classmate slinging a rubber band at a green scarab beetle resting on a windowsill. When

---

115 *Heterometrus longimanus*

Karl tried to put a stop to the torture, the other kid pulled out a shiv—a pencil with a small blade attached to the eraser. Karl managed to subdue his attacker before blood was spilled, but his school uniform suffered two slashes. The school was terribly embarrassed about the incident—this was the Lodge International School Kuching, after all, not some inner-city war zone with armed guards and metal detectors—and offered me to decide on the punishment. I did not want to add to the blade slinger's obvious mental issues and just recommended five demerit points and payment for a new shirt. The principal agreed with my Solomonic ruling and added, "by the way, Karl will receive five merit points for standing up for the beetle." (The Lodge School regularly rewards commendable behavior. Hans Jr. once received a framed certificate acknowledging his bravery in the rescue of a dog, which he had pulled out of a flooded ditch next to the parking lot.)

Karl's adjustment to life in the new country was expedited by a preexisting group of friends, namely those Hans Jr. and I had made over the past two years. Karl joined the rock-climbing group and hung out with his brother's buddies. We had also befriended quite a few émigrés. Many tropical backwaters have an eccentric resident foreigner or two, but Kuching boasted an entire community. Marius was a young helicopter pilot from former East Germany who earned an obscene income by flying the boss of a local banana empire around the state two or three times a month and doing exactly nothing the rest of the time. Marius was so bored that he seriously entertained the idea of going to Afghanistan to pilot giant Russian-made transport choppers for a Colombian mercenary outfit. James, a middle-aged Welshman and former IT manager, had come to Sarawak to help his company set up a project for the Malaysian government, but soon quit his job to start a career as a caving guide. "It was too good to ignore. Sarawak's caves are among the best in the world, and I had also realized that life is too short to waste in meetings with pompous prats in suits." Robert, another German and a passionate hobby cook, had arrived in Kuching to work as an engineer at a multinational semiconductor company. After marrying an ethnic Chinese local, he found his new relatives and their friends clambering over each other to get at his homemade Thuringian bratwursts. This combination of German food engineering and Chinese pork worship led to the foundation of GE Sausages "Made by a German", and the organization of Borneo Oktoberfest, an annual three-day bash complete with Bavarian beer, German meat products, and imported all-female oompah bands. Stephen Petersen was a retired marine geologist based in Fairbanks whose life's focus was the science of honeybees. Every Alaskan winter, he installed himself in a backpacker hostel at Kuching's Waterfront and roamed Borneo's jungles in search of his favorite insect family. He was jolly and gregarious but made it quite clear where bees ranked in his universe: "When I discovered the first hive in my garden, I fell in love with it. Then I bought a second. Then another. Then came a fourth. Then, of course, came a divorce, which I celebrated with a fifth hive."

If I had to pick a favorite among Kuching's lovable oddballs, it would be young Thomas Brabbs, the only child of a Czech–British marriage. His mother was a teacher at a local international school, his father was with the British Council, and they had arrived at the same time as Hans and me. Thomas was eight at the time, and his intelligence and curiosity were far beyond his years. On the first of our many jungle walks, he shocked me into awe when he picked up a big striped tiger leech and set it on his bare forearm. I was about to flick the thing off his skin before it could dig in, when I caught a glance of his parents' expressions. They were watching their son with serene smiles, as if petting bloodthirsty snot worms were a perfectly healthy activity for an eight-year-old. In a forced calm voice, I asked Thomas what he was doing. "Well, I know they suck blood," he replied, "but I don't know *how*. I want to see exactly how they go about it."

My wife also adapted well to her new surroundings. Our house and garden were more spacious than our place in Taiwan, and Lisa, ever the gastronaut, loved exploring the ethnic varieties of Kuching's food courts and restaurants. The magical wet market I had visited at the Waterfront during the 2007 Nepenthes Summit had recently moved to our neighborhood, and Lisa would sashay through the halls in the early mornings with her shopping sherpa (me) in tow, picking up seafood, fruit, and veggies she had never seen before, to experiment with later in our large kitchen. Like all of us, she loved the natural wonders of the island. After driving the boys to school in the morning, we would take forest walks in nearby Sama Jaya, and our family spent the weekends hiking in the hills around Kuching and taking cold dips under jungle waterfalls. All of us were endlessly fascinated with the rainforest, and our favorite time to explore it was after dark.

By day, Borneo's forests are magnificent by any standards, but at night they pull out all the stops. A great number of tropical animals are nocturnal. The air is cooler and more humid, and "Undercover of the Night" is not just a Rolling Stones song but a lifestyle. Smaller creatures seeking to avoid detection prefer to go about their business after lights out. Paradoxically, this often makes them easier to find. They will freeze in mid-motion when disturbed, in the hope the disturber will not spot them in the dark. In addition, many diurnal species of lizards, birds, and snakes can be found sleeping on low branches at night. A forest trail can feel like two different planets at daytime and at nighttime, from the visual surroundings through the soundtrack to the inhabitants. As wrong as it sounds, you *always* see more at night.

After dinnertime one Saturday we rolled up to the reception booth in Kubah National Park and picked up our keys. We had booked one of their cabins and were excited to spend, for the first time as a family, a night in the rainforest. There were two bedrooms, a den, and a fully equipped kitchen. This even came with a mortar and pestle, for those who like to create their curries from scratch. The freezer hadn't been defrosted in a while, and Hans and Karl took the rare opportunity of building a little snowman right by the equator. In the den, another visitor had already taken up residence. A male three-horned rhinoceros beetle[116]—mahogany-colored, and the size of a large, fat mouse—clung to

---

116 *Chalcosoma moellenkampi*

One of Borneo's countless waterfalls

[Left] Rhino beetle
[Right] Leaf katydid

one of the yellow couch pillows. His armament was extraordinary; each horn was almost as long as his body. Two of them swept down from his forehead toward the nose, where they were met by the third horn, which soared between them like a raised saber. We tried to pry the beetle from the pillow to return him to the jungle, but soon understood that he would rather sacrifice a few legs than give up his iron grip.

Rhino beetles count among the world's strongest insects, and I had already witnessed their brawn and determination a few months earlier. During a coffee stop at a small eatery in the border area, one of these giant insects fell out of the thatched roof and crashed on my saucer, spilling most of my drink. I took it home to photograph in my little studio the following day. I placed it in a Faunarium that I locked in my pantry for the night. Later that evening I was sitting in my office when I heard disturbing noises from the pantry: first a crack, then a crash, then a small propeller plane. The beetle had climbed up the dry twigs I had placed in the plastic tank, busted open the pop-on lid, and was now buzzing around the room like a very small Mitsubishi Zero with a very angry pilot. With this in mind, we surrendered the pillow to the bug and went out into the night.

Our destination tonight was the Frog Pond. The name is capitalized for good reason; calling the Frog Pond a frog pond is like calling the Grand Canyon a canyon. As frog ponds go, it is small; you can stroll around it in under three minutes. But with almost 70 species recorded in such a tiny area, and the frogs sitting on every surface from the trees to the boardwalk, the pond's amphibian diversity and accessibility create a true marvel. As we walked through the dark forest, katydids entertained us with their creepy music. Also known as bush crickets, katydids are mostly nocturnal, grasshopper-like insects famous for their unusual mating calls.[117] Among the commonly heard species

---

117 The common name "katydid" is onomatopoeic and comes from the loud, three-pulsed song, often rendered "ka-ty-did", of the nominate subspecies of the North American *Pterophylla camellifolia*.

here in Kubah were, in our family's parlance, the haunted cello, the door knock, and the water drop. The haunted cello sounded like the ghost of a tone-deaf cello player condemned to saw the same two bad notes for eternity. The door knock produced a sound like a bony knuckle asking for entrance. The frequency of the knocks was slow and irregular; just when you thought it had finally realized that nobody was home it would start knocking again. The water drop was weirdness cubed. Imagine drops of liquid falling into a glass of water at relaxed intervals, while you're standing in the dark, wondering how on God's green Earth a little boneless animal could make this sound just by rubbing two parts of its body together.

A shadow glided up a tree and stopped in the shine of our headlamps. A gray, shrew-faced thing with a feather duster at the end of its shoelace tail stared at us through a mess of bushy whiskers. It was going on 9 p.m., so we guessed it already had a blood alcohol level several times the legal limit in most countries. This adorable little animal, known as the pen-tailed tree shrew,[118] is the world's hardest boozer and doesn't even know it. Its tolerance for alcohol is so high that it lives on little else than palm wine. The flowers of the bertam palm[119] produce a fermented nectar with ethanol content equivalent to weak beer, and attract a wide range of insects and tree-climbing mammals. Most of them suffer from the effects of the alcohol, but not the pen-tailed tree shrew, though researchers analyzed its hairs and found clear evidence of chronic alcohol intake. It is not clear how the species copes with its bingeing, but we do know that tree shrews do not share the same enzyme-producing mutation as humans. Whatever the mechanism, something in their body breaks down ethanol with exceptional efficiency. As I hail from the Land of 1,000 Beers, the wastefulness of consuming alcohol in near-lethal quantities while being completely ignorant of the concept of inebriation somewhat saddened me.

The shrew's exit revealed, on a nearby leaf, a small huntsman spider that goes by the delightful name of *Heteropoda davidbowie*. Despite its vividly orange fur, ornate pattern, and relative abundance, the David Bowie spider was only described in 2008. Wikipedia explains that

> (t)he species name honours David Bowie, with particular reference to songs such as "Glass Spider" (…) as well as the 1972 album *The Rise and Fall of Ziggy Stardust and the Spiders from Mars*, and the resemblance of the frontal view of the spider to the singer's painted face in his early career.

The arachnid's spiky orange hair also played a part, as it looks like the hairdo of Ziggy Stardust, Bowie's alter ego. The spider's color was elegantly framed by two lime-

---

118 *Ptilocercus lowii*.

119 *Eugeissona* sp.

Leaf snail

green snails[120] on the same leaf, and we enjoyed the brilliant hues for a while before continuing uphill.

A small frog sat at the entrance to the Frog Pond, predictable and unexciting. But the black mass of ants swarming all over its body warranted a second look. It sat motionless like a Buddha statue; the only movement occurred when its tongue whipped out to catch an ant that strayed too close to its mouth. This was a sticky frog of the genus *Kalophrynus*. The members are distinguished by their weirdly small and pointy faces, and the glue-like substance they release through the skin to deter attackers.

A few weeks before I had found a black-spotted sticky frog[121] on the UNIMAS campus. When I got too close, it squeezed gray gunk from glands on its back. Unfamiliar with the nefarious ways of the sticky frogs, and too dumb to take a hint, I picked it up for a closer look. In response, the frog shot one last thick line of goo onto my hand and jumped back into the forest. The stuff was like plastic model cement and immediately glued my fingers together. I tried to wash it off with cold green tea (the only liquid I had brought), and tried scrubbing with towels and tissues, but that only served to transfer the glue to my other hand. I couldn't even drive to the nearest washroom and try soap, fearing my hands would stick to the steering wheel and cause an accident (what would I even tell the police? "Well, um, you see, officer, my hands got kinda shat on by this little frog, and then I just couldn't get them off the wheel, so there was no way to avoid the old lady ...") For what felt like a

120 *Rhinocochlis nasuta*

121 *Kalophrynus pleurostigma*

lifetime, I stood there like an idiot, shell-shocked and terrified of touching anything. Eventually the goo began to dry, and half an hour after I had picked up the frog it was finally safe to use my hands again. I didn't want to repeat the experience here in Kubah, so we just stepped over the ant-covered Glue Buddha and into the wooden rain shelter at the edge of the Frog Pond.

Just in time: we had barely sat down for a short rest when the bottom fell out of the sky. An almighty downpour lashed the forest, and the pond frogs, up to this moment only softly throbbing background noise, rose to the occasion. With the volume cranked to 11, and backed by the rain's thunderous percussion, an orchestra with thousands of players pumped out the grandest of symphonies. This is no exaggeration. In 2014, Australian nature sound recordist Marc Anderson won the Most Beautiful Sound in the World competition with an entry called "Dusk by the Frog Pond," which he taped where we were sitting now. We closed our eyes and immersed ourselves in this sonic natural wonder. Soon, we were able to make out individual calls from the chorus. Besides the standard croaking, squeaking, and barking one expects from frogs, there was a car horn, which our sons named Tarzan's doorbell. One species seemed to quack up and down a pentatonic scale, another snored like a drunken sailor. We heard cackling laughter, sheet-metal thunder, a broken telegraph machine, and a slowly opening trapdoor squawking for a drop of oil.

After the rain had subsided, we strolled along the boardwalk around the pond, careful not to step on the frogs sitting everywhere. Bornean file-eared tree frogs,[122] 4-inch bruisers able to swivel their heads, looked at us cockeyed from trees and saplings, our elbows almost touching them. The ground was littered with orange-pink harlequin frogs[123] with feet adapted to parachuting. There were green frogs, brown frogs, yellow frogs, and orange frogs, as well as marbled, spotted, and tiger-striped frogs.

Strangely enough, we didn't see any snakes partaking in this amphibian smorgasbord. The first serpent of the night didn't reveal itself until after we had left the pond, but it came in an interesting setting. We passed by a stand of green flask-shaped pitcher plants[124] and decided to check the pitchers for infauna. The pitchers of this species have no lids to speak of, so they are often filled with rainwater. They host a myriad of tiny, specialized creatures, and in Kubah this includes one of the world's smallest frogs. The entire life cycle of the matang narrow-mouthed frog unfolds in and around the pitchers of this carnivorous plant. Before their description as *Microhyla nepenthicola* in 2010, these frogs had been known for at least 100 years, but scientists had always assumed they were juveniles of another species. Professor Indraneil Das and his co-researcher, Professor Alexander Haas, recognized that they were looking at adults when

122 *Polypedates otilophus*

123 *Racophorus pardalis*

124 *Nepenthes ampullaria*

[Above] White-lipped frog (Hylarana raniceps) *and friend*

[Below] Harlequin frog

[Above] Bornean file-eared frog

[Below] Matang narrow-mouthed frog

they heard the frogs calling, because only adult frogs make calls. Half an inch of frog doesn't exactly roar at sousaphone level; to hear it you need to be quiet and close to the frog. After shining our lamps into a dozen plants, we found a male on the lip of a pitcher. Judging from the size of his pumped-up vocal sac, he was giving it his all, but even at grabbing distance we heard very little. The water in the pitcher also contained a few developing tadpoles, and the predatory pupa of an elephant mosquito, twice the size of the tadpoles.

Chien Lee explains the pitcher plant's open-lid strategy in an Instagram post:

> The plant benefits from everything entering the pitcher: detritus falling from the canopy above, insect prey that are drowned inside, or small visiting organisms ... that may help to break down the contents and leave their waste behind.

Life attracts more life: as we strained to photograph the minute creatures floating in the pitcher, a little brown snake with a red stripe down the back came slithering across the pitcher plants in search for prey. As it dipped in and out of the green jars, we could see flashes of its belly scales. Their black and white keyboard pattern stood in stark contrast to the subdued hues of the rainforest and clearly signaled danger. Small as it is, the banded Malaysian coral snake[125] packs enough potent venom to ruin anybody's night hike. The snake was not in a hurry, but still too fast for my amateur photography skills. I really wish I had a picture of that scene—two of my all-time favorite life forms in the same frame.

Red-bellied keelback (Rhabdophis conspicillatus) *hunting among* Nepenthes ampullaria *(photo, Ray Hamilton)*

---

125 *Calliophis intestinalis*

⚘ ⚘ ⚘ ⚘ ⚘ ⚘

We slept late the next morning. After a slap-dash breakfast of oatmeal, soy milk, and lady finger bananas, we said goodbye to the rhino beetle—still hugging its pillow— and drove to Permai Rainforest Resort, where Hans had once almost stepped on that huge python. Lisa and I spent the afternoon lazing in the cool breeze of the resort's open-sided beach restaurant. We read books, drank iced coconut water straight from the fruit, and watched our boys trying to drown each other in the South China Sea.

Most people love tropical beaches. They promise life-giving warmth, refreshing wetness, fun, and relaxation. I like them, too, but only from a distance—on a postcard, say, or from the comfort of a breezy beach café. Hate me all you want; I only step on beaches to board boats. The ocean mirroring the sun and the complete absence of shade makes for insufferable heat and dangerous radiation. (There is a reason many

Haaniella echinata, *mating*

folks in the tropics swim in t-shirts.) At the approximate temperature of baby urine, the water is *not* refreshing. There's sand everywhere, inside your bathing suit and in all your skin folds, and you're constantly grinding your teeth on it. Another mineral that's out to get you is the salt in the water. Sun-drying yourself after an ocean swim will turn you into a salt-crusted, sand-caked, overbaked grouper, even if you are wearing a t-shirt. And I haven't even started on all the marine life waiting to make you regret that urge to dip your toe in the ocean. (Sure, the resort staff hoists red flags to warn of stingers when the water is brimming with Portuguese men o'war. But the deadly creatures just titter and wait.) Lisa largely shares my sentiments about beaches, so we enjoyed our books and drinks while we waited for the boys to emerge from the sea and join us for dinner. They would be covered in sand, salt, and blood (from those sharp little rocks hidden under the sand), but too hungry to bother with a cleanup. Dinner was fried pineapple rice cleverly served in half a scooped-out pineapple, and there was chocolate lava cake for dessert. When the kids had hoovered up the last crumbs the sun fell into the sea, bats started hunting for bugs between the restaurant's rattan lamps, and it was time for another night walk.

We took the trail where Hans Jr. and I had found the giant python. When we left the concrete walkway and moved onto the narrow jungle path, we stepped into a different world. The giant trees that ran the show during the day were now reduced to background props. The leaves we rubbed shoulders with were now alive with bugs. Wherever you turned your headlamp, brilliant white diamonds shone back at you, the reflective eyes of spiders of all sorts and sizes. Walking sticks grazed on the leaves of the bushes, like so many miniature horses on a multi-layered prairie. Besides the traditional stick-like creatures that give the phasmid family its common name, there were also less orthodox clan members. A common sight was a stocky monster the size of a Jamaican doobie, the color of a wilted leaf, and with a battery of serious spines bristling all over its body.[126] As one of the world's heaviest phasmids, it lays the largest and heaviest eggs in the insect world. It also carries a pair of tiny, heart-shaped, and completely useless white wings on its back, a reminder that its ancestors probably once soared across Borneo's skies. Another regular on the phasmid freak show was a slender, less than pinky-sized fellow from the genus *Epidares*. Its species name, *nolimetangere* (Latin for "don't touch me"), carries a warning, in case you missed the six sharp spikes on its back.

Now a miniature train crossed the muddy trail. It was the larva of a firefly species, hunting for meat. Each side of its body was adorned with a string of yellow bioluminescent dots that looked like illuminated windows on a passing night train. We switched off our headlamps and watched the little soundless choo-choo creep along until its lights faded away in the distance. When we turned our lights back on, we were

---

126 *Haaniella echinata*

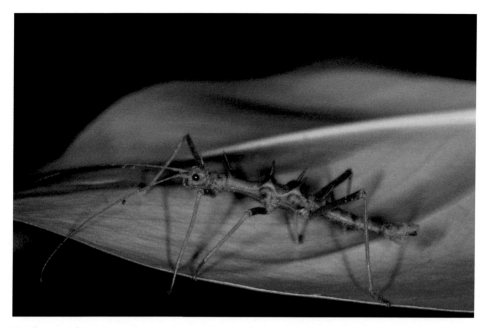

Epidares nolimetangere

met with a pair of dark eyes glaring at us from a scaly head the shape of an excavator bucket. Behind it trailed three chunky feet of Bornean keeled pit viper[127] along a dead branch. The snake's keeled, rhomboid scales were of the lightest green and yellow and stretched over the reptile's fat curves in an arrangement that reminded me of Victor Vasarely's Op Art. Its bulk and pattern marked the snake as an adult female from the same species that had given me such a deliciously horrifying experience during my first visit to Borneo. Seven years and thousands of snakes later, I now knew this animal presented no danger whatsoever to us (unless we messed with it) and wanted nothing more than for us to go away already so it could continue its ambush in peace. I explained to my family a few interesting facts about pit vipers (did you know they're the most advanced of all snakes and even have parental instincts?), and why they're called pit vipers (no, they don't live in snake pits—between eye and nostril on each side of the face sits a heat-detecting organ called a pit, which helps the snake detect warm-bodied prey such as rodents and birds). Then we left the snake to its business and headed deeper into the jungle.

About 300 phasmids and a second pit viper later, we rested on some boulders scattered along the shore of a dry creek bed. We turned off our headlamps, adjusted our eyes for a few minutes, and looked around for glow-in-the-dark fungi. We were lucky. Low on a

---

127 *Tropidolaemus subannulatus*

Bornean keelbacked viper
(Clement Sim)

tree close to us grew five small mushroom clusters. Each cluster contained of half a dozen mushrooms just a few millimeters tall, all emitting a pale green light from foot to cap. The fungus kingdom is comprised of about 85,000 species, but only 65 are known to be luminescent. Humans have always been fascinated by fungal bioluminescence, but even today, many of the big questions remain unanswered: why are there so few luminescent species? Why do they glow night *and* day? And why glow at all? We know that some glow to attract nocturnal insects to aid in spore dispersal, especially in dense forests with little wind. Some want to signal to predators of the insects that eat the fungi—the enemy of my enemy is my friend. And some glow for reasons yet to be discovered. We sat quietly in the dark, each of us absorbed in our own thoughts about these little green lanterns.

Our musings were brutally cut short when the gates of hell flung wide open in the trees above us. It sounded like a 12-foot gorilla engaged in a life-and-death fight with a bear-sized leopard, both combatants screaming and roaring and hissing and breaking branches in a terrifying pandemonium that had pure, naked fear surging through our veins. And the din was coming closer. Lisa and the boys looked at me in hope of a rational explanation, but all I could do was panic. "So this is how we all die," I thought. "Torn limb from limb by wild jungle beasts. But I needed to be closer to the snakes and pitcher plants, didn't I? How foolish and selfish. I should have listened to our Taiwanese neighbors, after all." During a sudden moment of clarity, I suggested we turn the headlamps back on. Whatever demons made that noise, maybe they feared light, as lions fear fire. I pointed my headlamp into the canopy. The first thing I saw was the entire crown of a slender tree bending over hard, then snapping back like a catapult. As the tree came to a rest, its neighbor began to whip forward and backward. Branches broke off and crashed to the ground. All the while, the terrible noise kept shredding the night. When a third tree started whipping around as if caught in a hurricane, I finally made out the animals on it. They had orange body fur, gray arms, legs, and tails, and they stood as tall as a human toddler. The smaller, slender ones had pointy, cut-off noses like victims of botched cosmetic surgery, but the bigger, potbellied specimens stole the show with their grotesque schnozzes. These were shaped and sized like blackjacks and hung over their owners' mouths in inexplicable bizarreness.

I told my family, "These are proboscis monkeys,[128] and I think we've disturbed their sleep. I've never heard of this species attacking humans, but I don't want us to become the first case on record. Let's get away from them, fast." We hustled down the trail, and the monkeys followed us in the canopy, easily matching our speed as they jumped between trees, breaking and throwing more branches, and growling and roaring in leopard-like fashion. The giant nose of the male proboscis monkey, a tool for sexual selection, has earned the animal the Malay name *orang belanda*—Dutchman. Proboscis monkeys are endemic to Borneo, and are among the largest monkeys in Asia. They survive chiefly on a diet of leaves, and to help break down this tough fodder, they have evolved a specialized three-chambered stomach that allows them to digest foods other primates cannot. Their bloated bellies are a result of their leaf-heavy diet, which also causes flatulence. If this troop hadn't started their noise terror, their farts would have probably revealed them to us.

Back at the beach, we slumped onto the benches in a wooden shelter, everybody shaken from the experience. The monkeys had kept up the harassment until we reached the end of the trail, and now we heard them retreating into the forest. The mellow sloshing of the surf in the dark, and the charming little tree-climbing crabs[129] in the bushes all around us soon helped us ease into a calmer mood. Back in the car, the boys fell asleep in an instant, but not before Karl managed to mumble: "No way my classmates are gonna believe this …"

*   *   *   *   *   *

"*Stay in the car*, for Pete's sake!" I shouted at Marcus, who was opening the passenger door and about to step out of my truck.

"I'll be fine, it'll just be a couple of shots," my old high school buddy replied with serene confidence.

---

128 *Nasalis larvatus*

129 *Episesarma* sp.

Male proboscis monkey (Elliot Pelling)

"He's going to tear you limb from limb, dammit—STAY IN THE GODDAMN CAR!"

My clenched knuckles were pale on the steering wheel, and I noticed Marcus clutching his Nikon a teensy bit tighter.

"As long as I stay outside a five-yard range, he's going to ignore me," he opined. "That's what the rangers said."

The 200-pound orangutan blocking the forest road with his presence dug his middle finger deep into his left nostril and observed our cabaret number with the jaded air of an old theater critic. I wondered if he cared about, or even knew, what the rangers had said.

"Don't soil your drawers, I'll throw in an extra three yards. Happy?" Marcus snarked, and opened the door wide.

The ape had now lost interest in us and instead turned his full attention to the rich green spoils he had unearthed from his nose. He was an imposing example of an adult male *Pongo pygmaeus*, the Bornean orangutan. His shaggy coat fringing down his muscular back like tangerine mammoth hair lent him a prehistoric air. If you squinted hard enough, you could just make out a Neanderthal hunter in furs hunkering down to start a fire.

"See?" Marcus called from outside the truck. "He's totally ignoring me!"

The orangutan peered at us with yellow eyes set deep between two enormous cheek pads that seemed cut from dinosaur leather. He gave his flaming-orange goatee a lazy stroke and yawned, peeling back his lips to expose a set of fangs for which any Siberian tiger would have gladly traded his stripes.

From the road, Marcus gave a stifled shout. I kept the engine running, just in case I needed to medevac my friend's mangled body, and thought about our magnificent cousin before us and the fate of his race.

Edward O. Wilson noted that "destroying rainforest for economic gain is like burning a Renaissance painting to cook a meal." Orangutans are among our closest relatives in the natural world. These highly intelligent great apes share more than 95 percent of their genetic material with us, yet their plight is one of the region's many tragic tales of greed and extinction. Three species are known—the Bornean, the Sumatran, and the Tapanuli orangutan, which was discovered only in 2017. A century ago, there were probably as many as 230,000 orangutans on Borneo alone. Now their numbers are estimated at around 10,000. The Sumatran species hovers at around 15,000 individuals, and we know of only about 800 Tapanulis. It is estimated that humans kill around 1,000 Bornean orangutans per year, with forest cleared for oil palm production being a major factor.

Earlier this morning, Marcus and I had come to Semenggoh Wildlife Center just outside Kuching to observe some of these great apes having breakfast. Semenggoh is the biggest orangutan sanctuary in Sarawak. It was established in 1975 for orangutans that are injured or orphaned, or have been illegally kept as pets. The apes spend most of their time roaming the surrounding forest but are trained to return to the center during feeding times when the caretakers offer them a spread of fresh food. Visitors can watch the feast from a distance. A pile of fruit and veggies sits on a wooden platform in a forest clearing, accompanied by a ranger who hollers the names of the apes into the forest to call them to the table. Eventually a treetop will wiggle on the far side of the clearing. Then, a little closer by, a whole tree bends and snaps back. More rustling of leaves and bouncing of branches, and an orangutan emerges from a tree crown and lowers itself onto the platform on one of the ropes that are tied above the clearing to facilitate ape travel. Depending on the day, you might be able to see giant males, smaller teenagers, and if you are lucky, a slender mother with a pale orange baby clinging to her chest. The apes do not linger on the forest floor. Their body design is unsuitable for moving on the ground, so they pick up some food and climb back to a safe height to eat. Their table manners lack refinement—bananas and papayas are chucked away half-consumed, and their preferred method of opening coconuts can only be described as brutally effective yet highly inefficient. They smack a coconut against a tree trunk, spilling the juice as it bursts open, and then use their fingers to dig the flesh out of the fragments that remain in their hand. They will descend again for

Female orangutan with baby,
Semenggoh Wildlife Center
(photo, Christoph Lepschy)

seconds and thirds, and upon departure carry food into the forest for elevenses. The show is usually over within an hour. Then an army of multicolored Prevost's squirrels[130] arrives to clean up the feeding platform, and the visitors are asked to leave.

We were driving back from the orangutan breakfast, still on the forested grounds of the wildlife center, when we met Ritchie sitting in the middle of the road. Ritchie is one of the oldest and biggest males at the center, and he commands respect. This is not an animal you can just pick up and carry to the roadside. Even an attempt to drive around the gentle giant may lead to disaster if he gets spooked. Marcus was back in the truck now (thankfully unharmed), and a line of cars, bikes, and pedestrians had formed behind us—other visitors leaving the center. We were on the only exit road and Ritchie had it bottlenecked. Two rangers arrived with bananas and tried to lure Ritchie off the blacktop. Ritchie ignored them. A female orangutan emerged from the forest on the right and sat next to Ritchie. Another female appeared and sat on his other side. The rangers looked increasingly hapless. After a short while, one, then a second, then a third juvenile ape appeared. As soon as the last youngster had joined the five other orangutans, Ritchie stood up, climbed over the picket fence that lined the road, scaled the next tree, and sat on the first branch low above the ground. His family followed

---

130 *Callosciurus prevostii*

suit, finally clearing the road, and the last thing I saw in the rearview mirror was the two red-faced rangers yelling and pointing bananas at the six great apes in the tree. During the pre-breakfast briefing, the staff had warned us: "Should you come face to face with an orangutan today, do not, repeat, DO NOT engage with it. Their bodies are stronger than yours, and so is their will. They do what they want and when they want it. You will always lose. Just back away slowly and don't make any sudden moves." I had a feeling the two rangers were going to be under that tree for quite a bit longer.

🐾   🐾   🐾   🐾   🐾   🐾

The orangutan breakfast show at Semenggoh Wildlife Center was the first stop of a weekend tour I often organized for out-of-town visitors. The second leg was a two-hour drive across the countryside, with stops at pepper farms, pitcher plant colonies, waterfalls, and an old Chinese cemetery. Our final destination was Borneo Highlands, a golf resort in the Penrissen Range surrounded by montane jungle around 3,000 feet above sea level. Here we would go on a night walk and do some birding the next morning at the Kalimantan Viewpoint at 3,300 feet.[131] The viewpoint is a large meadow

---

131 1000 meters

hemmed in by jungle on three sides; on the fourth side it drops off into a 2,000-foot cliff. The breakoff line runs on top of the Malaysian/Indonesian border (bring your passport in case you fall off the cliff) and allows spectacular views of the sea of clouds over northern Kalimantan. The Kalimantan Viewpoint has officially been named one of Malaysia's Important Bird Areas, and it is one of the few places in the world where you can watch flocks of hornbills from above.

This was Marcus's second visit to Borneo, and I was eager to show him the mountains. Our last stop in the lowlands before driving up to the resort was Kampung Sibakar, a hill village close to the border. Sibakar sits at the terminus of a switchback-studded and often very steep road. Today that road is paved, but at the time of Marcus' visit it still thrilled adrenaline lovers with a string of hairy sections best negotiated with an off-road vehicle guided by an optimistic driver. Sibakar is famous for the many waterfalls in the surrounding forests. The border is in walking distance, and the villages on both sides are populated by the same tribe. This creates vibrant cross-border traffic. There are no checkpoints, and no roads cross the border. The locals walk between the two countries on muddy jungle paths to hunt, trade, or visit.

I wanted to show Marcus a few of those waterfalls, and after parking outside Sibakar's community hall, we walked across the village toward the forest. The dwellings were mostly simple wooden affairs on short stilts. Most of them had front porches; bamboo platforms for drying pepper and winnowing grains decorated some of the yards. In a corner of one of the sun-blasted porches I noticed a cage cobbled together with the wire casing of an industrial floor fan and some chicken wire mesh. Inside squatted what could only be described as a bear the size of a young pug and the tragic expression of an Italian opera clown. It stared at us with sad eyes that were three sizes too large for the small face, and triggered flashbacks to my youth and the many times I had spent in the nocturnal houses of various German zoos admiring the members

Morning over Indonesia, at Kalimantan Viewpoint

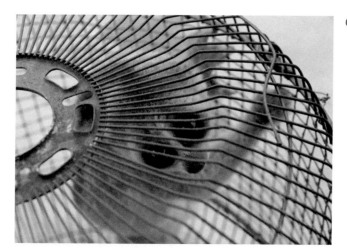

Caged slow loris, Sibakar

of the fascinating primate branch called *Strepsirrhini*. These include Madagascar's lemurs, Africa's pottos and bush babies, and Asia's lorises. The name loris comes from a Dutch word for clown and reflects the animal's facial markings as well as some of its remarkable behavior. The furry ball of cuteness in the fan cage was a slow loris,[132] and I had already met this species the previous autumn.

Slash & burn, or swidden, agriculture has been practiced in Borneo for thousands of years, and every autumn the hills are alive with smoldering fires that create space for more plantations. One September night I had been road cruising with my sons, and after hours of driving through endless smoke and burning bush we were all thoroughly depressed. This changed abruptly when a tan, cat-sized furball with the shape of a bear and funny white face paint crossed the road from the bushland on the left toward a cornfield on the right. It seemed to be in no hurry; in fact, it walked as if fording a river of molasses. Instead of running away when we approached, it stopped, threw its arms above its head, and started hissing at us. "What is this thing?" Karl asked. "Well, whatever he is, we need to remove him from the road. Can we just pick him up and carry him to the other side … or do they bite?" With its giant eyes, round bear ears, and tiny cat nose, the loris was an overdose of adorability. The white lines around its eyes endowed it with an air of profound sorrow, and everything about it just screamed, *"Please hug and love me!"*

"This is a slow loris, a close relative of apes and monkeys," I explained. "The size of its eyes tells us it's nocturnal, and although it moves awfully slow, it can travel in the tree crowns in search of fruit and insects for up to 5 miles a night. That's the good part." The boys looked at me expectantly. "The bad part is that it's a dangerous animal. Lorises

132 *Nycticebus menagensis*

are the only venomous primates in the world, and this one could dish out serious harm. So, we will stay the hell away from him." Hans' and Karl's skeptical expressions made clear what they thought of that. *Seriously, Dad? A poisonous monkey? How dumb exactly do you think we are?*

Their lack of trust stung, but I ignored it and continued. "There are open venom glands on the insides of his elbows, and he's getting ready for battle now. When push comes to shove, he'll lick these glands—that's why he has his hands in the air now—and then bite his attacker, transporting the venom into the wound with his saliva. Also, loris bites are among the most powerful in the world; their fangs can bore clean through your finger, bone and all. Believe me, I couldn't possibly make this stuff up." The boys stared at the loris with open mouths. A venomous teddy bear with hyena jaws? *Cooooool!* The loris had given up its fighting stance and decided to try flight instead. Arboreal animals tend to flee upwards, so it crawled up the next vertical structure. Unluckily, that structure was just a wooden stake on the side of the road, a visual aid to help motorists during the monsoon floods. The stake was only 5 feet tall, and now the loris clung to the top with nowhere to go.

Thanks to their over-the-top cuteness, slow lorises are a hot item in the illegal pet trade. Poachers disarm them by removing their fangs, which often leads to massive blood loss and infections. The majority of wild-caught lorises die before they reach a buyer. Even if we drove off now and left the loris where it was, hunters might find it. But how to remove it from its perch without putting ourselves in danger? When I explained the dilemma to my sons, Hans saved the day and the loris: "There's a woolen blanket in the back of the truck. Why don't we fold it for double thickness, wrap the loris in it, and carry him into the cornfield?" And that's what we did. We placed the bundle at the foot of a tree, carefully unwrapped it and took a few steps back. After blinking at us a few times, the loris climbed the tree as slowly as an overweight cat burglar and vanished into the foliage.

With Marcus in Sibakar now, I knew that loris poaching and cross-border trafficking had long been a problem for Sarawak's wildlife police. It was also no secret that Sibakar was a hotbed for animal poaching. At the entrance to the village, a man kept dozens of caged wild-caught birds in his garden, for everyone to see. But the animal Marcus and I were now looking at was the first poached slow loris I had ever met. It held a chunk of papaya in one of its chubby little hands, and a forest cockroach in the other, then bit the head off the roach and chewed slowly with closed eyes, as if savoring a great delicacy. Then it opened its eyes again and washed down the roach head with a mouthful of papaya. As it took another bite of the cockroach, a woman appeared in the door. In a spontaneous decision that I would later regret, I pulled out my wallet, took out 50 ringgit (about US$15 at the time), and offered her the money while pointing at the loris cage with the other hand. She took the 50 without further negotiation, smiled, and went back into the hut. The waterfalls that I wanted to show Marcus were forgotten. We had a brand-new agenda now: smuggle the loris into the resort, smuggle it back out again the next morning, and release it in a national park near Kuching. My reason for the purchase was simple. By buying the loris and setting it free, we would prevent its untimely and painful demise by botched dentistry. Even if it survived the butchery, it would spend its final years rotting away in a tiny cage lined with its own excrement. We would make sure none of that happened. We stuffed the cage in a big black garbage bag, drove to the resort, and checked in without raising suspicion. We hid the cage in our room under the bathroom sink, gave the loris some fruit and water, and went to dinner at the resort. After an excellent dessert of purple sticky rice with mangoes and coconut milk we went for a night walk, and the next morning we slept in, because heavy rain made birding impossible. We nixed all other activities I had planned for the day and returned to Kuching as fast as we could. That night, after a satisfying photo shoot in a friend's garden, we released the loris in a national park.

Later that week, still flush with excitement over our loris adventure, I wrote an exuberant post on an online wildlife forum and included a generous number of impossibly cute close-ups of the loris' heart-melting eyes. I was convinced the forum would explode with e-hugs and accolades, and fete me as Wildlife Avenger of the Year.

Reality was sobering. One of my father's favorite nuggets of wisdom is that "in any aspect of life, there's always at least one person smarter than you." And here were about a dozen people much smarter than me reacting to my post:

Released slow loris

Buying a Slow Loris, even with the intention of releasing it, creates demand. You also paid the foreigner price, which may lead its former captors to believe that there is a lucrative business in selling Slow Lorises to foreign tourists. The ideal course of action is to find someone who can confiscate and rehabilitate the animal. But even if you do, the guy would just go out and catch another one.

They were right on all counts. By reacting to the cute, dungeon-bound animal with my heart instead of my brain I had made a range of mistakes at once. I called Oswald Tisen at Sarawak Forestry, gave a full confession, and asked for his advice. "You're not the first one to make that mistake, and you won't be the last," Oswald said. "But at least you're willing to learn. I suggest you keep the number of the Sarawak Wildlife Crime Hotline in your phone and call us immediately the next time you see something like this."

* * * * * *

Next to orangutans and proboscis monkeys, no primate is as iconic to Borneo as Horsfield's tarsier.[133] The editors of the Lonely Planet travel guide series clearly shared this sentiment when they selected a photo of the kobold-like critter for the cover of the first edition of their Borneo issue. According to Hollywood lore, tarsiers were the inspiration for everyone's favorite sage, Master Yoda from *Star Wars*, and for the mischievous creatures in Steven Spielberg's *Gremlins*. Tarsiers are among the most fascinating mammals in the region, but their nocturnal habits, notorious cautiousness, and lightning-fast movements make them hard to find and even harder to photograph. Very few of my Sarawakian friends, even those with a solid history of nature photography and scientific work, had ever seen a wild tarsier, and neither had I. Since Day One in Borneo, the *kera hantu* (Malay for ghost monkey) had been on my must-see-before-dying list. My excitement was boundless when a friend informed me that a few mutual friends had spotted a tarsier in a nearby forest the previous night, and invited me to tag along on their next excursion. When I asked about the location, he said, "Oh, just in your neighborhood, in Sama Jaya." My excitement turned into euphoria. This legendary creature lived in the little jogging park just down the road?

Sama Jaya is not open to visitors during nighttime. But my friends had discovered a design fault in the security system: a substantial gap in the fence where the back of the park met a swamp. There was a night guard in the hut at the main entrance, though, which called for a stealthy approach. The following Saturday night, six black-clad nature nerd commandos armed with heavy camera gear gathered behind Sama Jaya. We slipped through the fence and split up into two groups. One group searched to the

133 *Cephalopachus bancanus*

western part of the forest; the other one went east. Fifteen minutes later my cellphone buzzed: "Get your butts over here; we found a tarsier. Better step on it; there's no telling how much longer he'll stay put."

We ran through the forest as fast as the darkness and my double-wideness allowed. When we arrived at the location we had been given, there was nobody—we had misunderstood their directions. Three more frantic phone calls and more wild panting through the nocturnal humidity finally brought us to the object of our desire. A tarsier is small enough to fit in your hand, but its hindlegs are formidable catapults. These primates possess the longest legs in the animal kingdom in relation to body size, and they can fling their owner 15 horizontal feet in one shot, about 30 times their body length.[134] Our friends had spotted the tarsier in a stand of saplings, and as soon as the flashlights had hit it, the little *mogwai* had leaped deeper into the thicket, hurling itself from trunk to trunk. One of our group had followed the animal off-trail, a move severely restrained by the deep leaf litter, the density of the trees and bushes, and the insidious creepers tripping him up at every step. At some point, the tarsier stopped its mad rocket trip and paused for a break, or maybe to take a better look at its giant, clumsy cousins. The moment I arrived, it swiveled its head in my direction at a sickening angle, Exorcist-style, and stared at me as if it had never seen anything this big on two legs.

The sensation was mutual: I had never seen anything like it either. It looked like—what? The result of a Star Trek transporter failure? A visitor from outer space? I settled for an animal made from spare parts. Paper-thin, transparent bat ears, a long spaghetti tail that ended in a toilet brush, and the giant, creepy-cute eyes of a Snapchat filter. These eyes are even more pronounced than in lorises. Each eye is bigger than the tarsier's stomach—and, indeed, larger and heavier than its brain. This leaves no space in the sockets for any muscles to move the eyeballs, a shortcoming compensated for by the ability to rotate the head up to 180 degrees in both directions. Its long, bony fingers and toes recalled those of Madagascar's aye-aye lemur, and I thought how perfect they were for catching insects (Bonus Crazy Anatomy Fact: a tarsier's third finger is as long as its upper arm). The creature's otherworldliness goes further than its looks. Tarsiers are the only primates that are purely carnivorous. With their strong jaws and shark-toothed smiles, they prey on a large variety of invertebrates, crabs, bats, birds, frogs, and reptiles, including the venomous kind. They prefer to hunt from positions not higher than 6 feet from the ground, and on occasion jump to the forest floor to catch things, which they chase by bouncing on their hindlegs like kangaroos.

My friends were already photographing the thing from all angles, but I was so mesmerized by the little night monkey that I had to be reminded to take out my own camera and start shooting if I wanted some souvenirs of the encounter. For the best

---

134 The name tarsier is derived from its elongated tarsus, ankle bone.

Horsfield's tarsier

part of the next hour, the tarsier sat there, revolved its head like an owl, occasionally circled the tree with the help of its nimble toes and fingers, and scrutinized the six higher primates around it with its saucer eyes. Finally, it released a commentary in the form of a huge turd, and with one giant leap that was probably just a small step for it, disappeared into the dark.

Like most living things in Borneo, tarsiers are playing on the losing side. Forest conversion, monocultures, pesticides, and even overhunting (in some parts of Southeast Asia certain "higher primates" actually eat tarsiers) are hitting them hard, and so is human ignorance. A 2015 article in Wired.com, titled Absurd Creature of the Week, quotes Myron Shekelle, one of the world's foremost experts on tarsiers:

> Perhaps the most ironic problem seems to be its villainization as an agricultural pest. "So, one of the things that I've done is try to work with [farmers] and explain: No, no, tarsiers are actually interesting. They're the only primate that doesn't eat any plant matter, none at all," said Shekelle. "If you see them in your crops, they're eating insects that eat the leaves on your crops, so they're actually good." His advice isn't always heeded, though. "One very memorable time, after we did this and the people were like, 'Yeah, yeah that's very interesting,' we came back the next day and the guy had cut down his own fruit tree that had the tarsier nest in it. Clearly he didn't believe a word that we said."

* * * * * *

In December 2013, the cover photo of the august *Herpetological Review* shook the world of reptile science to the core. It was of a brown lizard sitting on a bed of wet rocks, hind legs and prehensile tail partly submerged in clear, shallow water. Instead of scales, its leathery skin was covered in small beads. Half a dozen rows of large, triangular knobs running along the back of the beast gave it a dragon-like quality. Its head was thick, blunt, and heavy-jawed, and the nostrils sat on top of the snout, hinting at an aquatic lifestyle. In stark contrast to the animal's gnarly, prehistoric look, its tiny eyes surprised with the color of a bright blue sky.

The Malays call it *cicak purba* (ancient gecko) and it really is a remnant from the depths of time. To many reptile fanciers and scientists, this is the Holy Grail of Herpetology. Known in English as Bornean earless monitor, its scientific name, *Lanthanotus borneensis* (hidden ear from Borneo) also reflects the lack of an external ear opening. Together with the lizard's forked tongue, this strengthens the argument that monitor-like lizards were the ancestors of snakes. In 2013, the Bornean earless monitor was still a poorly known enigmatic species considered to be the only living represen-

Lanthanotus borneensis
(photo, Indraneil Das)

tative of the clade Lanthanotidae. The only other taxon allocated to this family is a fossil[135] from the Upper Cretaceous period, 100 to 566 million years ago, which makes *L. borneensis* a living compatriot of the dinosaurs. The Austrian herpetologist Franz Steindachner described the lizard in 1878, but for roughly the next 100 years, this obscure species fell off the radar before a few specimens reappeared in the 1960s. At the time, Tom Harrison, curator of the Sarawak Museum, obtained some earless monitors and published papers about their appearance and general behavior in the journal *Nature*, and further articles in the *Sarawak Museum Journal* and other publications. These were the only existing data on live specimens. A few monitors were kept alive for several years in captivity, allowing the first important behavioral studies of this rare species. Some mysteries could be lifted, but all further assumptions about the natural history, behavior, and specialized morphological adaptations of this unique animal remained speculative. The following decades revealed no additional knowledge on the lizard, and it remained hidden from the scientific world.

In 2013, lizard researchers and breeders alike still spoke of the earless monitor in hushed tones of nearly fetishistic adulation. And now, the cover of *Herpetological Review* rocked a photo of the world's rarest lizard in the wild, recently taken at an unknown location by Professor Indraneil Das. The saga behind the rediscovery of *L.*

---

135 *Cherminotus longifrons*

borneensis in Sarawak is as weird and wonderful as the animal itself, and I had the great fortune to experience it from a front row seat.

It all started with a cryptic WhatsApp text from Neil Das. As a reptile fancier, I was aware of the little dragon and its mythical status, but the only *Lanthanotus* I had ever met was a stuffed specimen, which had seen better days, at the Sarawak Museum. I had long made peace with my assumption that *L. borneensis* had gone the way of its closest ancestor from the Upper Cretaceous. Even if a few of them were still kicking around in Sarawak, I would never see one alive. This species had been one of the reasons Neil Das had moved to Borneo in 1991, and for 22 years he and his team had unsuccessfully tried to rediscover the reptile. If the pros couldn't find it in over two decades, what were my chances?

All this was radically turned on its head when my phone screen lit up with a message from the professor that threw me in a state of high confusion: "Going on a Lanthanotus hunt!"

I texted back for more details but received no answer. Neil called me two nights later to explain. A *Lanthanotus* had been caught in a border village two hours from Kuching, and would I like to accompany him next time he visited the lizard? *This can't be happening,* I thought. *Not in my lifetime. It's a prank.* But I pretended to take Neil seriously, and a few days later I collected the professor and his assistant, Pui Yong Min, at Neil's house, to drive out to the border and see the magic dragon. Over breakfast at a noodle stall, Neil finally offered an explanation. The *Lanthanotus* was held captive at a mom-and-pop shop in a tiny village on the Indonesian border, right by a steep, forested hill streaked with small, fast-flowing streams. Early one morning, the shop owner's wife had found the earless wonder perambulating the paved area in front of the shop that she was sweeping. Its native habitat was most likely one of the nearby hill streams. Speculations still abound on what exactly had possessed the lizard to leave the water and venture into the village, but the answer remains unknown. Luckily for the lizard, the shop owner and his wife were ethnic Chinese with strong traditional superstitions. They concluded that the animal had sought them out for a reason and would therefore bring them luck. Initially they housed it in an empty rat trap. Nobody in the village had ever seen such a creature or knew what it fed on. The elderly shop owner, whom everyone called Uncle, tried a variety of foods from carrots to instant noodles. The lizard rejected all nourishment until Uncle offered it a piece of raw fatty pork, which was gobbled up in two seconds flat. Uncle was a smart man and quick on the uptake. He sensed that a rat trap was probably not the most natural environment for his new pet, and somehow assumed it might be fond of a wetter place. He transferred the *Lanthanotus* to a shallow plastic container filled with an inch of water and two flat rocks for basking. He also experimented with other meaty fare such as earthworms and small fish, all of which the lizard devoured with great relish.

One day, a neighbor took photos of the beast and put them on Facebook asking for identification. The post immediately went viral, and within hours a friend of Neil's saw the pictures and notified the professor. Neil drove out to the village to convince Uncle to donate the lizard to the Universiti Malaysia Sarawak, to be kept in a large comfy terrarium and studied at leisure. Neil explained the animal's incredible rarity (at the time, it was the world's only known captive specimen), and its priceless importance for science. He had even brought a stack of scientific papers to support his claims. Uncle read them all, but his mind was made up. The lizard had come to his house on his own volition, ergo it would bring luck, ergo it was not to leave the premises under any circumstances. Uncle was so enamored with the reptile that he even took it for daily walks in front of the shop. Under Sarawakian law, *Lanthanotus borneensis* enjoys the highest protection, and anyone removing this species from the wild suffers the full wrath of the government. But one earless monitor at Uncle's shop meant there would be more where it had come from, and if Neil wanted to launch scientific expeditions on the hill behind the village he would need the cooperation of the villagers. After lengthy negotiations, they reached a compromise. Uncle's lucky pet would stay where it was, and Neil's team was granted unlimited access to it for further studies. The village's communal house would be repurposed as a makeshift dormitory for the scientists. (As mentioned earlier, Uncle was a shrewd man. A dozen hungry and thirsty biologists living in the village also meant brisk business for his shop.)

We were getting closer to the border now. While I tried to digest Neil's stranger-than-fiction tale, I noticed that the secondary-growth trees had disappeared from the roadside. We had entered an area that reminded me of old photos of the battlegrounds at Verdun. Trees and undergrowth had been cleared, leaving the earth denuded and vibrating in the heat air. We passed a stack of logs piled up by the road. A dozen indigenous and Indonesian men in black t-shirts bearing a company logo were loading the tree trunks onto a logging truck with the help of heavy machinery. An ethnic Chinese man in the same black company t-shirt watched the operation. He had his hands in his pockets, which indicated him as the foreman. I stopped, rolled down my window, and inquired what tree species those logs were. In lieu of an answer, he asked me—not unfriendly, but straight to the point—what business I had here. Instead of picking up on the vibe, rolling up my window, and getting the hell out of Dodge, I feigned ignorance. "Just curious, sir. Never seen these trees before, I believe. … What company do you work for?" I added unnecessarily because that information was clearly visible on the man's shirt. In a puzzling move, he turned to one of the workers and relayed my question to him. The worker shrugged and walked away.

This should have triggered a dozen alarms, but my curiosity benumbed me to the scene. I had to know. "Where are the trees from?" The foreman had now decided that there was no need to come up with an elaborate lie. He had marked me as a harmless foreign dunce whom he could trust with the full truth because I would not believe it anyway. He pointed at Indonesia. "From the inside." The fog in my brain started to lift. They cut down trees just beyond the border in Indonesia and dragged them out here to haul them off on Malaysian trucks. They wore shirts with the logo of a company they didn't seem to know. They were suspicious of strangers. My sense of self-preservation kicked back into gear. I thanked the man for his time and kindness, and hit the accelerator. Neil looked at me with an inscrutable expression that I interpreted as "You *really* don't know what a bonehead you are, do you?" His assistant, Pui, tended studiously to his own thoughts and avoided eye contact. I guessed it was true: God watches over drunks and fools.

The village sat on the edge of the wild. It looked as old as the hills around it but was kept trim and neat. A school, a small church, and a *baruk* (skull house), were the prominent features. Boulders lined the village trails winding between colorful stilt houses. The porches teemed with pets and children. I waved and said hello to a particularly sweet-looking little girl. She bolted into the house in naked terror, dragging her poor puppy along by the neck. Like the rest of the kampung, Uncle's shop was rustic, but squeaky clean. Apart from the drink fridge and the enormous freezer, all furniture was made from rough wood, from the floor-to-ceiling shelves to the large counter. A dozen people in traditional garb milled around the shop. They belonged to different tribes, including a few from Indonesia. The border was less than 500 yards away, and judging from their bare, calloused feet, some of these folks regularly hiked over from Kalimantan to shop here. A stocky woman in a Bidayuh turban was transferring hundreds of large, live, and presumably edible frogs from a big net into a waist-high gunny sack. The shelves overflowed with cheap snacks and candy, dried fish, canned goods, sacks of rice and flour, bottled beer and moonshine, farming tools, and a thousand other useful things. The shop was dark and swirled with aromatic scents. It transported you 300 years back, while always reminding you what century it really was. A 60-inch flatscreen hung on a wall between parang machetes and fish traps; and a group of rough-looking fellows, maybe plantation hands or loggers, were watching a home video of a traditional *gawai* harvest celebration in an Iban longhouse. As we entered the shop, one of the celebrants in the video vomited over the veranda railing, wiped his mouth, and reached for the tuak bottle again, cheered on by his equally hammered buddies. The video sound was muted; instead, indigenous *sape* music poured from powerful loudspeakers chained to the walls. The place and its patrons reminded me of the Mos Eisley cantina on Tattooine, described in the Star Wars Databank as "a dimly-lit tavern known for its strong drinks, hot tunes, and occasional outbreaks of shocking violence."

On the shop counter, next to a rosewood abacus polished to a high gleam by decades of daily use, sat the world's rarest lizard. It rested on two flat rocks in a transparent Tupperware box and soaked its tail in the surrounding water. A sense of unreality stole over me like a shadow. Time stalled. I pinched myself in the thigh.

Uncle's shop

Yep. Still awake. Not dreaming. Yes, Mr. Hans, you are looking at a genuine, breathing *Lanthanothus borneensis*. Few things could have excited me more at that moment, short of a triceratops crashing through the back wall and raiding Uncle's icebox. As lizards go, the dirt-colored critter wasn't exactly a thing of beauty. But its archaic ugliness was part of the legend. It was large for the species, about a foot and a half long. Its blue eyes were smaller than rice grains, the legs short and equipped with long sharp claws. Adding to this the knobby ridges and antediluvian head resulted in an animal that was simply beyond comparison. This was the greatest moment in my career as an amateur herpetologist, and I believe Neil was similarly enthused. The lizard did not reciprocate our feelings; the bipedal mammals on both sides of the counter were of supreme disinterest to it. When I picked it up with almost religious veneration, I discovered one of its most surprising qualities: its skin and flesh moved loosely against each other, like two independent entities. The wart snake I had found at the Serian market had provided the same sensation. Some believe this allows both animals to move easier deep inside narrow underwater cracks and crevices; according to another theory, it helps with oxygen uptake, as it does in certain cold-water frogs. Science is still unclear about the precise reason for the baggy skin.

Uncle watched us from under his bushy eyebrows with visible pride. We asked for and received his permission to take the lizard outside for a photoshoot. Ten minutes of wobbly walking on wet stones and roots brought us to a fast-flowing streamlet running over shale-like rocks. Pui was tasked with controlling the *Lanthanotus* while Neil photographed it. It was a thankless job. As soon as Pui set the lizard on the ground, it took off like a wind-up toy, not overly fast, but never stopping. Neil shot the animal in a dozen poses—in and out of the water, on a rock, on a tree trunk, and walking around. Walk around it did a lot, and Pui really had his work cut out for him putting the lizard back in focus times without number.

When we returned to Uncle's shop, the table outside was occupied by four sweaty soldiers in full camouflaged battle rattle. They carried Austrian submachine guns; the frag grenades hanging from their chests almost outnumbered their jacket buttons, and one of them packed an assault rifle with attached grenade launcher. They were chugging ice-cold liter bottles of 100Plus, that legendary Malaysian pick-me-up sports drink, and helping themselves to a small mountain of potato chips on the table. If you ignored the modern firearms and the Southeast Asian faces, you could easily mistake them for an American long-range recon unit heading into Laos, ca. 1971. They smiled at us as we passed by, and after returning the *Lanthanotus* to its Tupperware box, I went back outside and struck up a conversation.

They were indeed on patrol. "We just came out of the jungle after seven days of checking the border. We'll R&R here for a day, then go back in for another week." What were they looking for? "Smugglers with contraband like illegal firearms, drugs, protected animals, unlicensed alcohol and cigarettes, the usual stuff. But our main job is to pull out the border posts and plant them back in their original positions." That put a blank look on my face, and they explained: "The Indonesians remove the posts and replant them on Malaysian territory, to increase their acreage for farming, mostly rubber trees. But it's a tug-of-war we can't win. When we come back in a few weeks, the posts will be right back where we pulled them out, if not even deeper in Malaysian territory."

Neil instructed me to keep the *Lanthanotus* and its location strictly under wraps. For the foreseeable future, my photos were not to leave my computer, and under no circumstances was I to mention the lizard online or to anyone I did not trust. Poachers have identified sites from close-up photos by analyzing the leaves on the ground next to the animal, and the earless monitor was to be treated like an Area 51-level national secret.

This was still the status quo a few months later when I took two visiting American friends to see and photograph the reptile, and almost committed one of the worst blunders in the history of herpetology. Bill, Kevin, and I had taken the *Lanthanotus* to the table outside Uncle's shop. It slowly wandered around the surface, allowing us great close-ups from every conceivable angle. An hour later, we had taken every photo we could possibly want from the animal. It was resting in the middle of the table, flicking its forked tongue out in lazy intervals. We were chimping now, reviewing our photos on our camera screens like curious apes. Each of us had taken hundreds of shots, so the chimping took a while.

Then Bill looked up, surveyed the table, and said, "Where's the lizard?"

On that sunny morning in early 2013, that lizard was still the only living *Lanthanotus borneensis* known to science. Uncle, and by extension Neil, had trusted my friends and me with this one-of-a-kind reptile. And now, in an astonishing show of collective stupidity, we had managed to lose it. The lizard had never displayed any urgency in its movements; it was slow, if occasionally determined, and we felt it was too small and physically unfit to jump off a table. This had bred complacency; we had been duped into believing that we could afford to ignore the mini-dragon for a few minutes. We looked under the table. No *Lanthanotus*. Panic welled up in my stomach like hot acid. If we didn't recover this animal, not only would we get into serious trouble with Uncle and Neil (not to mention the instantaneous loss of our reputations as herpers) but I in particular faced possible retribution from the government. In my mind I already saw myself and my family getting deported, leaving behind forever the life we had carved out for ourselves in Borneo. My heart raced at a dangerous rate. Kevin ran into the shop to see if the lizard had tried to return to its Tupperware palace. It hadn't. I was approaching full-bore hysteria and felt I was about to black out. Bill and I looked around the corner of the shop, and there, 20 yards ahead of us and well on its way into the jungle, was the lizard. It was moving at a previously unrecorded pace, and by the time the two overweight pink apes—now panting hard and gushing sweat—reached it and picked it up, it was just a few seconds away from forever disappearing into the underbrush and from our lives.

Crisis averted, we brought the lizard back into the shop. As we placed it in its box, Uncle observed us closely. We were louder and giddier than necessary, and we bought way too many cold drinks. I bet Fort Knox against a rotten jackfruit that Uncle just *knew* something odd had happened. In future, he would be more careful around random tourists who wanted to take his lucky pet for a spin.

Not long after *Lanthanotus borneensis* had graced the cover of *Herpetological Review*, rumors about poaching operations began to materialize. A concerned friend wrote to me:

> It looks like illegal collectors are now finding *Lanthanotus* and smuggling them out of Borneo. I recently received this news from a German colleague: "Two Germans went to Borneo in late April and again in late May. During their first trip they poached 21 pairs of *L. borneensis* (we don't know whether in Sarawak or Kalimantan)—and the first online adverts for these animals appeared in May—asking for 7,500 and 8,000 Euro/pair." All the more reason to keep things close to our chest!

About the same time, a Japanese reptile magazine printed a multi-page story about the discovery of an earless monitor in a stream in Kalimantan, just south of the border from Uncle's shop. According to the article, the author had released the lizard in the stream after taking photos *in situ*. Curiously enough, a week later a Japanese reptile zoo announced that they had acquired a breeding pair of *L. borneensis* and would put it on display soon. Grapevine buzz about German and Czech poachers kept increasing, and a *Lanthanotus* pair was offered at the Terraristika Hamm, the world's largest reptile trade show, for €25,000. There is an ironic upside to wildlife poaching for the hobbyist market: as soon as people start to breed rare animals, the initially extreme prices implode. Today, various zoos and private reptile keepers around the world are running successful *Lanthanotus* breeding programs. The earless monitor is still not cheap by any standard, but the days are history when a single specimen could fetch US$28,000 in Japan.

Since those heady frontier days in 2013, field work by Neil and his team has produced support for the assumption that *L. borneensis*, while not directly threatened, must be seen as gravely endangered since it lives solely in riverine areas of Borneo where human activity has altered the landscape.

In other words, another not-rare-but-rarely-seen animal under pressure from habitat loss. The authors add a positive note:

> However, the earless monitor lizard can survive in high densities in areas surrounded by degraded habitats (including oil palm plantations), and rocky streams, possibly its preferred habitat, are relatively unaffected by humans.

At the time of writing, almost eight years after Uncle's wife rediscovered *Lanthanotus borneensis* for the scientific world, Neil's teams are researching the species at two sites in Sarawak's remote interior. They put radio transmitters on a good number of earless monitors to track their daily business and gain information on their ecology, thermoregulation, and other data. *L. borneensis* has long lost its ultra-rarity status, and that is good news for the species. But I must admit that I sometimes wish it were 2013 again, when the only live dinosaur that science knew of lived next to an abacus in a village shop deep in the heart of Borneo.

*   *   *   *   *   *

My uncle Jürgen is a retired physician and one of the world's great travel companions. An avid hobby sailor, nature connoisseur, and intrepid adventurer, he displays an exuberance for life and knowledge that is hard to find even in people half his age. Jürgen is a true polymath, a man whose interests reach from the breeding cycles of the birds in his backyard to the history of the Roman Empire, from photography and classic cars to enology and aeronautics. His idea of a well-spent vacation is crisscrossing the Arabian

Peninsula or the Australian outback in a rented off-roader, armed with little more than a map, a med kit, and an unlimited supply of optimism.

My earliest childhood experience with Jürgen's love for the natural world came during my first year of elementary school. Our family had met for Sunday brunch in his backyard. It was July, and the table was crawling with wasps. I was too terrified to even reach for my orange juice. My parents assured me the insects were more interested in the plum compôte and the apricot pie than in my sweaty flesh, but I just sat there petrified, clenching my armrests with bone-white knuckles.

My uncle said, "Let me show you something." He pushed his lower lip out and spooned a blob of strawberry jam on it. Within seconds, a wasp alighted on his lip and helped itself to the fruity treat. I stared at the beast in unbridled horror, expecting it to do—*any time now!!*—what I thought wasps do: unsheathe its stinger and turn my uncle's face into a swollen mess. But that didn't happen. After the wasp had had its fill, it gave itself a quick preen and flew off. Jürgen licked the remaining jam off his lip and turned to his shocked nephew: "See, Hans, it's just like your mom said: they're not looking for trouble, just for food. They only mess with you when you mess with them. Just avoid sudden movements."

Imagine this man's joy 40-odd years later, when the nephew announced his plans to move to one of the world's greatest biodiversity hotspots. Jürgen had never visited Borneo before, and it didn't take long for him to show up at Kuching airport with 60 pounds of gear and a huge expectant smile: "Greetings, my dear nephew! Which way to the rainforest?" For the next six years, he would visit us every February ("I need to get away from the German winter and see something green!"). We would take trips together on the weekends, and when I had to work, he borrowed my truck and went exploring by himself. Eventually he had seen all the highlights around Kuching, and during his third visit, we decided to take a little family vacation in the crown jewel of Sarawak's protected jungles—Mulu.

Gunung Mulu is Sarawak's largest national park and a UNESCO World Heritage site that wows the visitor with geological superlatives. Underneath the mountainous rainforest setting are 184 miles of explored caves. Among these are the Sarawak Chamber, one of the world's largest underground chambers, Deer Cave, the second-largest cave passage in the world, and Clearwater Cave, the longest cave system in Southeast Asia. The Sarawak Chamber is 2,000 feet long, 1,362 feet wide and at least 260 feet high, with a volume of 420 million cubic feet and an unsupported roof span of almost 1,000 feet.[136] The Deer Cave passage is almost a mile and a half long and 400 feet tall in the main chamber. As of October 2018, 745,000 feet[137] of Clearwater Cave's passages had been explored.

---

136 Sarawak Chamber: 600 meters long, 415 meters wide, at least 80 meters high, volume 142 million cubic meters and an unsupported roof span of 300 meters. Deer cave passage: 2.4 km long, 122 meters high.

137 227.2 km

In the sunlit world outside these gigantic holes, there is more to behold in wonder:

> 20,000 species of invertebrates, 81 species of mammals, 270 species of birds, 55 species of reptiles, 76 species of amphibians and 48 species of fish have been identified in the park area. The park has 17 vegetation zones, with 3,500 species of vascular plants and 1,500 species of flowering plants. There are 109 species in 20 genera of palms, over 1,700 mosses and liverworts, 8,000 species of fungi, and 442 species of spore-producing pteridophytes are recorded. Examples of vegetation zones found in the park are: peat swamp forest, heath, mixed dipterocarp forest, moss forest, and montane ecosystems. Lowland forest occupies 40% of the park area while montane forest occupies 20% of the park area. (Wikipedia)

The area is also home to the Penan, one of the last hunter-gatherer tribes in Southeast Asia. The Penan originally maintained a nomadic way of life, but since the 1970s, the Malaysian government has made it a priority to bring them into the fold of civilization. They were convinced to settle in longhouses, pick up farming, and send their children to schools.

The official reason is that Malaysia does not want to be stigmatized as a backward country where illiterate stone age tribes still roam. During a meeting of European and Asian leaders in 1990, Malaysian prime minister Mahathir Mohamad said, "It is our policy to bring all jungle dwellers together into the mainstream. There is nothing romantic about these helpless, half-starved, and disease-ridden people." Jungle nomads also stand in the way of progress. Over the past decades, the Penan have rebelled against logging activities in their traditional hunting grounds by putting up roadblocks and sabotaging heavy equipment. The Penan issue is politically charged. When a German television crew shooting a documentary about Sarawak wanted to include material about the conflict in their show, their local handlers told them in no uncertain terms that their filming license would be revoked if they so much as mentioned the tribe in their footage. A small number of Penan are settled near the western side of Mulu National Park, and a few hundred of them enjoy hunting rights for pigs and deer in designated areas. Many Penan work in the park as guides, boatmen, and mechanics, and there is a small tourist market where they sell handicrafts.

Mulu is remote and isolated. No roads lead to it, and it takes a full day by river to reach the park from the next town. The river is shallow, the boats are small, and travelers often spend less time riding in the crafts than pushing them. That leaves air travel as the only viable alternative. On the day of our departure we arrived at Kuching airport before dawn with our bags and 15 gallons of drinking water (All supplies are flown in, so in Mulu everything, including bottled water, is expensive.) The flight was memorable. I am as terrified of heights and flying as some other people are of snakes, and the ride in the small plane, constantly buffeted by brutal gusts, was one of the worst I can remember. Uncle Jürgen, the aviation nut, sat next to me with a Christmas morning grin and showered me with technical particulars about the death machine in which we would surely soon perish. Much as he tried to spark my interest in the aircraft—"Italian-made ART-72! Twin-engine turboprop upper decker! Short-haul regional airliner!"—all I wanted right now was a quick and painless end. Across the aisle, Hans and Karl weren't helping either. They were busy making fun of their dad's torment with cruel jokes about engine failures and fiery deaths. Lisa, as usual, slept through the whole flight.

I finally calmed down during the landing approach. The beautiful surroundings of the airstrip helped me forget that, statistically, the landing is the most dangerous part of air travel. We touched down in a lush valley surrounded by rainforested mountains. If you ignored the tiny airport, it felt like arriving in a lost world.

A local travel agent welcomed us to the park and ushered us through the airport formalities. Soon, all of us, plus bags and drinking water, were piled onto the truck bed of an old Toyota Hilux and bouncing toward our accommodations.

After a breakfast of *bee hoon* (fried rice vermicelli) at the park canteen the next morning, we went on a guided tour of the Deer Cave. Our two Penan guides—Harvey marching in front, Motang herding us from the rear—took us on a 2-mile boardwalk through pristine primary rainforest and along rushing streams. The air was filled with birdsong and the skirl of cicadas. I discovered a strange bug in eye-popping atomic pink sitting on the handrail. My highly inflammable enthusiasm often causes rash decisions, and without giving it any further thought, I picked up the insect and showed it to the group. After everyone had duly admired and commented on my lovely find, I put the bug back on the handrail. Karl noticed it first. "Dad, why is your hand orange?" A big ocher stain disfigured my right palm, and it smelled like burned garbage. Weeks later, an entomologist would educate me about the defensive secretions of *Pycanum rubens*, a member of the giant stink bug family (*Tessaratomidae*). The burnt-trash smell disgraced me for only a few days, but the stain stayed for over a week.

According to local lore, Deer Cave was named after the deer that visit it for shelter and its salt licks. We didn't see any deer, but maybe we just missed them in this vast cavern. The cave has ample room for a small town and even comes with its own river. After we had delighted in the colossal dimensions of the entrance chamber, guide Harvey described the next leg of the hike. Our destination was the Garden of Eden, a small circular valley outside the far end of the cave. There, among the rainforest trees and next to a beautiful waterfall, we would take our lunch. To reach the Garden of Eden, we would negotiate slippery trails, walk in a river, climb steep sections by rope, and squeeze through narrow openings. As he mentioned the latter, Harvey snuck a quick, doubtful glance at my ampleness. I caught his eye and said, "No worries, there's

Cicada

no need to tempt fate. I'll just stay outside and watch birds instead. See you guys in the afternoon!" Harvey thanked me for my understanding, and when the group continued into the guts of the cave, I walked back out into the sunshine.

Besides its dimensions, Deer Cave is also famous for its Bat Exodus. Every evening, unless it rains, a colony of around three million wrinkle-lipped bats[138] leaves the cave in tight formation to hunt for insects in the nearby forests. For better enjoyment of this world-class event, a bat observatory had been built outside the cave. A wooden shelter provides information about bats, and a concession stand sells snacks and drinks. The open lawn outside the shelter is framed by a seating area for convenient bat watching. It is also a perfect spot for birding the forest edges. (Finding and watching forest birds inside a forest is quite difficult. Your best chances are in open areas—parking lots, for example—from where you scan the forest from the outside.)

The birding bug had hit me not long into our stay in Borneo. I had arrived with a focus on snakes and pitcher plants but soon fell in love with everything else this biotic frontier offers. "The more you know about nature, the more you see, and this is enriching," Richard Fortey wrote in *Dry Store Room No. 1*, a behind-the-scenes look at London's Natural History Museum. In the 18th century, Laurence Sterne remarked, "What a large volume of adventures may be grasped within the span of his little life by him who interests his heart in everything." Borneo's embarrassment of natural riches accelerated my conversion to this broad-mindedness at warp speed. For the longest time, I had belittled birds as snake food, and birding as a hobby for middle-aged people too feeble to deal with real animals like snakes.

But my arrogance would not last. I was looking for flying lizards in Sama Jaya one morning, when a portly Westerner with a shock of white hair approached me. He carried a long-lensed camera on a monopod and inquired about my business with friendly curiosity. My answer provoked another question from him: "Why aren't you using binoculars?"

I explained that my main interests were reptiles and carnivorous plants, neither of which required visual aids.

"But flying lizards live in trees," he countered. "So do a lot of snakes. And many pitcher plants, for that matter. And, of course, over 80 percent of all orchids. The canopy is the business end of the rainforest, where most of life happens. I'm surprised you don't *sleep* with a pair of binocs next to you."

My ears reddened in shame. I was aware of all those facts, but had never considered purchasing binoculars, for the sole and simple reason that I didn't want to look like a birder. With an unreadable smile, the man unslung a pair of top-range field glasses from his neck and handed them to me. "Have a look. I'd wager this'll make your dragon hunt easier."

---

138 *Tadarida plicata*

I had never looked through a pair of expensive binoculars before. The effect was life-changing. Really good binocs do not just make things look bigger; they brighten dark areas and add vividness to the scene. Looking at the world through this instrument felt like discovering a fourth dimension. I was hooked right away, and when I spotted a flying lizard minutes later, I was converted.

"By the way," the man added, "when you look through binoculars from the wrong side, they work like a magnifying glass."

That's how I met Dr. Ronald Orenstein, a Canadian wildlife lawyer with a Sarawakian spouse, a Ph.D. in ornithology, and a slew of books under his belt: glossy coffee-table doorstoppers about hummingbirds, sleuthing work about ivory poaching, and children's books about extinct animals. His thirst for the natural world was unquenchable. We soon became fast friends, and I could not have wished for a better birding coach. Standing on the lawn of the bat observatory now, I silently thanked Ron for his tireless tutelage. The forest edge was dripping with birds, and I knew most of them.

Ron had used an almost unfair trick to fire up my interest in our feathery friends: "You know why herpetologists call them avian reptiles? Because birds are the dinosaurs that made it. Look at a newborn chick and dare tell me you're not seeing a miniature tyrannosaur!"

Fascinating morphological similarities aside, many of the birds here were simply gorgeous. I saw a pair of suitably named Asian fairy bluebirds, and a barrel-chested red-naped trogon bursting with colors. An olive-green long-billed spiderhunter dipped its saber beak into deep flowers, looking for nectar and bugs. Woodpeckers were busy everywhere, including a wren-sized rufous piculet, the smallest woodpecker outside the Americas. The bird was moving around a macaranga tree, pecking at its hollow twigs to drive out the ants that lived inside.

A length of snow-white toilet paper bobbed and weaved between the trees, and I identified it as the tail feathers of a male Blyth's paradise flycatcher, a small white bird with a pointy black crest and a body three times shorter than its tail. I heard the call of an ashy tailorbird, a drab, but loud little creature with an astonishing talent. It uses fibers and spider silk to stitch large leaves into cones. Inside the cone the bird then constructs a traditional nest. The stitching holes in the leaf edges are so tiny that the leaf does not wither and brown. This keeps the cradle identical to the leaves around it, for maximum protective camouflage.

When my stomach reported that it was time for the midday meal, I plopped myself on a bench and opened my rucksack to retrieve my packed lunch. Fragrant fried rice, a few pieces of fruit, and a juice box was exactly what I needed right now. My hopes were dashed when I looked through the bag and bitterly cursed my earlier decision to store my lunchbox in Karl's backpack to create more space in mine for my camera gear. I walked to the bat observatory in the hope of purchasing a snack, but the concession stand was dark and locked. The only people around were two men with carpenter tools fixing something on the back of the building, and they didn't seem to have anything edible on them. In my despair, I turned every pocket in my bag inside out. What I found, buried deeply under trash and lint, was proof that there is a God … but boy, is he a prankster. Until my family emerged from the Deer Cave in four hours, all the sustenance available to me would be five Fisherman's Friend throat lozenges with lemon-menthol flavor. At least they weren't the sugar-free kind.

As I slowly sucked on a cough drop, trying to make it last and wishing it were fried rice with shrimp, egg, and sambal sauce, loud barking came from the forest. I knew there were barking deer in Mulu, goat-sized ungulates with a piercing call that sounds like an ill-tempered corgi with severe bronchitis. I asked the two carpenters about it, but they nixed my theory: "Not barking deer. Gecko." I thanked them for their assessment but privately rejected it. No geckos I knew of were big enough to produce such noise. I put the mystery on the back burner for the moment, pending further research.

For dessert, I treated myself to a second lozenge, then walked back along the boardwalk to a wooden shelter I had noticed on the way in. If I couldn't have a proper meal, I could still enjoy a proper nap. With my backpack as a pillow, I lay on the shelter floor and was soon soothed to sleep by the gurgling brook outside. My dreams were infused by occasional comments from passing hikers about my snoring ("I thought chainsaws were prohibited here") and my appearance ("Didn't know that elephant seals live this close to the equator"). I awoke to the ungodly sounds of Donald Duck's unmistakable voice dressing down his three nephews. I rubbed the sleep from my eyes, stumbled out of the shelter, and looked for the source of the racket.

In the tree above me sat a bird, black all over and the size of a goose. It had short legs, not much of a neck, and a tail like a folded Chinese fan. Its huge white beak was shaped like a dragon claw and looked powerful enough to brain a yak. Atop the beak sat a bony, banana-shaped structure. This casque is the reason why this bird family is called hornbills. With eight species roaming its forests, Sarawak is known as Land of the Hornbills. They eat fruit but will take the occasional insect or small snake. Their feeding behavior is quite amusing. Their tongues are too short to reach the tip of the long beak, so they toss their food into the air and catch it with their throats.

Hornbills nest in tree holes, and they need big trees. The gradual disappearance of large rainforest trees threatens hornbill reproduction all over Borneo. Sarawak law classifies all hornbills as Totally Protected Species ("a species in danger of extinction due to hunting and habitat destruction"). Penalties for keeping hornbills as pets, killing, hunting, capturing, selling, trading, or disturbing them, or even possessing any parts of these animals, are severe—a maximum fine equivalent to over US$12,000 and three years' imprisonment. I wondered where the law stood on hornbills denying humans their rightful beauty sleep. The noise polluter above me, a male black hornbill,[139]

---

139 *Anthracoceros malayanus*

apparently did not care. Doing his Mad Uncle Donald impersonation, he hopped and fluttered from branch to branch like a neurotic chicken with an icepick tied to its face. Finally, he decided to change scenery and took wing. His flight across the creek into the jungle on the other side was spectacular. His motions looked like an animated woodcutting, and every stroke of his broad wings created a loud swishing sound. After he was well out of sight, I could still hear him rend the air with his squawks and screeches.

I was fully awake now, and flush with joy over this wonderful encounter. Whistling a jolly tune, I went behind a tree to answer the call of nature. I almost stepped on a large leaf with hundreds of wasps sitting on it. Like jet fighters on an aircraft carrier, they all faced the same direction—*my* direction. I had read somewhere that this was typical behavior for wasps when they sensed an intruder near their nest. I decided to ignore my pressing need for the moment and beat a strategic retreat to the bat observatory.

To my great joy, I found the concession stand open for business, and feasted on a late lunch of peanuts and Coke. When my family and the rest of their spelunking group returned from the Deer Cave, they were soaking wet and speckled with guano and dried blood from small nicks and scratches. They had traced a river and clawed their way up ropes and over rocks slick with bat shit. Everyone had slipped and fallen a few times, and they told me of a narrow passage that would have trapped me like a giant rat.

I felt like a winner.

The observatory area was filling up with people arriving for the Bat Exodus. At ten minutes to six, still in full daylight, the show began. Videos fail to do this spectacle justice, because they do not convey the time it takes to watch the entire migration to the end. Millions of bats, about 15 abreast, leave the cave in a thin, steady stream that sometimes morphs into parallel streams. These look like narrow bands of living smoke, swirling around an invisible core, and the bats' wings give off a whooshing noise like a distant waterfall. As they come out of the cave, the bats are attacked by bat hawks, raptors specialized in snatching flying mammals from the air. Thrilling as they are to watch, the hawks are just an insignificant sideshow; they do not make any detectable dent in the 3 million bats rushing from the cave. A full hour after it began, the bat stream finally dried up. The entire flight is calculated to be at least 30 miles long, and every night, the bats consume an estimated total of 9 tons of insects before returning to the cave. No wonder we hadn't seen a single mosquito during our stay so far.

On the walk back from the Deer Cave, everyone was caught up in their own thoughts. Witnessing one of the planet's great natural phenomena had left us in a humbled, contemplative mood, and we did not pay much attention to the nightlife around us. But the forest had one more surprise in store before we called it a day. Near the end of the walk, Hans and Karl discovered a giant gecko[140] sitting on a tree trunk close to

---

140 *Gekko smithii*

[Above] Bat exodus cave mouth

[Below] Bat exodus starting

Gekko smithii

the ground. The grayish-green lizard was over a foot long and had bright jade balls as eyes. When I took out my camera, the gecko lifted its head, contemplated me with those green marbles, and then shocked us with a string of loud barks identical to those I had heard in the afternoon. I really hoped to meet those two carpenters again, so I could apologize in person.

For the following day, we had arranged a boat trip down the Melinau Paku River to visit the Wind Cave and the Clearwater Cave. Our guide was a young Penan named Lucas whose bottle-blond fauxhawk nicely complemented his collection of tattoos, including one on his calf advertising Jesus is Love. We traveled in a typical Bornean longboat, a needle-shaped wooden canoe not much wider than an office chair. Inboard, six wooden crosspieces were set so close to the floor that I wondered why the shipwrights had bothered with seats at all. After many rainless days, the river had lost much of its depth. The boatman tried to pass the dodgier parts by gunning the outboard engine to rush across, while Lucas in the bow helped with elbow grease, poling the boat with a long, thin stick. Most of the time these maneuvers did not work. When we ran aground, which we did a lot, Hans and Karl were politely asked to step out and help push the boat into deeper water. On the rare occasions when the boatman's tough tactics did succeed, the boat would rock violently and threaten to spill us all into the river. Lisa would yell in terror, Hans Jr. would shout "Balance, people! *Balance!*", and then we'd float in deeper water again, taking a breather until the next shallow spot.

We first stopped at Batu Bungan, a small Penan settlement that consisted of a handful of clapboard shacks with a mountainous backdrop. Two concrete longhouses were under construction, most likely in recognition of the shacks' decrepitude. The Penan have been living in Borneo's rainforests for millennia. Before the arrival of civilization, chainsaws, and Christianity, they had been free-roaming folk who hunted with blowpipes and gathered what they could find. Hunting and gathering was governed by a concept called *molong*, which dictated never taking more from the forest than necessary. They used a bush communication system with over 100 signs made from bent branches and folded leaves. Their language included over 1,200 names for trees and their corresponding spirits, and they believed that theirs is only one of nine different worlds in the cosmos.

Only a handful of Penan still range free in the forests today, but the forests are dwindling,[141] and most of the tribe lives in settlements now. This settlement boasted two tourist attractions: a handicraft market and a blowpipe range. For a few ringgit, you could try your hand at blowing darts at Styrofoam cut-outs of local bushmeat: pythons, monkeys, hornbills, pigs, and bears. Hans and Karl immediately went into

---

141 In 2019, the Penan and Berawan natives near Mulu National Park staged a blockade against a logging company encroaching their lands for logging and oil palm plantations. The Sarawak government denied that the logging activities would affect the ecology of Mulu National Park. On March 15, 2019, the natives lodged an official complaint to UNESCO in the hope of bringing attention to the issue.

competition mode, each proclaiming himself the winner before they had even started. The shootout was accompanied by typical teenage trash talk and theatrics. In the end, neither boy won, but both had gained important knowledge. A dozen darts that all failed to hit any of the targets taught the kids a hard fact about life as a jungle nomad: food is not a given when you have to shoot it out of the trees with an unwieldy, 6-foot blowpipe that requires serious lung power.

The stands in the small market offered bead jewelry, rattan weavings, miniature blowpipes, and other handicrafts. The vendors, all women, wore glum impressions and only looked up when directly spoken to. An old lady played a direful melody on a nose flute. We had been told that the Penan in Mulu did not really like their jobs as guides, boatmen, and handicraft mongers. I was beginning to believe it.

We spent the rest of the morning climbing, descending, and climbing again thousands of steps in the Wind Cave and the Clearwater Cave, to see hundreds of stalagmites, stalactites, and other limestone formations. Many were illuminated by colorful mood lights, and in a subsection called the Lady Cave, we appreciated a stone pillar whose shadow resembled a praying Madonna. Pretty as the caves were, I was glad when the grueling Stairmaster exercise came to an end and we returned to the jetty for lunch. A long wooden table was laid out with a spread of chicken curry, crunchy eggplants, wild fern cooked with garlic, and other delightful dishes. After the meal, Lisa took a nap, while Uncle Jürgen, the boys, and I took a dip in the river. Using a mossy log as a diving board, Hans and Karl held a spontaneous cannonball contest, and I floated spread-eagled in the slow-moving water, at peace with myself and the world. The peace was disturbed only once, when a family longboat motored by, crammed with mom, dad, two kids, three dogs, and an ancient-looking grandmother with huge wooden plugs in her earlobes. When they saw the big white mammal in the river, they started a lively discussion in their native language. As of today, I still haven't learned whether the Penan also have a word for elephant seal.

We returned to our cabins in the late afternoon. Lisa and the kids wanted to take some time off adventuring before dinner, but Jürgen and I, looking to squeeze the most out of our visit, topped off our water bottles and went straight back into the jungle. We met a Canadian photographer couple, he with a formidable Santa beard, she with a cascade of white hair flowing all the way to her belt. They were setting up a complicated camera rig with multiple flashes and reflectors, all aimed at a tall ginger plant. In reply to my inquiry—"Whatchashootin'?"—the woman pointed at a 3-foot leaf that grew skywards from the plant. The leaf was young and still furled into a cone, and we were told to look inside. At the bottom of the cone was a little ball of fur, holding fast to the walls with delicate, almost transparent claws. "That's a Hardwicke's woolly bat,"[142] pronounced the man with no small measure of pride. "They

---

142 *Kerivoula hardwickii*

[Left] Nepenthes hemsleyana

[Right] Stinging nettle slug caterpillar

like to roost in these unopened leaves during the daytime. We've been looking for this for days!" We congratulated them on their find, and I mentioned that I had read about bats sheltering in *Nepenthes hemsleyana*, a pitcher plant species also found in Mulu.

"Oh yes, they do," the lady replied. "We found two bats in a *hemsleyana* just yesterday, and not far from here." This we had to see! The photographers gave us directions, and we hurried off to meet the pitcher plant that doubled as a bat hotel.

We never found it. Instead, we got lost, nightfall caught us without flashlights, and we were seriously late for dinner. But there was a consolation prize just before sundown. By the side of the trail lay a big green stinging nettle slug caterpillar[143] with strings of bright blue dots running along its body. Both ends were decorated with a pair of horn-like features, and little tapered nubs grew from the insect's sides. The thing looked lifeless, and I used a twig to inspect it for vital signs. The twig hadn't even touched its body when a forest of needles shot out from every part of the caterpillar and turned it into a cholla cactus.[144] The quill-like bristles are hollow and connected to sacs filled with poison that inflicts debilitating pain which can linger for days. Uncle Jürgen, M.D., was smitten by

143 *Setora nidens*, Limacodidae

144 A particularly vicious member of the family.

the caterpillar's toxicity and spiky defense system. For the rest of our long walk back to the cabins, he entertained me with horror stories about former patients who had met with disaster via toxic inhabitants of the natural world. It was all worth missing dinner.

The following morning, we joined another guided tour, this time to the famous Canopy Walk. The park's website explains:

> The Mulu Canopy Walk is a 480-metre walkway, suspended 25 metres above the forest floor and still one of the longest tree-based canopy walks in the world.
>
> Walk in the lush treetops with tranquil river views below and compare the vegetation of riverine forest floor to the understory, the treetops and nearby limestone cliffs. A unique opportunity to get closer to the rainforest 'web of life'.

This would be the highlight of our trip for me. A visit to the business end of the rainforest to see its inhabitants at close range would be any naturalist's Heaven on Earth. Our group was reinforced by three female senior citizens from Vancouver, and a shy German millennial in his Sunday hipster best. The guide was an equally young and quiet Penan boy with thick black spectacles. The Canadian women quickly outed themselves as the sort of traveling retirees who don't really know why they travel, with the possible exception of gaining bragging rights. Seeing our binoculars, one of them sneered, "I like birds only roasted." A while later, apropos of nothing, one of her compatriots ominously proclaimed, "I don't like bugs." She wasn't lying. Minutes after her confession, Hans Jr. found a dragon-headed katydid,[145] a large omnivorous cricket with a body like a dead leaf and a rusty iron bondage mask for a face. On the upper rim of the nightmare-triggering visage, two fish-egg eyes flanked a horn and a pair of antennae. A blood-red, botoxed maw and a row of gnarly spines on the neck perfected the hobgoblin look. Even hardened naturalists will admit that, fascinating as it may be, it is a face only a mother can love. For the entomophobic Canadian, the ugly bug was reason enough to cut the outing short and return to her cabin in a huff of disgust.

Her departure downshifted our group's mood somewhat, and the third woman decided to come to the rescue. Up to this point, she had not contributed much to the conversation, and now she attempted to start a new topic by sharing her thoughts about Borneo. "I found Papua New Guinea much better. The natives there are *so* much more interesting!" she babbled, trampling the feelings of the Penan kid who from that minute on only spoke to us on a need-to-know basis.

---

145 *Lesina blanchardi*

Dragon-headed katydid

The Canopy Walk is a series of footbridges suspended 80 feet[146] high between small platforms built around large trees. The bridges are just wide enough for one person, and the wire-mesh railings reach up to one's navel. Well, most people's navel. I am much taller and wider than the average Sarawakian, and my center of gravity rode well above the top of the railings. That was the first shock. The next one came when I started walking. The walkways are strong enough to hold several people at once, but they sway and wobble with every step you take. My fear of heights almost paralyzed me, and I turned around to step off the bridge and give up on this part of the day. But this universe of ours is cold and random: the guide informed me that once you set foot onto the bridge, there is no turning back. Traffic is only allowed in one direction. The quarter-mile walk to the other end was a traumatic experience that surpassed our flight to Mulu. For the next half-hour, I dragged myself across the shaky bridges in a low crouch, gripping the railing in constant terror. I expected the supporting cables to break at any moment, if the wobbling didn't pitch me into the abyss first. Mary Shelley must have been on the Canopy Walk at least once, for she wrote in *Frankenstein*: "My heart palpitated in the sickness of fear, and I hurried on with irregular steps, not daring to look about me."

During the whole horror trip my eyes were mostly closed, and the only memory I have of the wildlife I was supposed to watch and enjoy was the immense noise of the

---

146 25 meters

insects. If you think rainforest insects are loud when they're 80 feet above you, imagine the decibels when you're face to face with them.

After reaching solid ground again, I collapsed under the next tree. That tree happened to be a *binuang*,[147] a 200-foot monster popular with tourists, who like to pose for photos between its towering buttress roots. I fell to my knees between two of these wooden walls and ruined the spectacular forest giant for everyone by hurling my breakfast right onto the posing spot. My family found me leaning against a root, still panting from the experience, my face minty-green with nausea. Only my wife took pity on me. The boys, predictably, delighted in my misery, and expedition doctor Jürgen advised me—not without some amusement—to drink some water, man up, and enjoy the rest of the day. "You'll be fine. How could you not? We're in Mulu!"

Although they had kept their eyes open, my family also reported failure to find anything of major interest during the sky walk; one flying lizard, two little brown jobs,[148] and an estimated 11 trillion incredibly loud and miraculously invisible insects was all they had noticed. So much for that unique opportunity to get closer to the rainforest "web of life" that the website had promised. (To be fair, we probably just had a very unlucky day. Everyone else who has ever done the Canopy Walk will tell you the wildlife is so thick up there you have to beat it back with a stick.)

We spent the afternoon on the Botanical Heritage Trail where a series of large and beautiful signs explains the grand scheme of the rainforest's ecosystem and brings your attention to its finer details such as vines, parasitic plants, different layers of tree growth, and a forestful of other botanical points of interest. The narrative is spiced up with comments from a cartoon ant with a mischievous sense of humor ("*Nepenthes lowii* has formed a dependent relationship with a tree shrew called Bob ... no, of course it's not Bob, we're just trying another ant joke to see if you're still awake.")

The two Canadian photographers were also on the trail. Lost in concentration, they were taking pictures of a broken twig on the handrail. We kept quiet and studied the twig. It was the shape, size and color of a big cigarillo and looked for all the world like an ordinary twig. It was bent at a 45-degree angle, and two short shreds of bark hung from the middle. What was its significance? Did it come from a rare tree species? None of us could explain why the two Canadians would waste their time photographing a broken stick.

The question marks on our faces must have flashed like disco strobes when Donna, the Canadian lady, turned to us and laughed, "I know what you're thinking. We were thinking it, too. A ranger showed us this thing earlier and insisted it's a stick insect. We looked at it from all angles but found no reason to believe him. We wanted to pick it up to see if it's really a live animal, but the ranger wouldn't let us, told us our finger oil would harm it. We were convinced he was pranking us. But when he left, we

---

147 *Octomeles sumatrana*

148 a.k.a. LBJs; birder slang for any of the many species of small, dull-colored passerine birds, many of which are notoriously hard to distinguish from one another.

Karl, Hans Jr., Lisa and the author under a binuang tree

Karl with friend in Mulu (Pharnacia sp.)

Lonchodes hosei hosei

touched it with a pen. Would you like to see?" She took out a ballpoint pen and tapped the twig lightly. In addition to the pair of bark shreds in the middle, four more legs unfolded from the twig, and the thinner end split into a pair of antennae. Now we also discovered that the knothole in the middle of the twig was an eye, embedded in deep skin folds like that of a humpback whale. This[149] was the possessor of some of the most astounding camouflage any of us had ever witnessed. Still, it was just a tiny part of Borneo's unceasing parade of natural sensations.

We found a few more stick insects on the way, although none as amazing as the bent cigarillo trickster. There was an amusing *Marmessoidea* nymph, a young green walking-stick that stood out not only for its satanic-red eyeballs but also for its ability to use its starboard middle leg to scratch its head with great speed and intensity, not unlike a dog attempting emergency flea control.

We rounded out the day with the discovery of a creature fittingly named *Metallyticus splendidus*. Its common name is iridescent bark mantis, and it is arguably the most beautiful praying mantis of them all. It is also one of the oddest. The body is flat and oval like a cockroach, and glisters with red and yellow iridescence. The rest of the insect is metallic green—the legs, the typical mantis head with its huge, prey-seeking eyes, and the two forearms used for catching and detaining its victims. Praying mantises received their name for their erect posture and their habit of holding their long, barbed forearms up in a praying position. They are not known for running but tend to fly off when danger looms. The iridescent bark mantis breaks with all these conventions. It is built low to the ground like a sports car, its forearms are strangely short, and as I was about to find out, its escape technique is just as unorthodox.

Iridescent bark mantis

---

149 *Lonchodes hosei hosei*

The mantis was crossing the trail but froze when we approached. It sat there in a perfect photo pose, and I wasted no time in breaking out my camera and lowering my 300 pounds of joy into a prone position. As soon as I had set up the camera for the first shot, Mr. Full Metal Jacket ditched the fake-death tactics and raced off in short, zigzagging sprints, forcing me to lug my bulk after it in a jerky silent-movie fashion that would have impressed Buster Keaton. Whenever the mantis stopped between sprints, it would allow me just enough time to catch up, flop down on my belly, set up the camera, and frame the shot … and at exactly that moment, the bug would dash off again. After half a dozen of these episodes, the insect careened into a fallen, hollow tree trunk and disappeared. When I checked the shots I had taken, I found one single usable photo. All others were either highly blurred or showed—sharp as a tack and perfectly framed—the place where the mantis had been less than a second earlier.

The explanation for the unusual appearance and behavior of the iridescent bark mantis may be mimicry. Its hunting style has long been thought to mimic tiger beetles, which are known for their fierce predatory habits and their running speed of up to 5.6 miles per hour, or about 125 body lengths per second. The iridescent bark mantis is mostly found on and under the bark of dead trees, where it preys on forest cockroaches who favor rotting wood as their home. Dead trees are also frequented by some species of wood-boring jewel beetles (Buprestidae), a family of insects in brilliantly glossy colors similar to those of the mantis. Possibly, the mantis mimics their appearance to act as a wolf in sheep's clothing.

Walking back to the park canteen, we passed a Penan guide returning home from work. He walked slowly and his gaze was fixed at the treetops. After a friendly nod and a smile in our direction, he continued to scan the canopy. I wanted to ask him what he was looking for, when I noticed the blowpipe in his hand. Like us, he was thinking of dinner.

* * * * * *

It was a beautiful Friday afternoon at 1.510655° North, 110.375350° East, our house in Kuching. The 4 o'clock downpour had silkened the air, but instead of celebrating the coolness with a walk around the nearby forest park, with a possible chance of watching one of those equatorial fairytale sunsets later on, I was chained to my desk and slogging through a 2,000-word translation of a Facebook poker game. Gambling bores me silly and translating gambling software bores me sick. All the fun was outside while I was not, and with dinnertime fast approaching, I was at the gates of hypoglycemia, with dancing tandoori chickens teasing me before my inner eye. I wasn't feeling like a million ringgit by any stretch of the imagination.

Until Nicole called.

Nicole lives in Kuching and is a veritable fount of insight on everything Borneo. Flora, fauna, history, tribes, customs—her knowledge puts many longhouse folks to shame. A remarkable feat for any person, made even more remarkable by the fact that Nicole grew up half a planet away from the rainforest, in a small Bavarian village shadowed by the Alps. From there she worked her way east and eventually became the only non-Malaysian in Sarawak to work as a government-licensed tour guide. Nicole knows of my snake sickness, and now she was going to disperse the cobwebs of my working man's blues with a double-barreled shotgun.

In blessed innocence of the effect her call would have on me, she announced cheerily: "I'm just returning from Bako National Park. In the ticket office at the boat jetty, there's a big snake in a homemade cage. Some villager caught it in his house and brought it to the office; said he wants to release it in another national park next week. They say it's a cobra, but I can't verify that; couldn't see it clearly. It was coiled up pretty tight, but it's quite a thick snake, and I'd say at least 8 feet long. They say it's already been in that cage without water for two days. They plan to release it, but nobody has time for that before next week. Want to head over and see if they'll give it to you?"

A thick 8-foot snake, possibly a cobra? It couldn't be, could it …?

A mix of anguish and jubilance flooded my veins. "Nicole," I said in a pinched voice that strained against bursting out into a mad scream, "what color was the snake?"

"Darkish. But not really black, not like the spitting cobras."

There are only two kinds of cobras on Borneo. One of these, the equatorial spitting cobra,[150] glossy-black and seldom longer than 4 feet, is one of the most common snakes in the towns around the island. The other cobra, rarely spotted and even less frequently caught, is the King of Kings: *Ophiophagus hannah*. At a top length of 18 feet,[151] the king cobra is the world's largest venomous snake. The genus name *Ophiophagus* means snake eater, and reveals that the snake's diet consists almost exclusively of other snakes, including other kings, with the occasional monitor lizard thrown in for variety. A king cobra's bite can contain enough venom to kill an elephant. Female kings are the only snakes that build and fiercely guard nests for their eggs, and *O. hannah* is considered the most intelligent snake species in the world.

In short, they don't call it the King for its rhinestone-studded jumpsuits.

I had never set eyes on a live wild one, and to say that this species was at the top of my bucket list would be a serious understatement. This species *was* my bucket list. After years of stalking the island's serpentofauna, the only two king cobras I had recorded had been foot-long babies, each firmly pancaked onto a hot country road. With every kingless day I spent in the jungle, my unholy obsession with this creature grew. In comparison, even my notorious durian mania seemed like a casual diversion.

Immediately after getting off the phone with Nicole, I tried to call the ticket office at the jetty, but it was already five minutes to 5 p.m., and government employees as a rule

150 *Naja sumatrana*

151 5.5 meters

aren't renowned for their heroic dedication to unpaid overtime. I would have to wait until the next morning to find out more, and it would be an agonizing wait. Would the snake still be there? Would they give it to us? And, most importantly: *Would it be a king?* I notified Chien Lee, a man always keen on photo ops with our wild neighbors, then called Nicole back, and we all agreed to drive out to the jetty the next morning in the hope of a major scoop.

After a long and mainly sleepless night, I loaded Hans and Karl in the truck and we collected Nicole and Chien. On the way to the coast, we stopped at a random street stall to wolf down a hasty breakfast of Sarawak laksa (whose divine flavor was completely wasted on our preoccupied minds), and then raced through the coastal swamps to the Bako jetty.

To our immense relief, the reptile was still where Nicole had seen it the previous day in a dark corner of the ticket office building, less than a yard away from the bebirkenstocked feet of the backpackers lining up at the desk to buy boat fares to Bako National Park. A snake of solid proportions was crammed in a makeshift cage. Two sheets of chicken wire had been fastened to an upturned colander that served as the cage bottom, then tied together at the sides and the top with a few lengths of pink plastic thread. The snake was tightly coiled against the mesh, but in the dimness, we couldn't detect any details. What we did detect, in all its evil glory, was the smell. A heady sewage stench emanated from the animal, and blowflies were starting, landing, and marching all over its body. As Nicole had reported, the snake had already spent a few days in the cramped cage, without a chance to visit a lavatory.

Chien knelt by the cage, peered into the malodorous gloom, and spoke the magic words: "It's a king." My sons high-fived each other and yelled things unsuitable to be repeated here. Nicole beamed like a lighthouse. I took a few deep breaths, grabbed the cage, and took it outside on the lawn.

We splashed the snake with water to rehydrate it, and then took a closer look. The beast was as thick as my wrist, and I guessed its length at around 9 feet. Its huge, almost crocodilian, scales had occasional gaps between them and resembled coarse slate tiles stacked by a casual hand. Big armor plates also protected the blunt head with its watchful, birdlike eyes that brought to my mind a small carnivorous dinosaur. The low-slung supraoculars, or eyebrow scales, perfected the menacing, mess-with-me-at-your-own-risk aura that surrounded the animal. No two ways about it. This was a king cobra.

Now that we had established the reptile's identity, congratulated each other, and thrown fistfuls of imagined confetti in the air, reality began to sink in. Menacing aura aside, the snake neither looked nor smelled healthy. It made a listless impression, and several loose scales at the throat betrayed possible rough handling during capture. We needed to take the beast to the forest and release it at a safe location as soon as possible. Alas, we couldn't just take off into the sunset with the reptile; there were social complications to consider. The man who had caught and secured the king in his house was not currently present at the jetty, but local customs and village politics called for his permission for our plans. From a strictly logical viewpoint, one might argue that because *O. hannah* is a protected species under Sarawakian law, catching and detaining a specimen is a crime, which made the snake catcher the bad guy and us the heroes. But local reality scoffed at such straight reasoning. Bako National Park, the boat jetty, and the ticket office are all run by Sarawak Forestry. Forestry officials in sage-green shirts were milling around us, selling tickets, arranging boat rides, and taking care of the tourists. But not one of them had given even a fleeting thought to the legal situation relating to the protected species in the wire cage. In their version of reality, the guy who had caught the snake had done the right thing by bringing it to the jetty and promising to release it later in a location safe for both snake and humans. The fact that he had put the Protected Species into a cage instead of just removing it from his house (Wildlife Crime #1), and the fact that he had now delayed the release of the Protected Species by at least four days, without providing it with as much as a bowl of water, thus risking the demise of the Protected Species (Wildlife Crime #2), was completely lost on all of them. In their opinion, "He caught it, so it's his snake. Anyone wants to take it anywhere else; they need his permission."

Reluctant to draw the ire of the entire village, and possibly creating a parang-wielding flash mob, we stuffed our logic back into its pouch and opted to seek out Mr. Snake Catcher in person to engage in negotiations. A boy on a moped volunteered to show us the way to the man's house. After we had poured the king into a big red plastic bucket with a screw-on lid and stowed the bucket on my truckbed, we followed the kid to the snake catcher's house. It was deserted. Moped Kid had Mr. Snake Catcher's cell phone number, but only his voicemail answered. Inquiries with the neighbors did not reveal Mr. Snake Catcher's whereabouts, but someone produced the phone number of the man's wife. Mrs. Snake Catcher informed us that at this very moment, her husband was belting his heart out at some downtown karaoke joint, and that she would try to reach him on his second phone.

We waited for a long time, huddling from the boiling heat under a guava tree. I had taken the bucket from the truck bed and placed it under the car to keep the snake from frying alive. We wilted away in the tropical heat, kicking pebbles. The atmosphere was not unlike the opening scene of *Once Upon a Time in the West*, the keening harmonica replaced by an Islamic prayer station on someone's kitchen radio. Occasionally, a villager would bicycle along and inquire about the big bucket under my car. After learning about its contents, he would pedal off at a brisk pace, infused with a sudden sense of purpose and urgency. And we would go back to wilting and kicking pebbles.

Just as we started to melt into the asphalt, Mrs. Snake Catcher called back. Her husband had not answered the phone; it was probably too loud in the karaoke place. But he would definitely be back today. At some time. Before midnight, for sure. This put us in a bit of a pickle. Finally, somebody thought of a brilliant compromise: we would photograph the snake in the forest without waiting for Mr. Snake Catcher's consent, but we would take Moped Kid with us. He would act as Mr. Snake Catcher's representative and monitor our actions.

Moped Kid saw the wisdom in our thoughts, and soon our little roadshow was on the move again. A mile from the village we parked the car by the roadside and walked down a short trail through a nipah palm swamp to a patch of forest. Arriving at the clearing I had selected for our photo shoot, we readied ourselves to face the king.

In tropical forests, a clearing in the woods does not indicate a picnic greensward perfect for a spread of champagne and camembert where you serenade your lady (resplendent in a crisp white sundress) after lunch with a lute. In the jungle, a clearing is just a place with no trees. The ground is usually covered ankle-deep with leaves inhabited by a heaving biomass of creatures, and rocks and roots lie in ambush to make you rue any step taken without great care. I had chosen a spot in a lovely bamboo grove, which meant that instead of hidden roots, rotting bamboo poles hidden under dead bamboo leaves would trip us up. Not the best arena to spar with a large and potentially high-strung venomous snake, but it had the best light for miles around, and the temperature was bearable.

The moment of truth had come. My sons and I were about to photograph our first wild, live king cobra. Our lack of previous experience with the species had made me nervous. Just a few months ago, three friends had found and photographed a 12-foot king on a swamp road near Kuching, and from their account of the event, *O. hannah* prefers a proactive attitude when disturbed. With a snake of this caliber, this could lead to a disheartening episode or two. Thinking about that story now, I became even more nervous. But there was only one way to confirm the veracity of my friends' claims.

We had agreed that Chien would take the first round of photos while my sons and I handled the snake, and now we took up battle stations. I laid the snake bucket flat on the ground and prepared to open the lid. The boys, armed with snake hooks, flanked the bucket to prevent lateral escape. Nicole and Moped Kid stood in the back, smartphone cameras at the ready. Chien squatted 10 feet from the bucket and screwed a 70–200 mm zoom lens onto his Nikon. I thought *What's with the long glass, we're just shooting a snake?* and then recalled, not without trepidation, that Chien had photographed king cobras before, and probably knew exactly why to keep a distance. That brought my nervousness to an all-new level, but now it was too late to bail out.

I opened the lid and stepped back.

At first, the scene played out like with any other snake. The cobra cautiously slid out of the bucket, took a quick look left and right, then glided toward the closest tree line. I slid my snake hook around the snake's body and gently pulled the animal back. So far, according to script. Now the snake was supposed to slip out of the hook and retrace its

King cobra

path toward the trees, starting the usual flee/hook cycle that would soon end with the reptile tiring out and quietly posing for photos.

But at this point, the king threw away the script and started ad-libbing. It did slip out of the hook, but instead of running for the hills it turned around and came for *me*. It raised the first 3 feet of its body into the air, flared its hood, and rushed me in a straight line while its open maw brought forth the most chilling sound I'd ever heard coming out of a snake. I panicked backward, stumbling over hidden bamboo poles, while random thought fragments zipped through my synapses: *The boys are too young to lose their dad pity I never wrote a will I should have brought my long lens.* Just seconds before a huge load of king cobra venom was unleashed into my body, killing me on the spot via a massive heart attack … the snake stopped in mid-rush, cocked its head as if to say, "See what you get when you f**k with me, maggot?" and U-turned toward the treeline again.

This time it was Hans Jr. who hooked the snake back, and again it bum-rushed its aggressor in a fierce display of psychological warfare. The sudden blitz, the bone-chilling sound, and the subsequent escape while the victim was left with an urgent need for a change of underwear—it was a first-class strategy, carried out with guts and perfection. A large venomous snake coming at you with obvious hostile intent usually puts mortal fear into anyone, even if the snake is silent. But the king's sound effects elevated that fear to new heights. The noise it emits to command respect is a loud mix of hissing and growling, probably best compared to the explosive sound of a flushing airplane toilet. (For those who can't remember the last time they used the bathroom at 30,000 feet, just think of the vocalizations of Bilbo's friend Smaug. There's another reptile that makes you look under your bed at night.) From the Germanic tribes roaring out of the forests at Roman legions to Russian infantry waves disintegrating German morale at the Eastern Front with their terrible "*Uuuraaaah*," battle cries have always served two purposes: boosting your own confidence while destroying that of your foe. While I'm not sure how much courage the king cobra gains from its articulations, I can attest that it manages the morale-destroying part to stunning effect.

The boys finally calmed the snake down. It sat on the bamboo leaves, sides heaving. A more bass-heavy, less intensive, sound came from the snake now. The rumbling was synchronized with the cobra's breathing and seemed to emerge from everywhere but the mouth, as though a muscle car engine was idling somewhere inside the snake. We now discovered that the neck injury we had assumed earlier was real. Fearing the worst, I gave up the idea of getting any good shots and suggested to call it a wrap. Karl had taken a few dozen photos with my camera, so those had to suffice. To me, the whole experience was worth much more than a bunch of photographs. After all, anybody can take good pictures of a king cobra, but not everyone gets to be scared witless by one.

Putting the king back into its bucket seemed a no-brainer. I once watched a TV show about Rom Whitaker and his king cobra breeding station in India, in which he maneuvered a large king into a bag simply by showing the animal the bag's dark opening. The snake believed it would lead to a hiding spot and went straight inside. We positioned the bucket's opening on the ground in front of the snake and waited. Sadly, the hole was just a little too large and bright to make the reptile feel welcome, but at least we were treated to some interesting behavior. Chien used a long bamboo pole to maneuver the bucket closer to the snake, rolling it from side to side. The cobra immediately reared up and swayed its body in sync with the bucket's movements. A snake charmer trick as old as mankind—but I bet that was the first time anyone ever pulled it off with a 10-gallon plastic pail instead of a flute.

In the end, we hooked and tonged the king back into the bucket and drove back to the boat jetty in the hope that Mr. Snake Catcher had materialized by now. He had not, and neither had he called anyone back. Just then, a man with an extra-crisp starch job on his Sarawak Forestry uniform walked up and warmly greeted us with a thousand-watt smile. I couldn't have been happier if Santa Claus himself had appeared before us, for this was Abang Mutalib, the chief warden of Bako National Park, and our ticket to sanity. I pointed at the red bucket, gave the man a quick status report on the snake's health and the political situation, and asked him if he would give us permission to release the animal somewhere safe, right now.

Not only did Mr. Abang agree without any further thought; he also promised to explain everything to Mr. Snake Catcher should he come to the jetty later.

We thanked him for his help, bade Moped Kid adieu, and back to the swamps we went. There we released the king into the shrubbery on a creek bank. For a while, he just sat there, slightly dazed, then slowly crawled into the bush.

We celebrated the rescue with a few quarts of fresh coconut water from a street vendor. Chien explained to us the great health and rehydration benefits of the drink (add ice and some water for greatest effect), and the vendor taught my sons how to open the nuts with a parang without spilling the contents. We bought a dozen nuts for the kids to practice on at home, where Karl used one of our own parangs to extract enough coconut water to fill a baby bathtub, while keeping all ten fingers attached to his hands ... a lucky ending to a lucky day.

7 ... AND IN SABAH

About 600 miles northeast of Kuching lies Sabah, the other state in Malaysian Borneo. Sabah is only half the size of Sarawak yet offers natural attractions of the highest quality. Sipadan Island is hailed as one of the planet's best diving spots, and Sabah's rainforest treasures, such as Danum Valley Conservation Area, Tabin Wildlife Reserve, and the lost world of the Maliau Basin, are simply spectacular. High on the list of must-sees is Mount Kinabalu, at almost 14,000 feet[152] the highest mountain in Southeast Asia. It is protected as Kinabalu Park, and is a World Heritage Site. A combination of unique geographical and geological factors has made it rich in flora and fauna found nowhere else on Earth. And much of the mountain, especially the remote and inaccessible northern side, is still poorly explored. Botanists believe there may be as many as 6,000 vascular plant species, making Mt. Kinabalu's flora one of the most diverse, if not the most diverse, in the world. This botanical nirvana includes bevies of sensational *Nepenthes*, and in 2015 we went on a family pilgrimage to this pitcher plant paradise.

A 90-minute afternoon flight took us from Kuching to Sabah's capital, Kota Kinabalu. We stayed the night at a local hotel, and after an interesting breakfast of fish-paste noodles with fish balls, fish sausage, and fried fish we picked up our rental van and set out toward Mount Kinabalu. Sixty miles later and 6,000 feet higher, we arrived in Kundasang, a charming little town in a Swiss setting. Kundasang sits in a wide valley dominated by cow pastures, vegetable fields, and widely spaced farmhouses. At the far end of the valley, the stark gray walls and summits of Mount Kinabalu's thrusting hulk form an imposing backdrop. Kundasang was a climate shock. Compared with steamy, seaside Kota Kinabalu and steamy, seaside Kuching, the temperatures were ridiculously low. On an island that straddles the equator, Kundasang averages 70 F in the middle of the day, and night temperatures can drop to 55°F.[153] Instead of air conditioners in our rooms at the Cottage Hotel we found plenty of warm blankets.

Dinner at the hotel was a triumph of simplicity. There was a creamy omelet, and corn soup with crab meat, but the main attraction was the vegetables. They had been

---

152 approx. 4270 meters

153 21°C and 13°C

Mount Kinabalu

harvested in the valley that morning, and the cabbage, lightly sautéed and seasoned only with salt, was a culinary 15 on a scale of 10. This humble veggie may be a staple of peasant cuisine all over the world, stomped and pickled into kraut and kimchi, but at this altitude it becomes a very different beast, and one which deserves to be treated with respect.

Stuffed like turkeys, we gathered our night-walking gear and drove to Kinabalu National Park headquarters, not far from Kundasang. We decided to take it slow on our first night and forgo the trails in favor of the Loop Road which connects with the park's guest houses, the botanical garden, and many trailheads. One of the trails leads to Mount Kinabalu's summit, 8,000 vertical feet away. One does not simply walk up the mountain, though. The steep ascent involves a climbing permit, climbing insurance, a mountain guide, and an expensive fee for all the above. Only 165 climbers are permitted per day, and early booking is recommended. The climb takes two days and one night, which is spent in one of a number of huts and ends long before sunrise to allow enough daylight for the push to the summit and the descent. At the trailhead, we came across a wooden sign listing the ailments that prevent you from obtaining a climbing permit, among them diabetes, asthma, hypertension, fear of heights, and obesity. The last one hurt my pride a little, but we weren't here for the summit anyway. They could keep their barren rocks and freezing shacks, I huffed to myself. I would rather explore the mountain's unique plants and animals at a sane altitude, and in shorts.

On the roofed wooden gate to the Bukit Burung (Bird Hill) Trail hung a signboard with information about the path. Next to the letters grew a splotch of lichen, mottled green and gray. "Hey, that lichen's shaped like a lizard," remarked Karl. His brother agreed. "Yeah, even with five little toes at the end of each leg." The lichen's outline could indeed be interpreted as lizard-like, but it was fuzzy and expanded, like a lizard that had been flattened by a steamroller and then sprinkled with lichen flakes. As we examined the strange growth, one of the hindfeet lifted from the wood in ultra-slow motion. The toes curled upwards until we could see the gray underside, and then the foot descended again, half an inch ahead of its previous position. After a pause, the second hindleg followed suit, then the forelegs. Every move was executed with the lethargic precision of a three-toed sloth. I was hypnotized. What were we looking at? The answer came to me through the fringes along body and tail, and the big feet shaped like Mickey Mouse gloves. The Kinabalu parachute gecko's[154] flatness, body fringes, and oversized feet create lift when it leaps into the air and enable it to glide distances of up to 200 feet.[155] The gecko's sluggish movements assist its amazing camouflage in keeping out of sight of prey and predators alike. We watched the gecko for at least ten minutes as it crept toward its hiding hole in the roof of the gate, less than a foot away. The

---

154 *Gekko racophorus*

155 61 meters

Kinabalu parachute gecko

unusual performance even came with an unusual background score, a telephone that kept ringing off the hook. We never identified the creator of that sound—an insect? a frog?—but it was a fitting accessory to the gecko's bizarre locomotion.

Compared with the previous night's sublime dinner, breakfast at the hotel was firmly on the other end of the quality spectrum: sour coffee, cold chicken wieners, and scrambled eggs that took the term "soggy" to a new extreme. But it failed to sabotage our good mood. The view of the mountain from the breakfast room made up for it in spades, and we were excited about our day ahead. We were going to visit Mesilau Nature Resort, home to the only population of *Nepenthes rajah* readily accessible to casual visitors. This plant is endemic to Mount Kinabalu and neighboring Mount Tambuyukon, and produces pitchers that can grow well over a foot tall and up to 8 inches wide. It is one of only three *Nepenthes* species known for killing mammals. And there were hundreds of them growing on a hillside meadow in Mesilau.

The steep drive to the resort twisted through narrow valleys blanketed in oak and chestnut forests. It was a lovely day, and the crisp mountain air allowed clear and distant vistas. We stopped at an overlook and walked around to take pictures and see the oaks and chestnuts from up close. Over 40 oak species and 12 kinds of chestnuts are found on Mt. Kinabalu, and the forest floor was littered with their fruit. Acorns the size of small peaches lay around in clusters, while the chestnuts impressed with a dense cover of fearsome spikes that made them look like weapons-grade sea urchins and strongly discouraged handling without thick gloves.

It was here that a little bird introduced us to an interesting phenomenon. Many of the plants and animals up here seemed to be the species we knew from Sarawak. But on closer inspection they turned out to be montane versions of their lowland analogs, occupying the same ecological niches here on the mountain. A flight of yellow-vented bulbuls darted around the vegetation in search of food. These songbirds are the most common urban bulbuls in Southeast Asia, and we were not surprised to discover them here. But something seemed off. Tan back, lemon butt, white front, all the main markings were there. But what had happened to their black eyepatches? I fetched my dog-eared copy of *Phillipps' Field Guide to the Birds of Borneo* from my backpack and worked my way through the island's 26 bulbul species. I learned that the yellow-vented bulbul does not occur at these altitudes. The pale-faced bulbul on the next page, however, bore strong resemblance to it, *sans* the eyepatches. Unlike its almost-doppelganger found in our garden in Kuching, it is endemic to Borneo's montane forests and found at altitudes from around 3,000 to 11,500 feet.[156] During our time on Kinabalu, we would find these mountain analogs day and night. Insects. Geckos. Frogs. Ginger plants. And of course, more birds. When we arrived at Mesilau Nature Resort, two kinds of local barbets high in the treetops held a full-throated warbling contest. To our amateur eyes, they looked pretty much like their lowland cousins: lime-green bodies, mustachioed nutcracker beaks, heads painted with a mosaic of four or five colors. The only visible features that set them apart from their relatives in the flatlands were the different arrangements of these color patches, and to our rookie eyes they were hard to distinguish.

We walked to the resort office to arrange for tickets and a guide to the Nepenthes Garden, and were grieved to learn that it was currently closed for visitors due to a recent landslide. That was a gut punch. One of the world's most impressive congregations of one of the world's most impressive pitcher plants grew just a short, tantalizing distance up the hill behind the office, but we were denied access. I tried to guilt-trip the chirpy clerk into letting us in by explaining to her the all-important role tropical pitcher plants played in my life, and that we had moved to Borneo just to live among them, and how seeing all those *rajahs* would be the high point of my existence, even topping my wedding day and the births of my sons.

---

156 900–3,500 meters

When I mentioned my first visit to Borneo to attend the Sarawak Nepenthes Summit organized by Chien Lee, the woman became extra chirpy: "Chien Lee! Oh, he is such a nice man! Why, he was here just yesterday. He was guiding a Korean television crew, and they filmed our pitcher plants!"

Say what? Wasn't the Nepenthes Garden closed because a landslide had made it inaccessible?

"Strictly speaking, it is not inaccessible, but parts of the trail are damaged, and it's dangerous to walk on those bits. So we closed the trail for safety reasons. I'm very sorry for the inconvenience."

But ... but ... why were Chien and the Koreans allowed in?

"Oh, he has a permit."

A permit that made him indestructible? But I held my tongue. Up against such Kafkaesque rationale, I decided not to probe the matter any further. We inquired about alternative activities, and the clerk gave us a trail map and recommended the Kogopon Trail for its floral richness.

Ten minutes up the trail, all our sorrows were forgotten. At an elevation of about 6,500 feet,[157] the Kogopon Trail led us through a phantasmagorical jungle. Every tree was covered in a thick fur coat of mosses, and pale beard lichens spanned twigs and branches like cobwebs spun by dog-sized spiders. We walked through entire forests of ginger plants, 12 feet tall and with supersized lance blades for leaves. Some of their flowers dangled above us like pink, petaled pineapples; others huddled on the forest floor and looked like star-shaped alien probes in brilliant red and yellow. Ferns of all shapes and sizes, including scaly-barked 20-footers, intensified the Late Cretaceous vibe. There were wild bananas, the ancestors of our supermarket Cavendish. Inside their small fruit lurked raisin-sized seeds as hard as glass and capable of shattering a molar in one careless bite.

We watched a chestnut-capped laughingthrush, a bird with elegant gray plumage and a puce forehead, raid a banana flower as big as a mortar shell. We saw little indigo flycatchers and a midnight-blue Bornean whistling thrush, which picked its way through the leaf litter next to us, unafraid of the humans. A pair of grey-chinned minivets, dubbed Flame of the Jungle for the male's striking orange and blue feathers, held a lively debate in a tree, and just before the end of the trail we heard a strange bird calling in a rhododendron bush. Its song was an eccentric mix of sweet melodies and magpie-like cackling. I was unfamiliar with the call, and the bird stayed hidden, making identification impossible. When the song started to feature muffled snickering, I realized I would not find this bird in *Phillipps'*. "Nice try, silly," I said. "Now come out."

Hans Jr. emerged from behind the bush, grinning like the Cheshire cat. "Sorry to get your hopes up, Dad. I just wanted to improve your birding experience. How about some lunch?"

---

157 ~2,000 meters

[Left] Wild ginger (Alpinia sp.)

[Right] Butterfly ginger fruit (Hedychium cylindricum)

We had tiffin at the Renanthera, the resort's stylish restaurant. Its breezy veranda afforded fine views of the surrounding jungle, and the food was excellent. Fish & chips, a legacy of Malaysia's colonial history, were dished up here in generous portions. Each included two units of cod, lovingly battered and skillfully fried, and so massive they hardly fit on the plate. I only wished they had served them with more than six fries.

One of Mesilau's trails leads to Kinabalu's summit. The trail is famous for its orchids, and we wanted to spend the afternoon on the lower section. We knew that the trail gate closed at 1 p.m., and that hikers were not allowed in without a guide. But after years of experience with Malaysia's kind rule-bending officials, we were optimistic about our chances. Lady Luck smiled on us: when we arrived shortly after noon, the rangers opened the gate and allowed us to enter on our own. The only stipulation was to be back before 4 o'clock.

The Kinabalu massif is smaller than most English counties, but an astonishing number of orchid species can be found there. About 40 percent are known from only a single locality, and some have been collected only once. Along the Mesilau Summit

[Left] *Nepenthes tentaculata*

[Right] Bulbophyllum membranifolium

Trail, a mind-blowing potpourri of orchids grew on the ground, on rocks, and on the mossy trees. They ranged from Borneo's smallest species, the pinhead orchid,[158] whose 2-millimeter flowers were easily overlooked, to seagrass-like clumps of *Bulbophyllum membranifolium*. Its blossom consists of three wedges and a fat lower lip, and scores of them nestled between long, narrow leaves sprouting from tree trunks. They sported a pink-on-yellow cheetah pattern, a purple central column, and a clear lacquer finish that turned the whole construct into fancy candy. We noticed all-green dendrobiums, fragile, star-shaped *Coleogyne* flowers, and *Eria* inflorescences like snowy foxtails cascading off the mother plants. But most of the orchids were unfamiliar to us. The plant diversity started to freak me out. In less than four hours we had to be back at the gate—*what to photograph first?* The orchids? The 5-foot begonias? The clusters of potbellied, leopard-spotted dwarf pitcher plants?[159] Or maybe the little bristly forests

---

158 *Podochilus tenuis*

159 *Nepenthes tentaculata*

of *Dawsonia superba,* at 40 inches[160] the world's tallest non-climbing moss? Ultimately, my fear of losing out trumped all other concerns. Afraid I would miss more discoveries further up the trail by wasting too much time on setting up proper photos, I took a couple of hasty shots of everything and moved on.

Lisa, Jürgen, and the boys had moved ahead and left me to deal with my shoot-or-not-to-shoot quandary. Now I heard hiking boots galloping down the steep trail at mountain-goat speed, and indistinct shouting that sounded like "DAD WAIT SNAKE WAITWAITWAIT!!" Hans Jr. and Karl came into sight, skipping toward me two steps at once. Hans pulled a 3-foot snake from his backpack and panted, "We found two of these way up ahead, near the short forest. They were curled up on the trail, so we grabbed one and ran back as fast as we could, so we'd have time to photograph it and bring it back to where we found it before 4 o'clock!" I was deeply moved. The short forest was the domain of upper montane vegetation at an altitude between 4,000 and 6,500 feet,[161] where stunted trees grew among rhododendrons and thick mists swirled in the wind. Not only had the boys raced down the mountain just to show me the snake; after I was done with my photos, they would need to run back up to the short forest to release the reptile where they had found it, and then race down once more to reach the gate before closing time. A luckier dad was never born, I thought, and I told the boys as much.

Two fire-lipped keelbacks

---

160 just over a meter

161 ~1,200 and 2,000 meters

[Left] Expedition doctor Jürgen examining fire-lipped keelback

[Right] Golden emperor moth

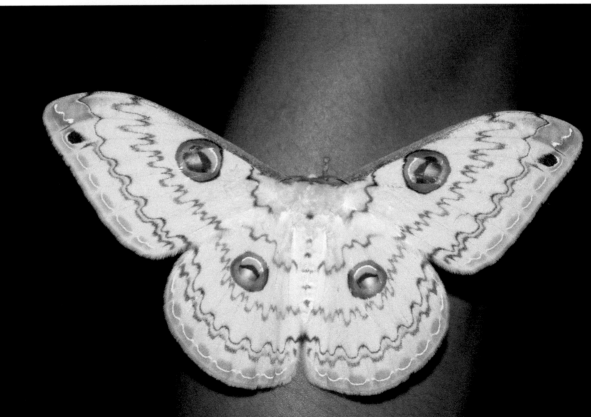

The snake was a fire-lipped keelback,[162] a comely creature endemic to northern Borneo's montane regions. Its olive body was ornamented with faint black and yellow spots, and segued into crimson toward the neck area. A blazing-red lower jaw contrasted the muted color scheme. The snake was in the process of shedding its skin; a few scales were peeling off the top of the head, and the eyes were milky blue. During shedding, snakes produce a bluish lubricant beneath the outermost skin layer which helps separate the old skin from the new. This fluid also runs under the transparent eye scales and clouds the eyes. At this point, the snake's vision is impaired, and it feels vulnerable. Snakes in their blue phase are usually ill-disposed for this reason, and so was this one. It had flattened its neck to appear bigger, enlarging the pretty red area behind the head. But the snake's spiteful demeanor and constant movements made it hard to photograph, and with our time constraints in mind I soon gave up on decent photos and sent the boys to take the reptile back to its habitat.

We all made it back to the gate with minutes to spare. In the parking lot I called Chien Lee to learn more about the magic permit that had granted him passage to the Nepenthes Garden.

"Sorry to hear they didn't let you in. But I don't have a special permit. I only signed a Release of Liability form that frees them from all responsibilities should anything happen to us during the visit to the garden. They have these waivers in a drawer in the front desk, but probably couldn't be bothered to tell you about them. Just ask for that document; once you've signed it, they're obligated to let you in. By the way, Pearl and I are still here on the mountain. You guys want to join us on a forest walk tonight?"

Is the bear Catholic? I grinned so hard my face hurt, and punched holes in the air with both fists. Our visit to the Nepenthes Garden had been thrown another lifeline, and the Exalted Grandmaster of Bornean Biology would show us Kinabalu's nocturnal wonders!

At 8 p.m. we met Chien and his girlfriend Pearl at Park Headquarters, outside the public toilet. He had selected the odd meeting point for a reason. "We'll switch on all the lights inside the toilet, and by the time we're back from our walk the place will be literally crawling with moths. There's also a resident cat that eats the moths, but hopefully we'll get some good shots in before he's done with dinner." Turning toward the lavatories, Chien found the first of many fantastic insects the night would present us with. From under a bench in front of the souvenir shop, he produced a golden emperor moth,[163] saffron-yellow with a 4-inch wingspan. Two parallel lines squiggled along the rear edge of the wings. The upper line was black, the lower blue, and if you looked long enough, they came together to form a horizontal ink scroll of a river flowing past a jagged mountain range. Above the landscape, a third line, this one as plain as an ECG printout, undulated in sync with the summits and the river. Amidst

---

162 *Rhabdophis murudensis*

163 *Loepa megacore*

the exquisite drawings, somewhat incongruously, were four eerily realistic eyespots of such vivid design that their gaze seemed to follow you wherever you went.

We turned on every light switch we could find in the lavatories, made sure all windows were open, and then hit the Silau-Silau Trail. Right off the bat, we spotted creatures left and right. Or rather, Chien did. Previous forays into Sarawak's jungles with him had taught me that in addition to his encyclopedic knowledge of Borneo's life forms he is gifted with a knack for finding them even in low light conditions. And tonight he was in fabulous form. As the designated journal keeper for our trip, it was hard enough for me to jot down the common and scientific names of all the creatures Chien discovered at seemingly every step, but the additional information barrage about their natural history and ecology was simply impossible to cope with.

Some of the highlights did stick in our memories, though. An entomology enthusiast (bug nerd) from early childhood, Chien excels at finding and identifying invertebrates. This forest was rich in phasmids, and by the end of our walk he had shown us at least 30 different kinds of stick insects in a broad selection of sizes and colors. Some wore conservative earthen tones, while others looked as if assembled from a bunch of glow sticks. A female *Calvisia conspersa* made no effort to conceal her presence and dazzled with an outré ensemble of blue knees, a fuchsia shawl, and a lime-metallic body dusted in red sprinkles. My favorite was *Dinophasma kinabaluense*, a mousy-brown fellow that appears quite dull. Get too close, however, and it will go full gangsta by spraying a defensive secretion at you that works like tear gas.

We were also introduced to some of Kinabalu's beetles, among them the entertainingly named handsome fungus beetles[164] and pleasing fungus beetles.[165] Regrettably, though, despite their brilliant monikers they were not much to look at. On the opposite end of the beauty spectrum was a muscular, show-stealing beetle in beautiful silky green. Its highly reflective eyeballs, rather than resting in sockets, sat outside of the face like black pearls, lending a new dimension to the term "bug-eyed". But everything comes with a price. Probably as the result of a Faustian pact, the poor insect pays dearly for its good looks with its tongue-crippling name: *Pseudochalcothea spathulifera*.

Chien had brought an intimidating camera rig that included two external flashes perched on the ends of mechanical arms mounted on the camera. Between the flashes and the subjects, Pearl held a diffuser, a light-softening screen made from the bottom of a plastic milk jug (no self-respecting macro photographer would be caught dead with a store-bought diffuser). More gear was waiting its turn in a trunk-sized camera rucksack. It was a master class in macro photography, and I tried to absorb as much as possible.

---

164 Endomychidae

165 Erotylidae

[*Above*] Calvisia conspersa

[*Below*] *Juvenile phasmid* (Necrosciinae)

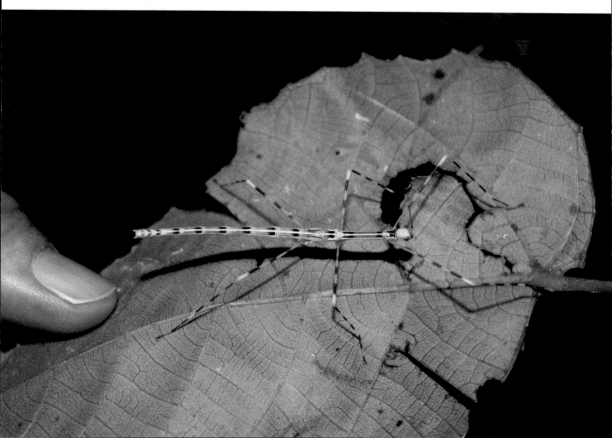

Chien and Pearl

Conogalactea imponens

Advancing further down the trail, Chien stopped in his tracks and said in a low voice, "Temminck's babbler." My eyebrows arched in puzzlement but I stayed silent. Chien slunk down the trail like a cat. We followed him as quietly as we could. Abruptly, he stopped again and whispered, "There's the nest. You see it?" Our headlamps were on, but all we saw was a lot of jungle. Chien skulked further ahead; we skulked along. He stopped a third time and pointed. "You see the nest now? Five yards ahead, at the trail bend, in a bush low on that slope." We shook our heads. Chien crept another yard forward. Like a bat out of hell, a tiny brown bird burst from the dark, hung a hard left and was swallowed by the night again. We were standing directly in front of the slope, now brilliantly lit by seven headlamps, but incredibly, we still saw nothing but a wild mess of shrubs. Only when Chien put his finger next to a small bird's nest half-hidden in a bush did we finally realize what he had been seeing and we had been missing all along.[166]

The last part of our walk treated us to a good variety of amphibians. The first one crouched on the trail and was so well cloaked that we almost squashed it underfoot. It goes by many common names, such as montane large-eyed litter frog,[167] and is closely related to the Bornean horned frog, which may explain its reliance on passive behavior and its coloration when approached. This one's brown body blended in well with the dirt trail, and only the bright reflections of our headlamps in its huge eyes saved it from being crushed. Like those of its flatland analog, the lowland litter frog,[168] its black-hole eyes carry a mournful expression seldom seen outside Japanese anime cartoons. We left it to its melancholy and immediately found another montane version of a frog we knew from Sarawak's lowlands. This one measured less than 2 inches and was all angles, like a Paleolithic arrowhead. I had never seen a Balu sticky frog[169] before but was well aware of its powers. As recounted earlier, one of its relatives[170] at the UNIMAS campus in Kuching had once taught me an unforgettable lesson about their clan when it temporarily denied me the use of my hands by shooting glue on them.

Just before our return to the lavatories, we came face to face with the fairest frog on the entire mountain, and possibly all of Borneo. It sat on a fern leaf and was easy to spot even for people without cat-like night vision. Colored like a ripe persimmon, the small, slender treefrog was bespangled from head to toe with little white spots. It wore campy white eyeshade, and a broken white line ran from each eyelid to the tip of the sharply tapered nose. A pair of arresting amber eyes bulging from the sides of its head inspected us with anticipation. The cinnamon frog[171] enjoys wide distribution from Thailand to the Philippines, but is not a common species. We all gave our cameras a good workout, and our lucky find cooperated nicely by staying stock-still the entire time.

Back at the toilets, an extraordinary spectacle awaited us. The white-tiled walls on the inside were abustle with winged things. About 10,000 moth species are estimated to exist in Borneo, around 1,000 of those on Mount Kinabalu. The diverseness of the moths sitting on those walls that night would justify a book on its own. We were captivated by the cornucopia of colors and patterns, yet the most interesting individual[172] did not

---

166 Chien will tell you with typical modesty that his detection skills are merely the result of many years spent in the forest looking for animals. But I strongly suspect that there is an owl somewhere in his ancestry.

167 *Leptobrachium montanum*

168 *Leptobrachium abbotti*

169 *Kalophrynus baluensis*

170 *Kalophrynus pleurostigma*

171 *Nyctixalus pictus*

172 *Dudusa vethi*

[Left] Cinnamon frog

[Right] Dudusa vethi

Nepenthes Garden, Mesilau

stand out by its artwork—it was mostly brown and gray—but drew attention with its structural design. The body was unusually hairy even for a moth, and at the end of the long thick tail perched a giant fluffy hairball.

Chien declared, "I'll show you something cool," and touched the moth's forehead. In response, the tail shot up, bent over toward the head, and tried to touch Chien's finger with the hairball. This quirky little contortionist act most likely causes attacking predators to hesitate and perhaps withdraw, giving the moth a chance to escape.

Early next day we returned to the park office at Mesilau: "We would like to visit the Nepenthes Garden, please. We heard you would allow us access if we signed your liability waiver."

The clerk shot a glance at her colleague, who gave an almost imperceptible nod, and five minutes later we were outside again, tickets in hand, and accompanied by a guide named Rose. A short walk took us into a valley with dense forest marching up its steep sides. A steel gate safeguarded a footbridge across a small stream cutting through the valley floor. On the far side rose a slope overgrown with scrubs and tall sedges and accentuated with thin trees. That was the Nepenthes Garden. Rose unlocked the gate for us, and when I stepped off the bridge an old dream became reality.

Ever since I had killed my first mass-market *Nepenthes* hybrid with inexperience a long time ago, I had been fantasizing about visiting this place. Eleven years had passed since the death of that first plant; eight years since my first visit to Borneo and my decision to sell my greenhouse plants and move to Sarawak; and four years since I had put that plan into action. A wave of emotions overcame me as I walked up the footpath that led through the garden.

But there was no time to ruminate on my feelings; the garden immediately commanded all my attention. The first length of the path was lined with *Nepenthes burbidgeae*, the painted pitcher plant. In 1858, Hugh Low and the British consul general in Brunei, Spenser St. John, were the first Europeans to lay eyes on the species. St. John later wrote of their discovery on Mount Kinabalu:

> Crossing the Hobang, a steep climb led us to the western spur, along which our path lay; here, at about 4000 ft, Mr. Low found a beautiful white and spotted pitcher-plant which he considered the prettiest of the twenty-two species of Nepenthes with which he was then acquainted; the pitchers are white and covered in a most beautiful manner with spots of an irregular form, of a rosy pink colour.

It was later named after the wife of Frederick William Burbidge, a British explorer who collected tropical plants for England's famous Veitch Nurseries. In an article for *The Gardeners' Chronicle* on January 14, 1882, he described the plant as

[Left] Nepenthes burbidgeae

[Right] Nepenthes rajah, *plant*

a lovely thing, as yet unintroduced: pitchers pure white, semi-translucent like egg-shell, porcelain-white, with crimson or blood-tinted blotches. Lid blotched and dotted with crimson-purple.

The ceramics effect of the large, tubby pitchers is rounded off by strawberry-and-vanilla candy stripes on the thick peristome, the hard rim of the pitcher. If not for the slimy mess of dead ants inside the vessels, they would not look out of place in any fine china collection.

We had now reached the landslide. It had started on the forested walls high above us and plowed a 20-foot-wide swath across the entire garden, including the path we stood on. We were relieved to find the mud avalanche not too difficult to cross, because on the other side waited the main attraction: the king of all *Nepenthes*, Rajah Brooke's pitcher plant. Hugh Low had collected the species on Mount Kinabalu in 1858, and British botanist and explorer Joseph Dalton Hooker described it the following year. He named it *Nepenthes rajah* after James Brooke, the first White Rajah of Sarak. Hooker called the plant "one of the most striking vegetable productions hither-to discovered".

The pitchers of these unearthly creatures were striking, alright. They lay on the ground between the tall grasses like footballs left on the field after practice, and tendrils as thick as my thumb connected them to 30-inch leaves. The younger traps were all-red, their flanged peristomes and inside walls a glossy bright magenta. The mature pitchers had taken on yellow speckles, and the rims were the color of dark garnet.

But as beautiful as their colors were, it was their impossible dimensions that brought us to gasps and shouts at every pitcher we turned up. Each of these killing jars can contain more than half a gallon[173] of digestive fluid and hold up to a gallon of water, which makes them the largest in the genus by volume. The pitchers attract some mammals, mostly rats and mice, who occasionally also drown in the liquid.

At least one mammal, though, has evolved a peculiar relationship with the plant. The pitcher lid is the shape of an upturned dugout canoe and can grow to the length of a large sneaker. The glands on its underside produce a sugary discharge, and to the mountain treeshrew, a furry cutie that looks like a squirrel but is closely related to primates, this stuff is what is Ben & Jerry's ice cream is to humans. The animal marks its feeding spots with scat, and as it sits on the pitcher rim and licks the sweet treat off

Nepenthes rajah, mature pitcher

173 well over 2 liters

the lid, the pitcher doubles as a latrine. The pitcher's size and shape force the treeshrew to do its business directly into the trap, providing the plant with valuable nitrogen, the lack of which being one of the main reasons why carnivorous plants evolved their meat-loving ways. Studies show that the treeshrew's behavior is habitual, and its poop makes up a significant percentage of the plant's nitrogen intake.

We did not witness any treeshrews using the king's pitcher plant as a powder room that day, but I could live with that. It was a perfect day: a light breeze whispered along the valley, and the world's greatest pitcher plants sat at my feet by the hundreds. I looked at the jungled ridges above me and thought about the discoveries they promised. Despite massive habitat destruction, Borneo is still an island of untold biological riches, and there are quite a few places that Marianne North and Alfred Wallace would still recognize today.

But Borneo's future is uncertain, and these places need help before we destroy them, too. With tropical rainforests disappearing at an ever-accelerating clip, the need for action becomes increasingly urgent. Rainforests all over the planet harbor an immense number of undiscovered species, and an equally immense number of creatures will undoubtedly have already gone extinct by our own doing before we've even had a chance to discover them.

"Save the Rainforest" is not about cute apes and pretty flowers, but about the survival of our own kind. Decades ago, the English naturalist and conservationist Gerald Durrell warned, "Many people think that conservation is just about saving fluffy animals—what they don't realise is that we're trying to prevent the human race from committing suicide."[174] Directly or indirectly, intentionally or not, *Homo sapiens* has effectively declared war on every single species that shares our world with us. If we cannot figure out how to turn off the chainsaw, we won't even show up as a footnote in the annals of this planet.

---

174 As quoted in *Gerald Durrell: The Authorised Biography* (1999) by Douglas Botting, ISBN 9780002556606

POSTSCRIPT

I will leave you with a selection of thoughts others have had about the topic. In this age of information overload, short attention spans, and real-time communication that is often limited to 280 characters per message, these quotes are of just the right essence and size to remember, inspire, copy, and forward.

> We are standing on an isolated rock of knowledge, gazing down into the vast abyss of the unknown.
>
> - Robert W.C. Shelford, *A Naturalist in Borneo*, 1916

> In the next 24 hours, deforestation will release as much CO_2 into the atmosphere as 8 million people flying from London to New York. Stopping the loggers is the fastest and cheapest solution to climate change.[175]
>
> - Daniel Howden, *The Independent*, May 14, 2007

> The silencing of the rainforests is a double deforestation, not only of trees but a deforestation of the mind's music, medicine and knowledge.
>
> - Jay Griffiths, *Wild: An Elemental Journey*, Penguin Books, 2008

> The practical importance of the preservation of our forests is augmented by their relations to climate, soil and streams.
>
> - John Muir, *Nature Writings: The Story of My Boyhood and Youth*, 1997

---

175 https://www.independent.co.uk/climate-change/news/deforestation-the-hidden-cause-of-global-warming-6262622.html

It is a sad fact that to many people the loss of a plant species is of less moment than the loss of a football match.

- Richard Fortey

Destroying species is like tearing pages out of an unread book, written in a language humans hardly know how to read, about the place where they live.[176]

- Holmes Rolston III

Man has been endowed with reason, with the power to create, so that he can add to what he has been given. But up to now, he has not been a creator, only a destroyer. Forests keep disappearing, rivers dry up, wildlife has become extinct, the climate is ruined, and the land grows poorer and uglier.

- Anton Chekhov, Uncle Vanya, 1898

We are destroying the world's greatest pharmacy. It is very important that we protect the rainforest in everything that we do.

- Chris Kilham

In Wildness is the Preservation of the World.

- Henry David Thoreau, Walking, 1851

Saving the environment is really about saving our environment—making it safe for ourselves, our children, and the world as we know it. If more people saw the issue as one of saving themselves, we would probably see increased motivation and commitment to actually do so.[177]

- Robert M. Lilienfeld and William L. Rathje

The forest is a peculiar organism of unlimited kindness and benevolence that makes no demands for its sustenance and extends generously the products of its life and activity; it affords protection to all beings.

- Unknown; sometimes attributed to the Buddha

---

176 *BioScience*, Vol. 35, No. 11, The Biological Diversity Crisis (Dec., 1985), pp. 718–726

177 https://www.nytimes.com/1995/01/21/opinion/six-enviromyths.html

THERE IS NO PLANET B.

- All of us

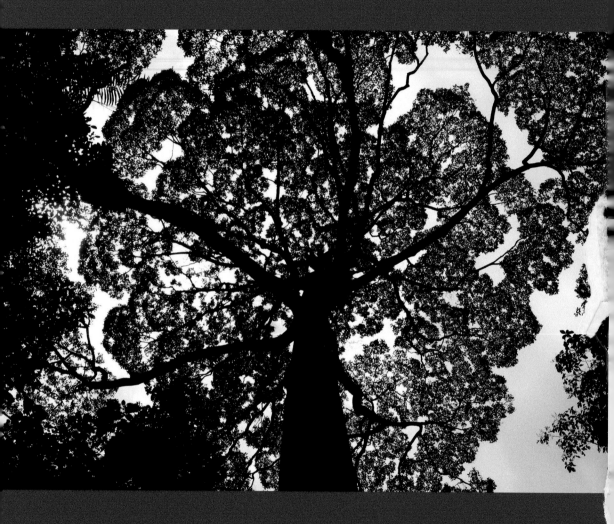